Peregrinations

Dear Mr. Meijjes,

Thank you for being – as I have discovered – such a good friend to my father for so many years.

You were right – an author should never edit his own work! But there was a point that dad would have seen the finished work & been the one ~~only~~ signing it for you. At least he got to see the proofs.

Kindest regards,

Eri

Peregrinations

A man's journey

Eric Grant

Writers Club Press
New York Lincoln Shanghai

Peregrinations
A man's journey

Writers Club Press
an imprint of iUniverse, Inc.

For information address:
iUniverse, Inc.
2021 Pine Lake Road, Suite 100
Lincoln, NE 68512
www.iuniverse.com

ISBN: 0-595-26817-X

Contents

Introduction 1

Prologue 5

CHAPTER 1 7

CHAPTER 2 16

CHAPTER 3 34

CHAPTER 4 54

CHAPTER 5 73

CHAPTER 6 95

CHAPTER 7 128

CHAPTER 8 168

CHAPTER 9 183

CHAPTER 10 204

CHAPTER 11 219

CHAPTER 12 240

Introduction

In 1984, a young adventurous Frenchman by the name of Patrick Bauer walked for twelve days in the parched heat of the Moroccan Sahara desert, carrying water supplies and food in a large backpack. It was the ultimate challenge to test one's limits, and at the end he was left—in his own words—"with a sense of meditation, of well-being and blessedness which far surpassed [his] own personal joy." He wanted to share this elation with as many people as possible: two years later, he inaugurated the first edition of the *Marathon des Sables* with twenty-six participants.

By 1995, it had become a well-oiled international race, despite the fact that an Italian disappeared for nine days the previous year (fortunately found across the Algerian border, forty pounds lighter), and that a twenty-three year old man had died of a heart attack induced by dehydration and heat exhaustion several years earlier. Over two hundred people signed up for this tenth anniversary of a hellish competition dubbed "The Toughest Footrace on Earth". My father, Cedric Grant, was one of them.

The Marathon des Sables is a 140-mile trek in the Moroccan Sahara over seven days in complete self-sufficiency; which means that each participant must carry his or her own food (a minimum of 2000 calories a day is required), cooking gear, sleeping bag, compass and race map, emergency flair, wind breaker, knife, flashlight, and mirror, for an average weight of twenty-two pounds. The organization supplies only nine liters of water a day, and open-air Berber tents which shelter each nine weary competitors every night. A fleet of Land Rovers, a helicopter, and a team of doctors, contribute respectively to moving supplies from one daily bivouac to the next, filming the race and evacuating seriously injured competitors, and attending to cases of dehydration, heat exhaustion, physically-induced depression, twisted ankles, and blood-filled blisters.

Flat terrain, low and interspersed sand dunes, and overcast skies colluded to make the race relatively easy in 1995; so much so that many complained. Over twenty participants still dropped out, unable to face the hardships, and on his first attempt, Cedric found himself sufficiently challenged. He managed to finish, albeit last, and was elate. The race had held its promise: the sense of risk, of adventure, of spiritual solitude, of challenge, of human bonding. He signed up immediately to return the following year.

Though he would fail to finish in 1996 and 1997, he managed once again to cross the finish line in 1998. He vowed to return every year as long as he could still put one foot in front of other.

◆   ◆   ◆

In April 1999, my father called me up in Los Angeles at a perfectly indecent time one Sunday morning to tell me that he had signed me up for the fifteenth edition of the Marathon des Sables. Well, I had seen the video-tapes of his previous races, and I had seen the fierce gleam of exhaustion and victory in the competitors' eyes at the finish line: they seemed like men and women in the throes of an epiphany, and a part of me at that moment wanted to feel the way they looked.

I had told my father this; I had never expected him to call my bluff. When he did, that early Sunday morning, I immediately wondered *why?* More frightening than the prospect of trudging through sand dunes with a twenty-pound backpack were the possible reasons my father might have for asking me to join him. And the only reason that came to mind was terrifying indeed: he wanted us to spend some quality father-son time together.

It was that and more: he also wanted to share his life.

The inspiration for such an idea came most likely from the fact that he was retiring from Citibank at the end of the year. Most naturally, he was now looking back and measuring the extent of his accomplishments. Several people within the bank had mentioned that he should write a book about his life. After all, there was no doubt that he had managed a remarkable career, met with some well-known personalities, and experienced the heyday of international banking. His life showed a real aspect of the American Dream—he had risen above his poor origins in Oregon to become the private banker of one of the wealthiest men in the world—peppered with his own unique adventures: a two-year backpacking trip around the world, a Land Rover crossing of the Sahara desert, life in Liberia and Saudi Arabia, and a plane crash that not only changed his life, but essentially gave him a new perspective on how a life should be led. I could not deny that his has been a unusual ride—like any son I felt the weight of surpassing my father's achievements and he certainly made the task difficult!

The *Marathon des Sables* provided the ideal setting, with ample time for him to tell me his story, though it would take two races and the intervening months for the whole story to be told. As I sat one night under the Berber tent in which we slept, having just covered fifty miles in 16 hours, I told my father what a thrill it had been to walk alone in the desert night. He didn't need to respond, he understood. And I realized that we were embarking on a fascinating adventure together.

My father, who believed until then that we had very little in common, learned that we shared more than just genes; and I learned that his achievements were not there to emulate or supersede. I discovered that he had been a son too, just as I might be a father some day with my own life to tell. But this is his, and I'm glad he was able to share it.

Prologue

For a long time he couldn't move, and for a long time after that he didn't want to move.

He'd broken every bone he could name on the right side of body, and many more that he couldn't name.

For several days he couldn't quite recall why he'd been in the plane and why it had crashed, and when he chose to remember again it was as if it belonged to someone else's past, someone to whom he was inextricably linked, but another person all the same. And if that person carried an engagement ring into the sky to then dive down and present it to the woman he loved, the person now lying on a hospital bed wasn't sure that marriage was what he wanted after all. There were many other considerations about his life and future but they had disappeared in the wreck of the Valiant, and his constant companions for several days were memories and dreams of Bible class and of paper routes, of his mother Marjorie and of his father Otto, of ship decks and breakfasts in an officers' mess, of long afternoons playing alone with two toy cars, and of the joy of receiving his first bicycle and of buying his first car and of traveling for the first time across the continent...And of Paris that he'd never seen and of New York that he hoped to see again.

Then the thought hit him at the end of the first week that now he could see New York again and Paris for the first time—if he wanted, if he tried. Memories of the accident started to filter back, and a weight dropped from his shoulders just as anxiety gripped him when he imagined what might have happened. He discovered with the lurching nausea of vertigo that the plane crash could have ripped his future, any future, from him and trampled it to a few insignificant days, hours or even seconds. Or worse: a paraplegic, turned every two hours to prevent bed sores...

Eventually the reality of his past reconnected with the possibility of his future, and he began to recast his job and his fiancée in a new light. He refrained from telling Katy what the purpose of the flight had been. The ring remained buried in his clothes and the few people involved in the plan were asked to remain silent. He was unable to make any decisions; he only knew that he needed time to collect his thoughts.

The plane crash tore a veil from his face and revealed the possibility of a future that remained to be imagined and created. Whatever had happened before the crash had defined who he was; whatever happened now would determine how he looked back on his life in later years…When he left the hospital six weeks later with his arms and shoulders in a cast, Cedric felt the dizzying power of choice without risk: he had so very little to loose in any decision he made, since he came so very close to losing life itself. ♣

1

On a gray Sunday April morning that felt nothing like spring, though it was quite typical of an Oregonian spring in its misty dismalness, Cedric was ushered off to Church with a quick push from his mother before she closed the door on him. He understood vaguely what was expected of him; at least he understood that something was expected of him. He wasn't quite sure what, but he decided that he'd walk first and hopefully find out later. Perhaps where he was supposed to go would give him some kind of answer. Why his mother, who had never expressed any particular concern for religion, would suddenly send him to Bible school was not a question that crossed his eight-year old mind. His mother had simply told him that this was something that he must do, and he assumed that she meant that it was something that kids just did as soon as they turned eight. She did not, of course, accompany him. He didn't question that either; not because he didn't have an inquisitive mind, but because that was the way his mother was. "There's the road to the church—now go join Bible school!…" she'd said. So he went.

His deep golden hair was dulled by the Portland sky; in any case it would grow darker with age. His first adult teeth had started to grow in, but the gap between the two front teeth—a later characteristic of his frequent smile—was not yet visible. Neither were the scar on his temple and the drooping of his right eye, remnants of a later plane crash.

Cedric could not imagine these things yet. Flying had not crossed his mind, but if it had, he probably would have considered it impossible. Flying *away*, however, in its figurative sense, was certainly in his dreams, even if it formed only a kernel of a dream so far—not yet a desire, and certainly not a goal. Newsreels were full of stories of the war in the Pacific, and among the battleships and aircraft carriers, some-where between Portland and Manila, his father had been at the helm of a navy transport ship. The cogs of Cedric's imagination turned and churned as he tried to place his father within the context of the stories he had read and the images he had seen; consciously or not, those sto-ries and images, and the projection of his father within them, became the pith of his desire to leave his hometown. Within ten years, Port-land would become a very small place indeed.

There was nothing lush, hip or trendy about the neighborhood where Cedric grew up: In the Thirties and Forties, Halsey Street cut through one of the poorer neighborhoods of Portland, a ghost town kept alive only by some invisible life support. It was close to the rail-road tracks—Cedric was frequently awakened at night by the rumble of a freight train since he slept outside on the porch, on an army cot—and an area dubiously dubbed the Gulch or, more ironically, Hooverville, home to pirates and bums, vampires and succuba, tooth-less hunchbacks and bearded bag ladies...Well, it wasn't exactly that dangerous anymore, but it had dragged an insalubrious reputation since the Depression. There were still a few desperate men whose ratio-nal minds had shattered after '29, drowned in rye and moonshine, men who'd slipped through the lines of the New Deal and had no money, no job, and little hope. Alongside and around this miasma of human misery were a few people who still wished to keep abreast of world events, and so Cedric would occasionally accompany his fifteen year-old cousin Roger on his paper route. They picked their way through pierced jerry cans, broken furniture, cardboard-tarpaulin houses, sheet-metal braziers and comatose bodies, while Roger clenched an old 38mm pistol to discourage the handful of perverts for whom the kids represented far juicier morsels than the wartime hard tack of sickly prostitutes.

That was his life at eight years old: fending for himself while his father—a captain in the Merchant Marine—was away at sea in the middle of a war.

◆   ◆   ◆

Otto Proschwitz was born in Riesa, Saxony, in 1904, into a family of Prussian military men. He realized early on that he could hardly hope to reach the level of achievement which his multi-decorated father and grandfather had attained before Germany was shattered and humiliated by the Versailles Treaty. Strongly attracted to the sea, he joined the German Merchant Marine in 1922. The ships on which Otto worked were mainly involved in trade with the Baltic nations and Scandinavia, but in 1924 he found work on a ship bound for the United States. Though little inclined to outrageous revelry or decadent partying (save for the blustering bouts of drinking for which sailors are infamous when on land), Otto could not help but marvel at the excitement offered by the United States during the Roaring Twenties, compared with the depression that weighed on an embolic and affrayed Weimar Republic back home. When his ship docked in Baltimore in 1926, he skipped off into the figurative countryside, obtained his American citizenship, and joined the U.S. Merchant Marine.

Otto remained at sea for several years, unwilling to settle anywhere, in part because firm ground made him uneasy (there was no *motion*), in part because there were too many exciting cities to choose from. As is often the case in such a situation (and as would be the case for Cedric getting a job in banking thirty-four years later) the choice was, to some extent, made for him. In 1928, Otto's ship docked in Portland, Oregon, but its departure was continuously delayed due to constant storm watches. After two weeks Otto had reached the end of his financial tether. He began looking for a job, and hit several brick walls. After the third consecutive day of rejections, he complained to his quartermaster about the situation.

"It's the name, son. Proschwitz don't sound too…Christian. Know what I mean?"

Otto knew what he meant. His former countrymen had been blaming the Jews for Germany's misery for years. He just didn't expect to find the same antagonism in the land of milk and honey, yet he came to terms with it with Teutonic practicality. He faced his quartermaster, raised the whiskey bottle in front of them and filled their glasses. He stared at the label on the bottle for a few moments, and said: "Then call me Otto *Grant*!" he exclaimed and they drank to the health of the departed President.

The next day he walked into the Lehigh Portland Cement Company and was hired immediately. His plan was to work for the next two weeks, then board his ship and steam off to a new destination. The frolicking figures of fate decided otherwise, however, in a rather painful way: three days before Otto's ship was scheduled to leave port, a crane cable snapped and lacerated his arm, almost ripping it out of its socket. Once he'd recovered from his injury, he found that his ship had sailed; so he returned to Lehigh and spent the next year contributing in his modest way to the fever of skyscraper construction that had gripped the nation. By the time he returned to the Merchant Marine, his name change had the official stamp of approval from the Federal government. And he'd met Marjorie Skei.

Cedric's maternal grandfather, Peter Skei, left Norway in 1895 on the *Norge*. After passing immigration in New York, he pushed westwards to Rawlings, Wyoming, where he pursued work as a logger. The following year, his friend Lars Nilsson convinced him to enter into a partnership. Land was still cheap and opportunities high in the Pacific Northwest and Lars had his eye on a sawmill. So Peter moved to Portland, where he met and married a certain Nicolina. The sawmill prospered and by 1908 the Skei family counted five additional members: two sons, Prescott and Kenneth, and three daughters, Dorothy, Alice and tiny baby Evelyn. Finally in 1914, Marjorie was born. That same year Peter and Lars decided to sell the sawmill and develop a larger timber business in the Pacific Northwest. But as soon as the sale of the sawmill went through, his partner scampered off with the proceeds, leaving Peter bereft and in debt. He quickly found new work as a logger, but he never quite adjusted to no longer being his own boss and to the simpler life into which he was now forced, further exacerbated by his investment in real estate across the Willamette River from Downtown Portland—an investment that would depreciate markedly over the years with the arrival of nickel and dime stores and burlesque houses.

For many years Cedric believed that his mother had been attracted to Otto's mercurial nature and restless sense of adventure, as his own wife would be thirty years later. Marjorie's consideration of Otto, however, contained a veneer of wishful thinking that the man would eventually settle down. While Otto might have considered the notion intermittently, he did not actually consider himself restless, indeed he found life at sea quite restful despite the hardships. Nor would Otto necessarily equate his love of the sea with a sense of adventure; it was simply something to which he was drawn inexplicably. He found lengthy bouts in port far more frightening, and he needed *motion* to feel at peace. Otto considered his life at sea to be quite normal; the excitement came from the fact that he loved his work. He could easily accept that someone else may not share his enthusiasm. But he didn't realize when he spoke to Marjorie of his travels at sea that her eighteen year-old ears found them to be more vivid and thrilling than the movies.

However much Otto may have loved Marjorie, she could not compete with the power that the sea held over him. Otto shipped off and returned to Portland twice in the next year and a half, and perhaps a few comings and goings would have sufficed for Marjorie to tire of his lengthy absences. Indeed the day he arrived on his second return, she tentatively asked him if there was any chance that he may wish to stay on land. He debated it, he considered the option, he staved her off; in the end he told her that they would discuss it after his next trip.

When he returned two months later, the decision was made for him: Marjorie was pregnant. Otto accepted the news in stride: he would trade off the excitement of life at sea for the pleasures of a family. Otto and Marjorie were married a few weeks later, and Otto set about finding a job in Portland. Fate, this time, worked in his favor. The New Deal had not yet gained momentum and FDR had been President for barely two years, still treading on a ground of volatile public opinion: Otto Grant was left with no other option in the midst of the Great Depression than to remain in the Merchant Marine. An option which he greeted with the same relief that ill-prepared students feel when they are told that their exam has been postponed indefinitely.

Cedric was born on March 20, 1934. Kurt followed three years later. Then war broke out in Europe and imperial Japan stared ever more fixatedly with inimical eyes across the Pacific. Otto joined the Naval Reserve Officer's training program on Treasure Island near San Francisco, and the family moved to Oakland. Soon he was sailing the South Seas and shuttling troops and equipment around Hawaii, the Marshalls, Wake, and Marcus.

In 1941, Otto became an officer on the SS Admiral Cole, one of the new welded Liberty Ships, those "ugly ducklings" spawned by Roosevelt. Then came the bombing of Pearl Harbor on December 7, and of Manila the next day. There was no news from Otto for several months and there was every reason to suspect that he and the SS Admiral Cole had been caught at one of the two ports, or in the subsequent cross-cannon fire in between. Marjorie had grown used to Otto's long absences. It didn't mean she had come to accept them, but she was now accustomed to the emotional rollercoaster ride that they entailed. Fueled by silence, Otto's absence this time was of a different nature and took on a more tragic meaning.

Marjorie did not particularly consider herself the wife of a war hero (a label deserved only when a war was actually over and the world had returned to some degree of sanity, she believed), and she was rarely, if ever, taken to wild flights of imagination, especially with regards to circumstances over which she had no control. That is not to say that she would be unaffected by her husband's death, certainly not, but she considered with Scandinavian stoicism that though she didn't wield the bow that slung the arrows of fate, she *did* have two boisterous children to raise. Plans were plans, and if Otto was still alive then their plans to move back to Portland should be followed (on his last home leave, Otto had mentioned that he wanted to find work in the shipyards in Portland, now that work was booming again in the shadow of war and in light of Roosevelt's sneaky lend-lease program with Britain. And if her husband were not alive, then Marjorie might as well follow them anyway, mainly because she'd rather be in Portland where she had been raised than in Oakland where she knew very few people. So in early 1942—despite Pearl Harbor, despite Manila, despite the Marshalls, and though she'd had no news from Otto in three months—she and the two children moved up to Portland, where they stayed with her parents and awaited news of Otto.

A telegram finally arrived in April stating that he had spent the last few months waiting for repairs on his ship, and he would be home very shortly.

◆   ◆   ◆

Cedric found his father sitting in the living-room with his mother and grandparents when he returned home from Bible School. He wasn't sure how to react. Otto was not a familiar face in the house, he was more like a distant relative who dropped in for a short stay now and then. But Otto broke the ice with some war mementos: a Japanese helmet, a diffused hand grenade, several bullets, a pack of army food rations and nautical drawings. He Otto explained that he had been in Manila when it was bombed, and he had been on one of the last ships to limp out and make it to safe port, where they then had to wait several weeks for repairs.

Otto remained at home for two weeks, and much of that time was spent hosting parties for his many acquaintances among the Navy officers and merchant mariners home on leave. Sailors of various nationalities would start arriving around eight or nine in the evening with a sack full of jokes, a pouch of pipe or rolling tobacco, and a bottle of something nice. There were always a few arriving in port that day, or departing the next, and for the latter it was often Cedric's duty to make sure that they made it back to their ships on time the following morning.

Otto explained how it worked and Cedric listened attentively. "Okay son, so you ask each man as he walks in whether he's leaving the next day. If he is, you take down the name of the ship and the time he needs to get there. Then the next morning you call Broadway 1234 and ask for as many cabs as you need—count three guys per cab, so usually you only need one or two—then take money from my wallet—it's about seventy cents to the port—and give the cabbie the names of the sailors' ships…"

Cedric took on the responsibility and soon came to enjoy it. The major difficulty resided in getting the sailors into the cabs, but his cousins Donald and Roger lent a hand when they were around, and the cabbies were almost always happy to help also. He felt grown-up and responsible, but it was for the breakfast and that moment on deck with the kind officers in starch that he returned. Especially the British—they thought think it was a kick to have kids bring back their drunken sailors. Cedric even took little Kurt along a few times, and his brother became more boisterous than usual. At four, Kurt was perfectly capable of coherent speech, but on the ships he returned to a cooing and gargling mass of happiness running up and down the gangways, crawling through portholes, and sniping food from the kitchen. Cedric would just stare out at the sea shimmering in the morning haze like a mirage in the desert heat.

Then Otto received his new orders: he was appointed first mate on the *Rufus King* bound for the South Pacific and tentatively Australia.

Cedric wasn't exactly sad to see his father go. It wasn't bad having him around, but it was almost a disruption to the usual routine around which his extended family organized their lives. The house on Halsey Street, with its five rooms and one bathroom, was home to fifteen people: Cedric and his mother, his grandparents, his uncles and aunts and his cousins. One more person just added to the crowd.

Yet that was set to change. Before his departure, Otto told his family that he had bought them a house on Arletta Street, in a better part of town. "You're the man of the house now, Cedric," he told his son. And in the lurching consciousness of his future, Cedric knew he'd be doing a lot of coping on his own.

2

Along with most of the other kids in grade school, Cedric took manual training classes: woodwork, carpentry and model construction, among other things. Their teacher, Simon Lovegrun, worked outside the class for a freely circulated newspaper called *The Shopping News*. Since the paper barely survived on advertising, Mr. Lovegrun came up with the idea to hire a few of the more dependable kids in his class to help with the paper route. Though it meant that Cedric had to wake up every Tuesday and Thursday morning at six o'clock, wrap the papers and deliver them before school, the company supplied Cedric with a rusty old bike, and that almost seemed payment enough. At the end of the year Mr. Lovegrun, impressed with Cedric's diligence, recommended him for a daily route with a subscription paper, *The Oregon Journal*. Cedric was promoted to station manager three years later, a job that consisted of supervising the unloading of the truck when it arrived from the printers at five thirty in the afternoon, and distributing paper routes the following morning to the twelve kids he had working for him. If someone didn't show up, Cedric had to know their route and make sure the papers were delivered.

His friends and acquaintances were always struck by his joviality and optimism, and indeed he tended to meander through the Dedalus of life with a joke and a heart-warming smile, keeping the more morose thoughts to himself. Otto and Marjorie were hardly the most emotionally expressive of parents, after all, and it takes time—if ever—to emerge from the shadow of one's upbringing. But soon after he turned fifteen, Cedric found himself drifting—aimless, uninspired and, though he would not admit it, bored. With school, with boy scouts, with his paper route...Sometime after Christmas 1949 Cedric inquired for a job at several drugstores. But it was just a pretext: he was more interested at this point in increasing a hundredfold the necessary components for gunpowder which he had read about in his new chemistry set. He walked into the first, bought a pound of saltpeter and asked if there was work available. He went into the second, bought a pound of sulfate and asked if there was work available…

By early evening he'd been turned down by all the drugstores that he'd visited but he had all the components he needed to make several pounds of gunpowder. He spent the next day calculating and cutting wick lengths, so that he could set off separate loads of gunpowder simultaneously. That afternoon he went into the backyard with his homemade one-item chemistry set, divided the gunpowder into five equal parts and affixed the wicks. He then lit the first fuse with his right hand, and started the stopwatch that he held in his left. He moved onto the next fuse and lit that twenty seconds after the first. He proceeded until he'd lit all five wicks, then he moved quickly away as the five lengths of string sizzled and sparkled down towards the batches of gunpowder. He had little time to wonder what he had got himself into when the they exploded—to his immense satisfaction—almost at the same time.

When the smoke cleared he realized that the garden was torched—no more tulips, no more rhododendron bushes, just a large patch of pummeled brown earth. He heard a whistle and a cough, and turned to see his mother and brother standing in the doorway. His smile faded: Kurt was beaming, Marjorie's stare had turned glacial, and Cedric knew that if he hadn't been too big to get spanked, he'd would've been be a wick's length away from getting the beating of his life.

He was grounded for a month. As much as his mother approved of his usual initiative to find work, she wouldn't even allow him that possibility for fear that he would cheat on the hours and sneak off with his friends. She knew his daily schedule, and how long it took to for him bike back from school or boy scouts. She set an alarm clock with a two-minute leeway, and told Cedric that if she ever heard that alarm clock go off…She never did. She would continue to use this practice every evening her son went out, up until the time he left for college.

There was little time to mope, however, and the pain of his grounding was eased by the news that he would soon be leaving Oregon and traveling by train across the United States for the first time in his life. Cedric had joined the same cub scout den as his childhood friend Dean McMullen almost six years before. There they met Paul Amort and Walt Jaspers, and the four of them formed an odd quartet of friendship. By the age of twelve they had all obtained the highest cub scout award, and entered Boy Scout troop 424 as Tenderfoots. After three years, they received their Eagle Scout distinction, and soon afterwards, there ceased to be any real challenge. Faced with several defections from the troop of the fifteen and sixteen year olds, their Scout Leader Ormond had called upon his friend John Miles, a half-Iroquois who spent his summers on Indian reservations, to help him galvanize the scouts with something new and appealing: Miles formed the Iroquois Clan with a group of sixteen older boys, including Cedric and his friends. The Patrol, as they later called it, started a fundraising campaign, and bought the necessary items to make their own Haudenosaunee regalia: kastoweh headgear, shirts and sashes, quilled and beaded bibs, kilts, leggings, breeches, and moccasins. They performed for birthdays and special events, half-time football shows and high school graduations, and acquired a statewide reputation. The kids became part of something special.

Then came the announcement that a National Boy Scout Jamboree was to be held at Valley Forge, Pennsylvania, end of June 1950. It was to be the first Jamboree to be organized since 1937. John Miles and Ormond Doty had convinced a few political bigwigs to have the City of Portland sponsor the participation of the Iroquois Patrol and have it perform at the convention. Cedric was finally going to travel beyond Oregon—all the way across the continent.

In June 1950, Cedric Grant left the state of Oregon for the first time since moving back there from Oakland at the age of seven.

An old steam train with lacquered and brocaded Pullman coaches had been specially chartered for the several hundred scouts traveling to Pennsylvania from the Pacific Northwest. It pulled into the station like a unicorn appearing in the Everglades—magnificent, ethereal, and not quite believable. Their first stop after picking up scouts in Seattle and Vancouver was Saint Louis. There they visited the Anheuser-Busch brewery, went to a jazz concert, and contemplated the cleared forty blocks of riverfront that had been chosen for Eero Saarinen's future architectural marvel, the Gateway Arch: a monument to the United States' westward expansion, the symbol of Manifest Destiny. Then they stopped in Washington D.C., and the White House...And the Capitol, the Washington Monument, the Lincoln Memorial...

The train finally chugged into Valley Forge on June 30, and few kids slept that night upon hearing the news that President Truman would be a speaker at the Jamboree on July 3, and General Dwight Eisenhower on Independence Day. And what a jamboree it was! More than a hundred thousand people—including 47,163 boy scouts—were gathered at the historical site where General George Washington's Continental Army had camped for six months before moving on to a definitive victory at Yorktown. Thirty-five separate camps sites circled the park's National Memorial Arch and were connected by temporary roads. Primary electric lines and water pipes had been installed, and the brown uniforms of the Scouts stretched as far as the eye could see.

On July 3, the Iroquois Patrol gave their performance on the large stage that had been constructed on the park's Grand Parade Ground. Later, Cedric had the honor of holding the United States flag, standing near President Truman while he gave his speech. It wasn't a long speech, and Truman didn't venture into esoteric politics, though he did make an oblique reference to the war in Korea which had just begun for the United States: "Scouting is based on the ideal of human brotherhood...There are movements in the world that would deny this fundamental ideal of brotherhood..." The scouts remained a full week in Valley Forge, before the Pullman coaches chugged north to New York City, sending black smoke into the humid heat of early July. This was the last stop before the train headed back home to Oregon. As soon as the scouts stepped onto 33rd Street outside of Penn Station, they could barely lower their heads. Cedric and Dean looked at one another and knew they were feeling the same thing: the invisible but vibrant energy of the City. "A *real* big city," Cedric sighed.

They spent three days there, and it was a struggle for Dean, Paul and Cedric to stay with the group, they wanted to head off into the urban jungle instead of just visiting the Empire State building, the Statue of Liberty and Ellis Island. On the morning of the third day, Dean convinced the two others to skip the group breakfast and branch out on their own. "The Waldorf-Astoria is right across the street—come on guys, let's live it up! Let's be Rockefellers just for one day!" So they slipped into civilian clothes and out of their modest hotel, stormed into the luxurious lobby of the crown jewel of hotels, and stood gaping for a short while on the carpeted mosaic, staring up at the massive chandelier. Dean boldly walked up to the Maître d' in the breakfast lounge and asked for a table. Their breakfast cost them four dollars apiece, almost half what they spent on the entire trip, but it was well worth it. "This lifestyle... *This*, I could get used to!" Cedric said to himself.

On the trip home, the train passed through Montreal, Detroit, Santa Fe, Albuquerque, Flagstaff, Los Angeles and San Francisco. When Cedric reached home on July 16, he found a note from his mother stating that she and Kurt had gone to the beach for a few days. "Food's in the fridge," the note ended. Cedric shrugged and walked out of the house. He decided it was time to look for a job, something that would enable him to buy at the end of the summer that hot-rod he'd seen at the Ford factory in Detroit.

The next day, he and Dean headed out of Portland, drove alongside the Columbia river, and soon come across a *Help Wanted* sign at the entrance to the L&H bean farm on Marine Drive. They located the field manager and were hired on the spot to load the bean bags onto the flatbed trucks for a dollar an hour.

They worked six days a week for the next two months until they entered their junior year of high school. They arrived at the farm full of energy at 6.30am, and left at 7.30pm depleted but still smiling, hearing war stories from the disgruntled field hands reduced to picking beans after their exciting roles in the Pacific. By the end of the summer Cedric found a 1934 Ford coupe for $125, and since that was considerably less than he'd anticipated, the money that remained was more than sufficient to carry him through the school year without having to work. It was the first time since he'd started delivering papers at the age of ten that he'd had such a long stretch without a job and without having to look for one. It would also be the last time for many years, until his plane accident had the side-effect of encouraging him to travel around the world.

He spent his junior year as if he were graduating that spring—he paraded the Ford coupe and attracted girls, he went to all the dances in the neighborhood (facilitated by one year of lessons and a tuxedo that his father had brought back from Hong Kong), and generally acted as though nothing really mattered. He wasn't *popular* in the classic high school sense of the term, but was well known—he was considered something of an oddball, a characteristic that would follow him for the rest of his life. The story of the gunpowder had circulated quite rapidly, and at one of the school dances Cedric showed up with a feather hat rigged with lights hooked to a battery pack around his waist. "Trying to liven things up!" he said, then added facetiously, "And get people to talk to me..." He was becoming more himself—gregarious and energetic and a little bizarre. To fill the hours freed up from not having a job, he went to a gym to lift weights. Since he couldn't get Dean, Walt or Paul to join him, he teamed up with a man in his early twenties, Gene, who happened to be taking flying lessons on the G.I. Bill. They would spot for one another on the free weights, and Cedric would ask Gene all about flying. Finally Gene invited Cedric to attend a ground course flight at his flying club one night a week, and told him that if he enjoyed it, he could take flying lessons that summer.

As soon as he finished his Junior year, Cedric was back at the L&H bean farm. Mornings he would take a flatbed truck down to skid-row to pick up any vagrant who was willing to hoe the fields and could haul himself onto the truck at six a.m. In the afternoon, he would load the flatbeds. He worked six and a half days a week, and began taking actual flying lessons on Sunday afternoons. He managed to find a few moments here and there for his girlfriend, Diane David, but otherwise his social life was negligible. This hardly bothered him—he was already thinking of college and beyond, and out of Portland.

Early in the fall of his senior year Cedric hurt himself badly enough in a football game to give up the sport. To compensate he began boxing lessons, and after his first fight—where he was pummeled into submission after three grueling rounds—he chatted with the guy who beat him. They got on well, went out for lunch, and in the course of the afternoon Cedric found out that his erstwhile opponent had just been drafted for Korea. He'd held a job in the stockroom at Nicholas Ungar, the number one perfume and cosmetic store for women in downtown Portland: he offered his position to Cedric. Senior year went by swiftly but dully and Cedric was itching to get out. Perhaps college wasn't a ticket out of Oregon—he would be attending the University of Oregon in Eugene—but it was a step out of Portland.

He attended his high school graduation, received his diploma, bought a carnation and took Diane to the prom. At two o'clock in the morning, Cedric drove Diane home, and four hours later he was at the L&H farm reporting for work his third summer in a row. Within a week the field manager promoted him to supervisor, and Cedric's physical workload dropped as his responsibilities increased. He was soon bored, however: the heavy rains of the past few days had made picking impossible, and there was little to be done. Cedric decided to get another job. He hopped in his Ford Coupe, and on his way back into town he passed a *Help Wanted* sign outside the American Can Company. He inquired within, and fell upon a startled employer who told him that that the sign had been put out only five minutes earlier. He liked Cedric's initiative, as haphazard as it may have been in this case, and as Cedric was halfway through listing his past work experience, the manager interrupted to him to ask him his age. All he needed to know was that Cedric was eighteen, and he hired him immediately to work the night shift on the steel slitter starting the following night. So from eight to four, Cedric worked at the L&H bean farm; and from midnight to seven, at the American Can Company, he lifted sheets of metal with a magnetic handle and slid them into the cutter, trying not to lose any fingers in the process. He learned to fall asleep inside of thirty seconds, wherever that might be.

For his first summer out of high school he was making $180 dollars a week, more than his father after thirty years at sea, and in a month he would be the first person in his family to enter University.

◆   ◆   ◆

Cedric started classes at the University of Oregon in the fall of 1952. Just before he left, his father gave him three pieces of advice: "Don't get married till you're thirty, don't have children till you're thirty-five, and study a subject in school that you'll never be able to take again." Well, he wasn't too concerned about the first two issues, but Cedric had no idea what he should choose as a major. What might be a good foundation for a future career? What career? Did he have to decide now? He began to lean towards the negative…Perhaps that was the point of all these choices. Cedric thought of a novel he'd read recently, *The Sheltering Sky* by Paul Bowles set in the Sahara desert: he considered the title wholly inappropriate for the setting—here in Oregon was the sheltering sky, a constant bleak tar-streaked white that shut out the rest of the world and pressed down on you and curbed your spine until you were sucking on your shoe laces…He wanted his life to mean something. Perhaps he needed more time, more exposure. Perhaps to get out of Portland permanently, he needed to leave Oregon for a while and finish his education later with a better idea of where he was heading.

A thought struck him immediately: why not enlist? Go fight Communism in Korea and come back on the GI Bill!

His trip that very same afternoon to the Marine Recruitment Bureau soon dispelled any hopes he may have had. "There are better ways to pay for an education, and I've filled my quota for the year," the sergeant told him, "Besides, we need officers, not canon fodder. Stick with ROTC, get a college degree and an officer rank, and come back and see me then." Cedric trudged back to his dorm room unable to decide if it was for the best. There wasn't much choice and it still left him stranded. And still unsure of how to pay for his next semester in college.

Soon after he'd arrived in Eugene, Cedric found work as a slash-burner, tramping around the Oregon forests every Friday and Saturday night, scorching the earth to prevent fires in logged areas, and to help the ground rejuvenate during the winter. His earnings over the summer and as a slashburner were already depleted, however, and if he managed the bean farm-American Can rotation again next summer, he would be able to pay for another two semesters, but the problem of the immediate next still remained. As undecided as he was regarding a course of study, he didn't want to start taking time off from college this soon in the game. Of course he could always borrow money but where to find the loan? His father immediately came to mind, but he dismissed it quickly as a last resort.

That Christmas, Paul Amort decided to marry his pregnant girl-friend. It was a dismal affair, Cedric thought with the sadness he felt for a friend marrying his first girlfriend through some conceptual accident. But he maintained a smile throughout and sipped the Californian bubbly that passed for champagne. If he were to be absolutely honest, however, he had to admit that there was something about the wedding that tugged on an emotional rope. The fact of the wedding itself, the ritualistic process of entering adulthood, compounded Cedric's uncertainty about his own future. He recalled the conversation with his friends at Amort's father's ski cabin on Mount Hood where Dean had said that none of them would never escape Portland. He remembered Paul and Walt's reaction—how they didn't have the urge to *escape*—and he felt almost envious of the certainty they displayed in their view of life.

At the wedding, he sat with Diane and her parents at the table closest to the bride and groom and their families. Inevitably, Diane's father asked what career he was considering. "I haven't even chosen a major," Cedric said.

Dr. David clapped Cedric on the shoulder. "I'll tell you what's made *me* happy for the past twenty years, Cedric: it's *medicine*! Medicine is detective work within Nature, studying the elements, trying to find a *pattern*...And yet there's the human contact, and the satisfaction that you're making *people's* lives more comfortable. You should consider becoming a doctor, Cedric. Study pre-med, go to U of O medical school, and you'll have a practice waiting for you with me very soon after that!...You'll be *settled*, make good money..."

Cedric drained his champagne glass and fled.

A few months earlier, Cedric had taken a weekend off work to go to a fraternity party with Diane at Theta Chi. It was probably the only time he'd been to a frat party, and since it happened to be an informal rush party—and since he was his voluble self at the party and his vivacious girlfriend impressed many an upperclassman—Cedric found himself asked to pledge Theta Chi. He pondered the issue for two weeks. Two weeks where he began a job as a houseboy at the Alpha Chi Omega sorority (and the sight of those beautiful women growling on Sunday morning, their hangovers illustrated by smudged make-up and knotted hair, further entrenched his temporary vow of civil celibacy), and decided from a housing point of view at least that the pledging made sense. He also perceived, albeit hazily, the possible contacts he could make, even if the term *networking* hadn't yet permeated the undergraduate job search culture. He stayed at Theta Chi for just over a year until his various jobs provided him with breakfast, lunch and dinner, and he spent so little time at the fraternity house that he moved out at the beginning of his Junior year. He no longer needed the room, and he failed to see the possible advantages in knowing a bunch of kids who got plastered every weekend.

That summer, and for the next four summers until he graduated, Cedric fell into an exhausting work routine: he supervised the picking of beans and loading of bags at the L&H farm from eight in the morning till four in the afternoon, then separated steel sheets and fed them to the slitter at the American Can Company from midnight to seven with quarter-hour catnaps at two and four in the morning. This rotation left him so little time for extracurricular activities that he and Diane agreed that it would be best if they split up.

At least he had made enough money to purchase a 1941 Buick convertible with a powder cerulean blue exterior and cordovan leather upholstery that made him an instant prized star when the women of the Alpha Chi Omega sorority found it parked in front of their house. It was not a splurge of pride or the result of boredom with his previous car, but a case of pure necessity. Before heading back to Eugene, Cedric had prepped his old Ford for the winter by re-filling the radiator; unfortunately, to save money, he had replaced the use of antifreeze with alcohol, and a few miles out of Portland when the car died, Cedric found the radiator blocked with black sludge that made the car irrecoverable.

Upon his return to campus sophomore year, Cedric postponed his choice of a major to keep his options open. Despite his initial reaction, Dr. David's words had their effect, and Cedric found himself enrolling in courses that would fulfill the pre-med requirements. He also figured that the perfect place to learn up close what a doctor's job entailed would be the school infirmary. He was aware that theoretical classes in biology and chemistry could not really allow him to judge the medical profession, and he had found little information on the subject from the people he knew, including Diane's father. He dropped his work at the Alpha Chi Omega sorority when he found a job in the university infirmary washing dishes and delivering meals to patients, morning, noon, and evening.

Through his work he met a young orderly who worked at the local Sacred Heart Hospital, and for over an hour Cedric listened to him brag about his wonderful job—fraternizing with the doctors and nurses, attending to the patients, and basically getting paid good money for not a whole lot of work. The next day, Cedric visited the Hospital reception, spoke with the nurse in charge, and was harshly rejected: their waiting list was two hundred and fifty applicants long. He returned two days later armed with forty-eight hours of reflection: he offered his services for free. It was done without machiavellian intent—he'd simply gambled on the fact that no-one could refuse a volunteer—but the Head Nurse liked his initiative so much that she fired the other orderly and hired Cedric instead.

He would keep the job until the end of his college career, emptying bedpans, answering phones, prepping patients for surgery, turning the paraplegics every two hours to prevent bedsores. Towards the end of his time there, he even performed catheterization and cast-cutting which he learned from befriended interns. It wasn't quite legal, but the interns only allowed him to don the white coat and handle patients when they were confident that Cedric wouldn't screw up. As much as he enjoyed the job, however, Cedric was thoroughly disillusioned with any idea he may have entertained of studying medicine by the end of his sophomore year. He found that few doctors were dedicated professionals, most were uninspired at best, and a good portion were arrogant and prissy, and cared more about money and social prestige than their patients and the Hippocratic oath.

Cedric eventually dropped pre-med classes and concentrated on philosophy and religion, finally taking his father's advice to heart: expand the mind and soul, he thought, there would always be time for numbers and statistics and budgets and market strategies later. He was now making enough money to cover all of his college expenses (as well as purchase a 1952 MG-TD convertible), and at this rate he would graduate only a semester late.

◆   ◆   ◆

The same year Cedric graduated, Marjorie and Otto decided to divorce. Neither Kurt nor Cedric were particularly surprised, and both their parents seemed happier in their own way after adjusting to life apart—love might fade away, but proximity can become a habit harder to break. Marjorie found work with the immigration bureau, and Otto moved to Los Angeles.

In December 1956, along with his Bachelors of Arts, Cedric obtained the rank of Second Lieutenant of the US infantry. He remained on campus and worked in the infirmary and at the Sacred Heart Hospital until the spring of the following year, and attended his graduation ceremony with a mixture of refulgence, sadness and nervous anticipation: it was the culmination of a series of achievements, but the moment itself seemed void of promise, or rather it seemed to encapsulate a collection of memories upon which to reflect. Cedric wanted to look forwards not backwards and that took energy and confidence.

He had interviewed on campus with the American Can company, and had been offered to join their management team. But Cedric first had to deal with military service. A few days after his graduation, he packed his affairs and headed to California to visit his brother who, as a Marine, had been selected to join the Radiological-Safety personnel in Operation Plumbbob. That summer, Kurt would be sent to Yucca Flat, Nevada, to monitor radiation and operate Geiger counters in two atomic testings. On June 24, at Camp Desert Rock, Kurt witnessed his first explosion in Area 5—a thirty-seven kiloton bomb named "Priscilla" that formed a blinding seven hundred foot balloon. On July 15, the second seventeen-kiloton bomb was detonated in Area 2B, and the thermonuclear tower reached five hundred feet into the air. With his back turned to the explosion, Kurt could see the X-ray image of the man standing in front of him.

In the mean time, Cedric sweated out as a paratrooper at Fort Benning, Georgia, in the middle of a sweltering June. The Army was exactly as he imagined it—stale male bonding, a lulling sense of disciplined adventure, mild hazing, and recondite orders followed without question. He learned the recoil of every possible weapon—from a .45 caliber and the carbine, to the 105 Howitzer—absorbed attack/defense tactics, experienced the thrill of his first jump, confronted the fear of the second (he found it more terrifying when he knew what he was about to face), and then the excitement of those that followed.

One of them was planned on the night of a perfect full moon to take place over an abandoned landing strip—the elements were all there, but trouble might possibly have been avoided if the plane hadn't dropped the paratroopers precisely when the moon was aligned in such a way as to bounce off the tarmac in a shimmering water-like induced reflection. The paratroopers swooped down, assumed they were jumping over a lake, and released their chutes twenty feet above ground. There no were deaths but many shattered bones. Cedric escaped with a broken foot and a nasty case of poison ivy that had him nailed to the hospital bed and covered in chamomile lotion for a week. It was during this time that he began to consider the possibility of an Army career. It was a life that could suit him well…

Then he heard the incapacitating news: Sergeant Jameson had been wrong, there had been little need for more officers; in fact the end of the Korean War had created a surplus and the ensuing reduction in forces effectively demoted officers—they maintained their official rank but assumed duties far below their status. There was no room for people like 2nd Lieutenant Cedric Grant. His two years of military service were cut down to six months and he was shuffled into the reserves by the end of the year. In early December he loaded the MG and drove seventy-two hours straight across the country with two other west coast victims of the RIF's, heading home to uncertainty.

By the time he reached Portland he'd decided to join American Can Company's Management Trainee program. He knew the work, the people and the company—and they had plants operating around the country. The money was good, the chance of traveling and living outside of Portland were a distinct possibility, and Cedric knew that those reasons were as good as any to embark on a career path that he now realized did not necessarily have to be permanent.

The American Can Company in Portland, Oregon, had been rocked by a series of strikes and spontaneous walk-outs. Over the years, management and the United Steel Workers Union had exchanged bitter words. By 1957, grievances were being submitted on a daily basis, and labor-management relations remained tenuous at best. The policy of American Can until then had been to hire graduate engineers to oversee aspects of their plants and increase worker efficiency. These diligent worker bees of management had little experience with the nuts and bolts of the industry, and if one of them were to attempt to feed a sheet of metal into the cutter, they were likely to end up with a few crushed digits. Not the most effective way to impress labor. On top of the labor strikes, American Can soon suffered a wave of resignations in management.

The company decided to change its policy. It began hiring people like Cedric who'd spent time in the factories while acquiring a college degree, and trained them in engineering principals. Cedric was assigned to plant 92A in Portland where he knew most of the men and women in the Union. His fears of envy or resentment were quickly dispelled when he realized that the company had gambled correctly—his former fellow workers considered him proof that it was possible to be promoted from within, and that the company had listened to their complaints and put in charge someone who knew their work and the fundamentals of the industry. Cedric was one of them, and though he wore a suit and tie, his tie was loose and his sleeves were rolled up to the elbows. Within six months he was promoted to Acting Night Foreman.

A chance encounter in early 1958 led to Cedric's transfer from the Airborne Infantry Reserves to Military Intelligence where the presence of a 2nd Lieutenant was required. A wild notion germinated in the minds of Cedric's friends when they took a hard look at his varied activities, though Cedric remained blissfully unaware that anyone could consider him a spy. He believed that his employer's deference at work was due to his hard work, he considered his girlfriend Katy Rapp's subdued awe to be the result of his charm and wit, and he considered Dean's insinuations to be innocent banter, until it finally dawned on him that people thought he worked for the CIA. Russian language courses, flying lessons, military intelligence—it all added up, and once he was aware of the fact Cedric did nothing to dispel their illusions. The charade allowed him to lie to himself about the fact that he was actually feeling more comfortable about settling in Portland. Dean was speaking of fatherhood, Amort's wife was expecting her third child, and even Walt was engaged. So when Katy announced that she was pregnant, just as Cedric was about to board the plan to Signal School at Fort Gordon to earn his commission as First Lieutenant, he took the news in stride and accepted the prospect of marriage almost with relief. For three hot weeks he thought about it incessantly but without alarm. He envisioned his life in Portland with Katy and a baby serenely, or at least so he imagined. He was in fact continuing to lie to himself, to convince himself that this is what he wanted, simply because no other alternative presented itself immediately to his mind. As a result, a frustration of which he was not even aware began to build within him.

When he returned to Portland and heard a sheepish Katy announce that it had been a false alarm, Cedric vented his bottled up emotions in an unusual burst of anger. "You could have called me in Georgia to let me know! It's not easy coming to grips with the fact that you're going to be a father, especially when the news is thrown at you as you're boarding a plane!" When Katy asked what he planned to do, he suggested that they don't rush into things. Katy agreed. Cedric later realized that she had been as unprepared to be catapulted into family life as he had.

A few months later, and without the added pressure of an unplanned pregnancy, they'd both agreed that marriage might not be such a bad idea after all.

Once he'd made up his mind, Cedric knew that his marriage proposal could not simply be made on his knees in a classy restaurant at the end of a candlelit dinner. It had to be something unique—like jumping out of a plane over Mount Hood.

The plane that he'd learned to pilot, and therefore the one he planned to jump out of, was the BT13 "Valiant", a World War II low-wing cantilever single-engine plane used for training pilots, and not specifically designed for parachute jumping. But it had the advantage of seating a crew of two in tandem, and though the pilot and co-pilot were covered by a transparent canopy of thermoplastic, they each had separate sliding panels. Still, Cedric was not sure he would be able to jump out of such a plane. He spoke to Elliott, the person he considered to be the most proficient pilot at their club, and presented his idea. Elliott was excited, and assured Cedric that they could pull back his portion of the canopy in flight, while he flipped the plane upside-down so that Cedric would simply drop out and dive down. The plan was set: the following Sunday, he arranged with Dean to convince Katy to join him on an excursion to Mount Hood. He would tell her that Cedric had a surprise for her—she would most likely guess the reason for the surprise, but she would probably not guess the method in which it would be presented. By the time the deadline arrived, the only thing Cedric was worried about was losing the engagement ring during the jump.

He and Elliott took off just after ten o'clock one September Sunday morning. The climb was unsteady due to some heavy wind currents, but finally they leveled out at eight thousand feet and headed east. They passed Mount Hood, flew over the Columbia River, then adjusted the flaps to circle back west. The weather could not have been more propitious.

A sharp rattling sound like a spanner caught in the cogs of a wheel jerked Cedric back to his surroundings. They had just passed back over the Columbia River when the Valiant sputtered and faltered, and, after a few stretched-out agonizing seconds, died in ominous silence. Cedric fumbled with his controls and Elliott did the same—instincts born of many lessons kicked in and they both assumed their respective tasks in trying to keep the plane steady and glide down as safely as possible. They were now at five thousand feet and dropping fast.

Everywhere below them timber stretched for miles. Cedric grappled with the controls but now the situation was beyond his knowledge, and even Elliott had done everything he could to avoid disaster. The plane was shaking heavily as they hurtled to the ground.

Then the moment passed, and they dropped with a sickening lurch as the trees came rushing towards them. A clearing suddenly gaped open on their right like the mouth of a sea monster but it was too late to direct the plane—they came within a few hundred feet of the clearing when Cedric heard the sound of torn and twisted metal of the right wing being ripped from its socket, and his head slammed against the controls—the seatbelt split, Cedric burst through canopy, and he felt the right side of his face melt away as he crumpled on the ground fifty feet from the plane…The Valiant lay on its right flank, the nose a mass of twisted iron, the tail jerked high in the sky.

3

It took several months for Cedric's body to heal, but he left the hospital after only six weeks thanks to an already muscular build honed by paratrooper training and frequent gym sessions. After the bones mended, he was left with only a few scars, some mangled veins, a drooping left eye, and the need to wear glasses. Elliott, however, was not so lucky, and Cedric returned to the hospital to visit his friend destined to be confined to a wheelchair for the rest of his life.

Cedric's visits passed in awkward silence spattered with infrequent one-liners, until finally Elliott told him to stop blaming himself. "I've done hundreds of flights like that, and it could've happened on any one of them. We didn't even flip the plane! It's not because of your wacky idea to propose marriage by jumping out of a plane that the accident happened. It was motor problems. It's the risk we take…" Cedric knew all that but he couldn't help but think that the accident occurred on a flight which *he'd* asked Elliott to make, and though hearing Elliott's words did alleviate some of the weight, the guilt was impossible to shake entirely.

Cedric returned to work at American Can in late autumn. For several days everyone expressed their sympathy and understanding, but within a week he was expected to function at full capacity. Yet he found his concentration faltering and his mind wandering—he needed a break. Memories of the plane crash came back to haunt him: he could feel the full extent of his mortality, and death was no longer an event that might occur at some point in the distant future, but a reality that could well have taken place just a few months before. He felt at times a survivor's exhilaration, and if his nights were sometimes filled with nightmares drawn from the crash, at least his days were buoyed by the surreal sensation of having come to grips with a life that might not have been. And it was too early, it was too much, to return to a daily routine as if nothing had changed. He decided to travel to Europe, a decision he relayed to Katy only on the eve of his departure.

He arrived in New York and took the first ship heading east, an ancient Italian steamer named *SS Vulcania*. Ten days later he was in Lisbon. For the first few days he thought of nothing and did nothing but lie on the beach outside of Lisbon and stare out to sea and let the tide wash away his past and bring in something new. Then he traveled south to Gibraltar and jumped across the strait and finally found in Casablanca among its desert dusted streets and alcoves some kind of liberation.

He drank mint tea and read a book, one of five that he'd brought along with him. He immersed himself in the story, became friends with its characters, and tore up the pages as he progressed, believing that his bag would be lighter and that he could always find an American library or books on sale and a PX store on a U.S. Army base somewhere. He spent Christmas in Morocco because Christmas there meant nothing really, and then he stayed for New Year's because he'd never passed from one year to the next under a bleached blue sky and a star-filled night while bathing in the Mediterranean.

He finished his book and all that remained were the front and back covers. So he traveled north to Madrid, but as soon as he arrived he knew he would find no inspiration within the washed yellow walls and the rubbed-raw cobblestones of the old city. He decided that he didn't like Madrid much and that it was the wrong place to be, so he caught a train the next day to Barcelona—a city ignored by Franco and an Old Town divided in two by the Ramblas—a city that suited his mood—and he ambled through the impressive harbor of Barceloneta, the geometrically perfect Ensanche quarter, the flower markets of the Ramblas, where he took a room, midway between the sea and Plaza Catalunya for a buck a day. He remained in Barcelona for three weeks.

Finally, when he'd torn out the last page in the last book he brought with him, and since there were no American bookstores or US Army bases to be found in Franco's Spain, he knew it was time to pack up and leave. *Today is January 20*th, he wrote in a postcard to his mother. *Tomorrow I am going to the Southern Coast of France, then Italy (Rome) and make it as far as possible.* He still carried with him the engagement ring that he'd meant to offer Katy as she walked out of church to see him fly down from the sky, and he decided in Rome that he could return to Portland for her and settle there with her, and that the ring was still meant for her. Then he found a few more books to read in a musty library and decided to continue traveling east. He crossed the Adriatic to make his way through Greece and paused briefly in Athens to finish another book and write another postcard to his mother. Eventually he boarded a ship chartered to carry convicted criminals to a high security prison in Alexandropoulos. He arrived in Istanbul, and found a cheap room in a youth hostel not far from the Hagia Sofia. He remained there for several days, scouring the sprawling city on foot until he reached exhaustion, and then he walked some more until he felt the need to return home.

It was not homesickness he was experiencing, but the desire to finalize the decision he had reached in Rome. At the end of February, he booked a second-class passage on the Orient Express and enjoyed a semi-luxurious trip back to London. Upon his return to Portland, he resumed his work at the American Can Company with renewed energy and decided to present Katy with the engagement ring on the midnight that separated their two birthdays, March 20–21.

Five days before that fateful day, however, on a Monday that effectively and decisively changed the course of his future and realigned it with his earlier visions of living far from Portland, Cedric was called into the plant manager's office and told that he was one of twelve people specially selected for a "Time-and-Motion study program" designed to increase productivity at American Can plants around the country. The program was two years long and would take him to several factories around the country. Cedric readily accepted the position. Two weeks later he took off for Kansas City without ever telling Katy about the ring which he left in the kitchen drawer of his mother's apartment on the eve of his departure. When he returned to Portland on July 4 for "home leave", Katy confronted him with their decision to get married. The answer came to him immediately and clearly: he had no wish to get married just yet. He told Katy that she should perhaps look around for someone a little more stable, a little more conventional. He just wasn't willing to settle down.

Cedric was soon making more than he was spending—saving his eight hundred-dollar monthly salary, and living off his six hundred-dollar expense account. He became good friends with two of his fellow trainees, Russ Taylor and Harry Overtoom. But they were soon separated when their training time ended after six weeks, and their real jobs began on their next posting—Harry was sent to Chicago, while Russ and Cedric went to New Jersey.

On their first tour of the plant accompanied by the manager, they arrived dressed in coats and ties and clipboard in hand, to assess how the plant could be rearranged to improve productivity. They were eyed suspiciously by the men working the machines, and for the first time Cedric realized the human impact of his mission. His job was to submit reports on how to decrease extraneous time between shifts and within a worker's own movements around the machines: the impact could mean cutting labor costs. He knew from the look in the factory hands' eyes that he and Russ belonged to a branch of management for which they had very little love. To ingratiate himself, Cedric handed his clipboard to Russ and walked over the cutter, the same machine he had worked for five summers in a row back in Portland. He asked the man in charge if he couldn't try his hand at feeding steel sheets into the cutter. The man laughed loudly and exchanged knowing glances with his colleagues. The plant manager tried to tell Cedric that he would more than likely slice a few fingers off, but before he could finish his sentence Cedric was feeding the hungry machine faster than most of the men working in the factory. His instincts kicked in, and soon he was lost in a series of automatic motions that took him back momentarily to those long summer nights in Portland, plant 92A. Finally the man in charge of the cutter tapped him on the shoulder and asked if he would join the guys for lunch.

This graphic introduction made Cedric's later suggestions much more easily accepted. His knowledge of the workers' job helped him and Russ build a rapport with labor that reflected well on their status sheet, and Russ was grateful to Cedric. When their time in New Jersey came to end (Cedric was slated to go to Indianapolis while Russ was transferred to company headquarters in Chicago) Russ invited his friend to spend the weekend with him and his family in Connecticut—which is how Cedric discovered that Russ was the son of the man next in line to assume the chairmanship of American Can Company, Russ Taylor Sr., an association that would serve him well when he began looking for a job after traveling the world for two years.

When he arrived in Indianapolis, Cedric and Harry decided to room together. But very soon, the responsibilities of his job began to weigh on him: he never quite recovered from the first time he was forced to consider a reduction of the labor contingent, and he began to wonder once again why he remained in a job which held less and less appeal. On Thanksgiving Day, 1959, Cedric rented a car, drove into the countryside, and spent two days in a motel staring at the ceiling, flipping through the Tibetan Book of the Dead, and finding himself flooded with renewed thoughts of his plane crash. He told himself that he had not capitalized on the freedom it should have provided him. Cedric knew that he owed it to himself and to Elliott to leave American Can Company, to avoid spending any more time doing something he didn't like if there were other options.

A month later, Harry came home one evening to find Cedric, brow furrowed, surrounded by colorful brochures. "See, that's Perugia, Italy, there's Vienna, then of course the Goethe Institute in Rotterdam, the Sorbonne in Paris, and here's Santander, Spain..." He looked up at

Harry with blazing eyes and the story came pouring out: he had almost ten thousand dollars in his bank account, and he wanted to travel, to see Europe again, to feel that he was expanding and not just around the waistline. There was little Harry could say or do faced with Cedric's determination except give encouragement and wish him good luck. When Cedric was slated for transfer to St. Paul, Minnesota, in January 1960, he resigned. And on the first frosty day of March, Cedric set foot on European soil at Bremerhaven, West Germany.

◆   ◆   ◆

Over the next year and a half, Cedric followed a circuitous route through Europe—hitting Perugia, Vienna, Leningrad, Rottenburg, Paris, and Santander—before heading to the Middle East, Africa and finally Southeast Asia. The only time Portland entered his mind, after he'd settled in for the long haul, was when he wrote postcards home to his mother or to Dean, and even then he had difficulty placing himself within the context of that far-flung western town. His time was here and now, wherever that may be. Homesickness remained a word nestled in the dictionary between 'homerun' and 'homespun'.

He arrived on a cold Sunday in this small town nestled in the hills between Florence and Rome. The storefronts were shuttered and uninviting, and only a few forlorn souls wandered the streets. Cedric had sat down on an Etruscan wall, unable to marvel at the 2500 year old seat he had chosen, remembered the well-paying and travel-friendly job which he had left behind, and for one moment wondered what the hell he was doing in such a godforsaken place. But his spirits lifted as soon as began classes at the "Università Italiana per Stranieri".

Dear Dean and Karen,

I've finally settled down, and I feel as if Perugia and the Umbria region were my home. I live with an Italian family consisting of mamma, pappa, a twenty-year old son, an eighteen year-old daughter (wow!) and a fifteen *year-old son (none of whom speak English). We live on the top floor of a new apartment building (nine floors) and it has a wonderful view of the medieval city and the Tiber River Valley. There are very few Americans here at the university, though I've met an International Correspondent for the Associated Press taking courses here, and I will be riding with him to Rome or Florence every weekend to see the sights and meet some of his friends. My classes are at the University for Foreigners, founded in 1921 under the auspices of Mussolini himself—interesting paradox! I'm really enjoying the whole works, and able to live on less than $75 a month.*

The fact that Cedric's host family lived in a "new" apartment building meant that there were no leaks when it rained and they had use of a refrigerator—the presence of such an appliance was finally starting to grow in Perugia—yet Cedric still needed coins to take his shower in the morning, and he had to join the women on their trek down to the icy-cold streams to do his laundry every other weekend. When he asked Pappa in his gradually improving Italian why he didn't buy a laundry machine for his wife, Pappa almost choked on his rigatoni. "What? And have her around all day? No, no! And her friends' husbands—they would never speak to me again. They would *kill* me!"

The AP correspondent sold Cedric his Lambretta motoscooter when his own language course ended, and from then on Cedric roamed the countryside with the wind in his hair and the sun on his face, feeling very content at having left time-and-motion studies four thousand miles away. He obtained his Basic Italian language certificate at the end of May, packed his army duffel bag, strapped it to the Lambretta, bid effusive farewells to Mamma and Pappa and headed to Vienna, where he spent sunny days and weekends reading in the Mozartgarten or strolling around the city. Within a week he had toured the traditional sights—Mozart's home, Stefanskirche, Schönbrün Palace…Most often he went riding on his motoscooter or joined acquaintances from the language program for extended dips in the Danube. He took advantage of the rainy days to visit the museums, and as often as he could afford it he went to the opera.

The idea of writing home came to him less and less frequently, but he managed a quick card to his mother, and then a longer letter to Dean upon his return from a organized trip to the Soviet Union that had been advertised on the language school bulletin board. *We visited Minsk, Smolensk, Leningrad, and Moscow…Moscow is a drab, sprawling city, although maybe that's because we were taken everywhere by the hand like the cub scouts we used to be. But the Kremlin and the size of the Red Square are mind-boggling! In Gorky Park we saw the remains of the U2 spy plane which was of particular interest to me. Wonder what has happened to Gary Powers?…I provoked a scene in Gorky Park! Just before getting on this huge Ferris Wheel, some of my classmates jokingly made machine-gun motions and sounds "Amerikanski! Amerikanski!"—I'm the only American in the group—and when I got off the wheel I was mobbed by a group of kids. You'd think they were seeing an extraterrestrial!…*

The program in Vienna ended after two months, and Cedric had a few weeks before the next program started in Rottenburg. He decided to pursue his explorations behind the Iron Curtain, notably Hungary, Bulgaria, Romania, and Yugoslavia. The drab and dismal surroundings of Budapest made him so depressed, however, that he decided not only to leave after two days, but also to forego the rest of his East European excursion: if Hungary was considered the most open and westernized of the Soviet bloc, as he had been told, then he had little desire on this trip and on the eve of autumn, to visit the other countries. He hopped on his motoscooter and fled west, leaving behind as the only highlight to this foray east of the Iron Curtain the memory of a beautiful Hungarian girl with stainless steel teeth.

Cedric reached France thirty hours later in utter agony. As he was traversing Germany, boils began to appear on his legs. Large, ugly, itchy welts, that made him scream in pain every time he hit a bump in the road. Despite the physical annoyance he was not overly concerned—there were only a few at first—but by the time he reached Luxemburg, they had multiplied all over his body. The welts achieved a deep crimson before bursting and releasing noxious pus. So once again he shunted his plans and headed to the one place he hoped could cure him of whatever ailment he was afflicted: the U.S. military general hospital in Würzburg. But to no avail: the doctor examined him cursorily and gave him some penicillin that did nothing to clear up the pus-oozing welts. When he arrived in Rottenburg three days later to start at the Goethe Institute, they not only hadn't cleared up, but now numbered ten, and Cedric was starting to worry. The boils were a result of *something* he had done, something real, something physical, like eating the wrong food. He hated not knowing, as much as he hated the pain resulting from the boils, and was afraid that it might be something serious.

Like in Perugia, the Goethe Institute in Rottenburg had assigned him a *Gastfamilie*, a host family that took in students to supplement their income. Within two hours of Cedric's arrival, his affable host mother asked him why he was walking funny. Cedric shed his shame and removed his pants to show her the despicable blistering boils. She immediately dragged him to the family doctor, who almost immediately assessed that Cedric had contracted a spore swimming in the Danube in Vienna. The doctor drew blood from the vein in Cedric's arm, and injected it into his hip muscle. Then he threw away the syringe and smiled at Cedric. "Good! Finished! That is all…" And true enough, the itch quickly faded, the welts surrendered and beat a hasty retreat. Within a few days only some minor scars remained as witnesses of the savage attack, but even they disappeared in time.

The experience forged a link with his host family, and particularly with his host father, Herr Brunig, with whom he spent long evenings exchanging views on their respective countries, before Herr Brunig felt comfortable enough to recount his tales of the Eastern Front during World War II, and the horrific retreat from Stalingrad. They skirted the issue of Nazism; nevertheless, Cedric couldn't shake the proximity of history, of a time when two monstrous personalities grabbed the conscience of the twentieth century at both ends, and like a chicken wishbone snapped it in two. He would never forget those evening conversations with Herr Brunig, and for the first time he thought about perhaps writing some stories on the people he met on his travels.

Cedric left Rottenburg reluctantly. But the language program there ended with the month of November, and a new one awaited him in Paris. He found in the French capital a good deal of interest in his native tongue, despite France's growing antagonism towards the United States under President de Gaulle, and very quickly he was able to fill his mornings before class with group English language lessons for company executives: Otis Elevator, Colgate, Palmolive…Once his own classes began, he moved to the Cité Universitaire, which was further from the Bohemian lifestyle of the Latin Quarter but which enabled him to live for less than a hundred dollars a month. Thanks to his tutoring, Cedric was once again earning more than he was spending—adding to, rather than depleting, his travel funds.

For New Year's he avoided the party organized in the American Pavilion where he lived, as well as the throng of revelers on the Champs-Elysées. He shared instead a bottle of Moët Chandon with his new girlfriend Susan—a fellow language student from London—and they sat sipping the champagne on the Pont Neuf looking at the lights lining the Seine. When they ambled back to the Pavilion in the early morning hours, Susan pointed at a notice on the billboard hanging in the commons room and jokingly told Cedric that here was another experience for him to indulge in: *Major French/Italian production is seeking two English speaking men to play talking roles as American GI's.* Yes, well, Cedric with his Fifties crew-cut and powerful build could easily pass for a GI, but he dismissed the notion as a fantasy. Yet he couldn't help to contemplate for a brief instance the possibility of appearing on screen, and he found himself two days later at the appointed place and time with a book under his arm to see if, perchance, there wasn't room for a neophyte like himself.

Two hundred hopefuls were milling around, chatting nervously, parading their portfolios, trying to ascertain whether their neighbor had more or less experience. One man stood out from a the rest, tall and good-looking with a brooding assurance that made everyone think—at least Cedric certainly—that there was only one role left. Cedric sat down next to him against the wall and started reading a book. Twenty minutes later, French director Jean-Pierre Melville entered the hall. Everyone fell silent as he walked through the throng, observing the candidates. He asked no-one for the portfolios, he paused briefly before the tall man, and then before Cedric. Finally he pointed to both of them and said, "You and you—you are my soldiers. Everyone else: thank you for coming. That is all."

Cedric's elation was short-lived. For four days he listened to Melville's constant drone—two days of shooting separated by two days of loafing around while other scenes were being filmed. A fun, interesting, and educational experience that emphasized the "making" in movie-making and stripped "movie" of its magic. On the movie set of *Léon Morin, Prêtre*, Cedric befriended a priest, Pàl Zölt, who had been hired to coach the lead actor, Jean-Paul Belmondo, in his role as a priest who falls in love with a Parisian mother just after the war. They continued to meet after Cedric's two scenes had been shot, and for the first time since Bible School, Cedric found himself going to Mass given by Pàl on Sundays, followed by lunch at the monastery where the priest resided.

He had reached that stage in the art of travel when the time to look back on his life in Portland had long since passed, and his existence had become very much his life in Paris. He worked, studied, and *lived* there; gone was the desire for motion. Yet the city remained foreign to him nonetheless. The cobblestone streets and old buildings of Paris contrasted sharply with the broad avenues, strip malls, and expanse of Portland. Cedric experienced a curious state of mind that excited and galvanized him, a curiosity bordering on hallowed ground which he bared for examination in lengthy discussions with Pàl.

Pàl Zölt was born in Hungary at the end of the Twenties. The deformity of his club foot, which prevented him from serving in the military, as well as his penetrating dark looks and ubiquitous rolled cigarette between his lips, lent him an aura of romanticism and a resemblance to Lord Byron. Pàl became a teacher after the war, but the pressures of the Communist régime, and then the crushed hopes of the 1956 uprising, forced him to reconsider his options. "There were three ways to succeed in Hungary," he told Cedric. "And by succeed I mean leave the country. I could not stay—it was as if the communist dictatorship had usurped the soul of Hungary itself. Since military life was out of the question, and I refused the political option, all that was left open to me was the clergy. But I have the faith, it was not mere convenience…Would I have chosen that path if our revolution had been successful? I don't know. But I am not unhappy…"

Through Pàl Zölt's acquaintance and friendship Cedric listened to Gregorian Chants and read Thomas Merten's *No Man is an Island* on the struggle to find the meaning of human existence. He bought a used copy of Shakespeare's complete works on Rue Royale, but set it aside temporarily to delve into the Book of Genesis. He often shared his insights with Pàl, and the swarthy Hungarian would listen attentively, offer advice, and continue to fill their glasses with Unicum—a Hungarian spirit made of nettles, *urtica*—which they both agreed was foul indeed but in which they both indulged lightly on occasion. Cedric was not particularly troubled but intrigued, and in a constant state of excitement at the new thoughts swarming in his mind. As the language courses at the Sorbonne drew to an end in the middle of April, he realized with a sinking feeling that he would soon be facing yet again that choice—a dilemma even—to leave or to stay. His Hungarian friend proposed a timely retreat to a Trappist monastery for a week at Easter in Chateaubriand, in the Loire-Atlantique.

The Spartan, frugal and silent atmosphere of the monastery was the ideal setting for Cedric's contemplative needs. For a week he divested himself of thoughts and anxieties and attempts at problem solving, and rather allowed solutions to present themselves to him. He immersed himself in the lives of the monks—five prayers a day, Gregorian chants, and silence, silence, silence. The first few days were almost maddening, but then the experience became liberating, and Cedric stayed an extra week, attending Easter high mass with its impressive décor, the pervasive incense, the ornate clothing of the monks that contrasted with their austere daily wear. By the time he left, Cedric no longer doubted the road down which he needed to travel. And travel he must, he realized. That was why he had left Portland: to keep moving until motion itself was self-perpetuating and he could continue on the strength of his convictions alone, to keep moving until he was living at the same speed as the existence unfolding before him.

...all I can say right now is that I'm having loads of fun and feel fully relieved of all responsibilities. It doesn't seem like such a bad thing...When I returned to Paris from the Trappist monastery, there was a postcard from my dad (he must've been back in Portland recently and it's good to see my mother's keeping up with my whereabouts!) telling me he would be in Le Havre, which is only a hundred kilometers or so from Paris. So I made that my last trip before leaving France. Dad and I spent the afternoon walking about, talking a little. And then we went for a few beers. He told me Kurt was alternating a year of college with a year in the Merchant Marine. At this rate it will take him over eight years to get his degree, but at least he'll be getting one.

I sold my scooter in Paris before heading to Santander, Spain (knew it would be a problem selling it there!), where I took classes at the University of Mendes Palaö. Santander is a beautiful town on the Atlantic ocean with plenty of white sand beaches. There's also a prehistoric cave south of the city, 14,000 years old!.. But almost more impressive is state of near-nudity of some of the girls on the beaches. They wear those two piece bathing suits, "bikinis"...

Now I'm on my way to Beirut, Lebanon, and then Israel, and Syria maybe. I boarded this boat in Marseilles and the sight of the Mediterranean, the Greek Islands somewhere north..., well I'm not very intellectually inspired to read, so I have all this time to kill which explains such a long letter to you. And maybe you're hardly interested in any of it! So I'll sign off now. I hope you're all doing well and enjoying the four and a half days of Portland summer sunshine. I guess the best place to write me and be sure I get it would be American Express in Hong Kong. Not sure when I'll get there, but I'll get there!

◆   ◆   ◆

Cedric posted his letter to Dean upon his arrival in Lebanon, on August 12, 1961, from the same city in which his daughter would be born eight years later, and exactly ten years, day for day, before his son's birth.

He had omitted to mention to Dean the aborted plans to travel through West Africa. A game of cards with three other residents of the American Pavilion—John, David and Melvin—had led to a discussion about missionaries, which in turn had led them to contemplate a trip to Tunisia, Algeria, Mali, Upper Volta, Ivory Coast, Guinea, Senegal, Mauritania, and Morocco. Foremost in their minds was the crossing of the Sahara, Northwest to Southeast, with John writing up articles for Time Life, David recording sounds and discussions for RCA, and Melvin filming. Cedric was in charge of the itinerary, organization and logistics, and by April he had a flexible schedule that allowed leeway for visa delays and other imponderables. They planned to head to Tunisia in June, but the kidnappings of oil expatriates on the Mauritanian-Moroccan border, the boiler situation in Algeria, and the revolt in Tunisia, made North Africa too volatile a place for travel and the plans were shelved.

Cedric didn't take well to the Middle East in the beginning. He discovered with a degree of surprise that the chaotic laxity that reigned in that region made him uneasy, and the inability to be certain of anything destabilized him. Perhaps also the heat of summer—despite Cedric's insatiable love of the sun—made his head swim. In any case he began looking east then, towards India where he had enrolled in a university outside of Bulpur near Calcutta, and considered its reputed intrinsic chaos as a charm rather than a hindrance. But Egypt first, he decided, a country he found inescapable, drawn to it as he was by the mysterious allure of ancient monuments, so ancient that they seemed not only to defy time but to exist on a plane entirely different from the world around them.

"Nice view," Cedric heard as he stared out at the desert from the top of Cheops pyramid. Cedric looked up at a man in his late twenties, prematurely bald, and recognized a fellow traveler like himself: gregarious and quick to engage in conversation. They shook hands, and Les introduced Cedric to his traveling companion, Michiel from Rotterdam. The three descended Cheops pyramid together, and found a tawdry bodega that served up a surprisingly tasty dinner. Les and Michiel revealed their current plan to hitchhike down the continent's spine to South Africa, and at the end of dinner, they asked Cedric to join them.

The Tudor edition of Shakespeare's complete works became his journal, each play corresponding to a new country, a new town, another portion of the red dusty road south. *The Tempest* and *The Rape of Lucrece*: Wadi Halfa, Sudan; *Antony and Cleopatra*: Malakal; *Troilus and Cressida*: Bor; *Pericles* and *Prince of Tyre*: Juba; *Timon of Athens*: Masindi, Uganda; *Othello the Moor of Venice*: Murchison Falls; *Cymbeline*: Eldoret; *A Midsummer's Night Dream*: Nairobi, Kenya. The trio traveled by packed train from Cairo to Luxor, standing for twenty-four hours in a dry heat that seemed to only get worse at night without ventilation in the train car. In Luxor they rented bicycles and toured the city and the temples for three days before embarking on a river steamer to Abu Simbel, enjoying the still thriving city of Wadi Halfa before it was partially engulfed by Lake Nasser after the construction of the Aswan dam ten years later. Here Michiel decided that it was all too much for him (too much heat, too much fatigue, too much potential danger) and returned to Cairo.

October 2. 9:23am
Les and I finally managed to obtain our Blue Nile visas, and arrived in Juba, Sudan, yesterday after an eventful trip, surrounded by ethnic tensions between Christians, Moslems and Animosts.

*We almost got trampled by a herd of elephants on our first night camp-
ing out at Murchison Falls. The game warden had allowed us to sleep
under a thatch roof deep in the park, but like dummies we left food out
that attracted wart hogs, and they attracted other animals. Larger animals.
Or maybe it wasn't really our fault and we found ourselves on the elephants' path to the watering hole…Whatever it was, Les and I woke up in
the middle of the night to the ground shaking and a rumbling sound as
loud as an earthquake…We scrambled onto the roof and prayed that the
beasts wouldn't actually run across it or that we wouldn't tumble through
it…We watched it all and came out unscathed—laughing nervously with
uncontrollable relief…*

October 5. 4:40pm
*In Mombassa for a few days. Have decided to drop Les here and let him
continue on his own. South Africa holds no particular interest right now,
and the travel south from Kenya seems to be tame—White Paper of Independence in progress here but no upheavals, Tanganyika also going through
peaceful democratic elections. Northern Rhodesia, Nyasaland and Southern Rhodesia are all safe and sound apparently. And in any case, India
beckons, I'm now anxious to get there.*

*It's strange how safe travel seems, unexciting and uninviting…Maybe
I'd appreciate the Middle East more now. It's true that after Europe, especially stringently ordered Spain, it was a bit of shock. After Africa, however, I could probably deal with the chaos. Plenty of that in India…*

October 9. 6:30am.
*And still another Monday morning, but a bit more exciting. I am
finally on my way to India. Twelve hours outside of Mombassa on the SS
Amra, a British-India steamship line. "All of Neptune's multitudinous seas
cannot (at this moment) cool these sweaty hands…"*

Shakespeare continued to accompany Cedric through India and Malaysia. *King John, King Richard the Second, Coriolanus, Titus Andronicus*: Mombassa to Karachi, Pakistan; *King Henry the Fourth*: Karachi-Bombay; *King Henry the Fifth*: Calcutta; *King Henry the Sixth*: Chittagong-Rangoon-Penang...By the time he reached Hong Kong, Cedric was able to stow the book away at the bottom of his bag with an undeniable sense of pride.

The ship *SS Amra* was huge, and his steerage class ticket bestowed a bunk in the massive sleeping quarters that resembled those of a troop transport, one bunk among endless rows of bunks welded to the deck—four hundred aft and three hundred astern. He took one look at it on the evening he boarded the ship, imagined what night would bring, and decided to spend the next twelve nights sleeping in a life raft.

Once he arrived in Bombay all his senses were assailed by the smells and spices of India that made those of the ship seem bland in comparison. He stayed for several days at a University hostel, then continued on by train to Nagpore, Calcutta, and finally Bulpur where he switched to a pedi-cab to reach the University. Once there, Cedric was submerged by a wave of cruel disappointment: the place was a dust ball, a few wooden shacks in a dry and desert landscape. Well, no use dwelling in a place that didn't speak to him, there were far too many other regions to discover. Two days later he returned to Calcutta and hopped on the first ship heading East to Singapore.

Until his arrival in Beirut, Cedric hadn't really felt he had been traveling. Other than the language classes around which he'd organized his time in Europe, he had left Portland without a clear intention of what he'd be doing or for how long he'd be gone. It wasn't until his trip with Les that he had felt himself rid of the desire to settle in any one particular city and do something. Now he felt truly free, coasting along with all senses alert and as innocently curious as a child. The ship to Singapore took him to Chittagong, East Pakistan, then Rangoon, Burma, and Penang, Malaysia. He did not remain long in each place. None of them caught his fancy in any particular way, and if he'd been willing to remain longer in Malaysia it was because of an Australian girl he'd met and whom he'd gotten to know rather better than the rest of the group with which she was traveling. But they were a student group invited to Malaysia by the local government, and their tour guide in Penang made it blatantly clear that Cedric could not tag along. So he caught a clean and comfortable train ride through the jungle to Singapore, before catching up with his ship and continuing on to Hong Kong, where he arrived end of November, 1961.

Now Hong Kong caught his fancy...The first night he shacked up in a hotel that turned out to be a brothel; the next day, while sipping a cold beer at the Mayflower bar in Kowloon and wondering where he was going to sleep next, he engaged an elderly whore in conversation, and within ten minutes she offered to rent him a room in her apartment, in a massive living complex in Kowloon, on Nathan Road. Cedric stayed there for almost two months. The apartment was clean and comfortable, ideally located near the Star Ferry that linked the mainland with Victoria Island, and the kindly prostitute never bought back clients. Cedric ate his meals for one U.S. dollar at the Star restaurant down by the port, and spent his days checking out books at the US/British library on Victoria Island, reading in the Ling Tao monastery, or bussing to Repulse Bay to sit in the sun all day.

By January he realized that he would soon be out of money, yet he had no real desire to leave Hong Kong, and none to return home. In almost two years since he'd left Portland, the only moment when he had felt anything vaguely resembling homesickness had been his first rainy day in Perugia. So he started perusing the newspapers for odd jobs and found an ad claiming to offer work for ten thousand dollars a year tax-free. Cedric went to the appointed place at the appointed time and met with a man named Bernie Cornfield who spoke enthusiastically of his company, International Overseas Services, and explained descriptively how Cedric could become a high roller in the sale of securities worldwide. Through the bombast and bullshit, however, Cedric realized that this was a commission-based job, on top of which Bernie would be getting a substantial cut. He would have to open his own markets and hire people to work for him. He would in turn earn a cut of their sales in a pattern that would later become known as the pyramid scheme. After a brief internal debate, he declined.

He flew to Manila and then on to Formosa, Okinawa and Tokyo. There he was offered a job teaching English to Japan Airlines employees. Once again he hesitated—it was hard to bury so easily after two years an existence that was relatively free of responsibilities. On the one hand he could learn Japanese and martial arts and lead a comfortable and financially secure life, peppered by the exotic appeal of Japanese women...On the other hand, he could find himself ten years later stuck in a job that had lost its luster, with little chance of upward mobility, and a poorly saleable CV upon his return to the States. He wasn't like Kerouac, and didn't want to be a be a bum. He'd met the head of the Berlitz office in Rome, and he didn't want to turn out that despondent and dreamless at forty-five.

He knew he had to get out. And once he'd reached that decision, his desire to return to the States became anchored in his mind. He had been traveling for just long enough, it was time to embark on a career.

In February 1962, Portland greeted a weary and weathered Cedric with a grim cloud cover that made him realize that in two years, he had missed absolutely nothing. Portland still had nothing to offer, yet Cedric found himself searching nonetheless, like a gold-digger searching for nuggets in a coal mine. He kept his eyes peeled and ears tuned for news of a job, but it was a half-hearted attempt prompted no doubt by his poor financial situation, and soon he was gasping for air amidst conversations on the price of plywood, gossip about who was screwing whose neighbor's wife or husband, complaints about recent local tax hikes, and an apathetic interest in his two years of travel. Amort and Walt, even his parents, were of little comfort, but Cedric understood that their reaction was more due to an inability to comprehend what he had experienced rather than jealousy or disregard. Eventually he brushed off the disappointment and decided that it didn't matter much anyway. He returned to his old adage: something only held intrinsic value if you could never tell a soul about it.

Dean was interested in his stories, however, and Cedric indulged him for several evenings running. Afterwards Dean delved into his own life: his brief job on the creative team of the Young & Rubicam advertising company, before establishing himself as a freelance artist; and especially the child that his wife was expecting in two months. Finally Cedric revealed the uncertainties about his own future, talked about how two years abroad hadn't brought him more insight as what career he might want to follow, or what life he wanted to lead. Dean told him exactly what he needed to hear: that it didn't matter, that he had already taken the biggest first step: figuring out what he *didn't* want, and that was to stay in Portland. "Go to New York," he said. "because it is certainly the only city that can provide you with an answer. Perhaps you can't think of what you want to do, but I'm sure you'll recognize the career you want when it comes knocking. And in New York, it will definitely come knocking."

Three days later Cedric was on the train to Chicago to visit Russ Taylor. Three days after that, he arrived in New York. He calculated that with some tight budgeting he had enough money to last about six weeks, and banked on finding a job before the beginning of March.

4

"So you really don't know what you want to do?" Russ Taylor Sr. asked.

"No. Anything that will take me abroad."

They were sitting in a raucous beer hall on 86th street, in Germantown, Manhattan, between Third Avenue and Lexington. It was Sunday evening and Cedric had been in New York for a day and a half. His brief stop in Chicago had resulted in Russ arranging for Cedric to meet with his father, now Chairman of American Car & Foundry, to see if he couldn't help him on his job search.

"I had an interesting meeting on Friday with one of our bankers," said Russ Sr. "He was a young guy, a few years older than you and Russ, and I asked what had tempted him to go into such a—well, such a dull profession. I was curious." Mr. Taylor paused and Cedric waited expectantly, as if Mr. Taylor were about to hand him a map that would expose the mystery location of his future. "This young man told me that the industry was changing. Banking was becoming more aggressive, with young kids going up against the Securities Act, looking for ways to circumvent legislation and find new avenues to expand. The old rivalry between Chase Manhattan and First National City is flaring up, and both are challenging the preeminence of Bank of America. And one place they're looking is abroad…So? What would say to a career as an international banker?"

Cedric almost toppled off his chair laughing. Banking?! Cedric knew nothing more than clichés about banking, but he had to admit that it had a ring of adventure to it, not to mention a lustrous veneer—especially from the way Russ Taylor Sr. presented it. Travel, overseas experience, people, and most certainly financial security. The previous evening he had outlined a modest plan of action to approach those companies like American Express and Pan American that seemed most likely to promote jobs overseas. But a banker, an international banker...? Why not? Five more weeks and he would be out of money anyway.

"Very well then," Mr. Taylor exclaimed energetically, "I will set up some interviews for you. Come to my office tomorrow morning at nine."

On Monday morning Mr. Taylor introduced him to his treasurer, a middle-aged man with sharp features and an efficient look who had been asked to arrange interviews with some of the more important banks in the City with whom American Car & Foundry did business. The first was at Bankers' Trust at ten o'clock the next morning, and four more followed for the rest of the week. It all seemed too easy.

Two days later, Cedric listlessly cracked six eggs into a mug, churned in a half-pint of orange juice and a half-pint of vanilla ice-cream—his "Royal Orange Julius concoction"—and tried to buoy his sinking spirits. None of the interviews were panning out. Immediately he'd sensed the foreign world into which he was hoping to enter when he had stepped into the lobby of Bankers' Trust, and then Manufacturers Hanover. There was a bustle of activity from important-looking, important-acting, young men of his age, or younger, who strode with confidence around the plush halls. Cedric maintained his poise throughout his interview despite the coolness of his interviewers and their forced politeness: he knew that neither bank would call him back. He consoled himself with the fact that both Bankers' Trust and Manufacturers Hanover had only less than a half a dozen overseas branches between them, and therefore offered very little chance for him to work abroad. They didn't want him? He wouldn't have accepted him anyway.

Two out of five: no worries. Still on the list were Chase Manhattan, the illustrious Morgan Guarantee and finally First National City Bank. Chase, however, was another dismal affair. He was greeted (if such a verb can characterize the guttural moan by which some human icicle indicated that Cedric should sit down) by a reedy type in his early thirties, clammy faced and thin lipped. Cedric tried to shake off his incipient gloom and responded with a benevolent smile to the undertaker's barked questions. Then there was a lull during which Cedric was sure that he would be asked to leave; instead Mr. Reedy shifted in his chair and asked with obvious exhaustion what were some of Cedric's activities in college. He recounted his jobs as a slashburner, a bean-picker, a sheet-metal feeder, a sorority houseboy, a hospital orderly and his brief activity as dorm president. Noticing his interlocutor's bored expression, he realized that Mr. Reedy was not impressed. Until he casually mentioned that he'd been a Theta Chi.

"Ah, you were Theta Chi?" he heard Mr. Reedy gasp after a sharp intake of air. "So was I, so was I…It's always nice to meet a brother," he said. His arms jerked to life, and he extended his arm to shake hands. He smiled. Cedric found it a sickening sight. "I was Theta Chi too," he repeated. Then he dragged Cedric all around the bank and introduced him as a fraternity brother and a good bloke. It didn't help Cedric get a job, however, since at the following interview he was told that he would be kept on file, but that unfortunately there were no openings available at the current time.

Try as he might to explain away the rejections and perceive the situation as his own refusal to accept the first job that came his way just because he was growing nervous and soon out of money, he could not help but doubt the sanity of doggedly pursuing a path that now seemed rashly chosen. Entertaining the thought of a career in international banking was ludicrous, he thought as he glanced in the mirror at the reflection of a dispirited young man in a coat and tie that now seemed shabby in comparison to the tailored suits he'd seen on his interview forays. An hour later, Cedric stared up at the building occupied by Morgan Guarantee, unable to repress a surge of wonder. "Next-to-last chance," he said, finding within him some new reserve of unwavering optimism.

He felt a difference with the other banks minutes after the first interview began. He sensed *interest*. When he gave succinct reasons why he felt that his background might be conducive to a successful career in banking, his interviewer seemed to nod with approval. He was given a favorable review and asked to await a second interview with three bank officers. Cedric returned to the lobby, drank a cup of coffee and welcomed the renewed sense of belief with open arms. The industry might be filled with young men of better social standing and higher levels of traditional education, but Cedric knew that with hard work and his personable disposition he could progress. And if it meant working abroad, he would throw his whole weight behind the endeavor.

He was never given the chance. The second panel fired away questions of economic and financial nature, and remained unimpressed by Cedric's down-to-earth answers. He knew they wouldn't get back to him; he knew what their conclusion would be: *a friendly kid but he'll never cut it...*

Could he in fact cut it? He walked to Central Park after the failed interview, and flopped down on a bench. He watched the silver waters of the lake shimmering in the sunset as he tried to regain some control over his emotions at the twisted turn that fate had taken, deciding to strip him of his streak of luck at a time when he felt he needed it the most. It was a bright, beautiful, freezing day in March, and he drew his coat tightly around him as he traipsed down Amsterdam Avenue a few hours later. His steps were slow, his feet dragged, he coughed with a pretense at illness, his head slunk in his collar...Finally he looked up, tired of his own despondency. He looked around and thought of all the places he had traveled to...And he had a college degree, was a First Lieutenant in the Reserves, knew more than a smattering knowledge of four foreign languages, and was only twenty-eight years old...He observed the immigrant community around him, their energy, their faith in the future and in those elusive concepts of the American Dream: they were starting out with so much less. What did Cedric have to be depressed about?

The following morning he was revved to go at six am. He reached the new offices of First National City Bank at 399 Park Avenue two hours ahead of his eleven o'clock interview, and he took advantage of this time to visit the exhibit held on the ground floor entitled *The Story of Banking*. The only line he would remember later was the definition of banking: "Service to the clients and profits to the shareholders."

Cedric was greeted by Jimmy Griffin for his first interview, and immediately he recognized the type of person he'd met at the other banks—a guy his age from a good family, with a framed degree from Princeton that hung on the wall behind his desk and attested to his proper education, with a tailored suit and Omega watch that were emblematic of his social standing and success. Yet as the interview proceeded Cedric sensed none of the condescension and superiority exuded by so many of the other interviewers at the previous banks. Griffin asked him about his background in Oregon, his work at American Can, and his long trip around the world, and then went on to tell him about the myriad offices in dozens of countries run by the Overseas Division of the bank. Cedric felt a curious mixture of excitement and serenity course through him—it was as if he had worked through a batch of keys to finally find the one that fit the lock. And when asked to think about where he might eventually like to work, Cedric said—restraining himself from appearing too precipitate—that he would go wherever they thought he could be of most use…"That's just the stuff we like to hear," Griffin said. He showed Cedric through the building, introduced him to five other people who would spend time with him that afternoon, explain facets of the job, answer questions, and of course evaluate him as a prospective Executive Trainee.

Cedric never ascertained the fact, but he suspected that he had impressed Griffin favorably enough to be introduced to five people that Griffin liked and who he assumed would like Cedric. He was told to enjoy his weekend and return on Monday to meet Ed Thorn, the Senior Vice President in charge of Europe, Africa, and the Middle East. This was the division that—in Griffin's view—best suited

Cedric's background. Why not? He hadn't just been coy and utilizing a subtle interviewing technique: he really would gladly accept to go anywhere. The more he slipped into the glittering world of International Banking, the more it appealed to him. And he was anxious to start as soon as possible.

The smooth ride into First National continued with Ed Thorn the following Monday. Cedric entered the Senior VP's office and found Thorn ruminating over his résumé. After a few minutes he looked up, smiled broadly, and exclaimed: "Well, you wouldn't believe this, Cedric, but I took the exact same trip as you in 1937, except in the opposite direction. Started out in New York, headed west, went to Asia, ventured into China…There I got locked up by the Chinese because of some argument over a bar-room bill. I was a little drunk…" He paused, then waved a hand. "Well, anyway!…Oh! And you're a pilot too! Love planes—do you know, when I was at Yale, I would fly my Stinson down to New York to visit my girlfriend on weekends…" He spoke for most of the interview. Cedric patched together that he was from a very wealthy New England family, but again—like Griffin—he sensed none of the arrogance displayed at other banks. It would come, surely, but for the moment Cedric felt that he was accepted here. After a half an hour, Ed Thorn handed back his resume. "Well, all that's left now is to meet our big boss. Executive VP, Walter Wriston. He's on a business trip right now and won't return until next week. Tuesday. I'll set up an interview. Walt likes to meet and personally approve any new recruit to the Overseas Division!"

Cedric was elated, but he couldn't shake a latent anxiety, the fear that Wriston would walk in the following Tuesday after a row with his wife or losing several million dollars on a deal, or both—and blackball him immediately. As soon as he emerged from Thorn's office, he bolted to the lower floor where he found the executive trainee with whom he had had lunch the past Friday, and asked him to lend him any and all information he could regarding the history and current situation of First National. The trainee gave him a few documents, then added a sheaf of papers to the pile: "It's about Wriston. He's worth the read."

The history of the bank was a tortuous account of mergers and acquisitions from the moment it received its New York charter in 1813 until the Great Depression, followed by a period of slumber after Charles Mitchell, Chairman of the bank in 1933, was indicted by a jury anxious to publicly pin the blame of the stock market crash of 1929 on high-profile financiers. Then the Securities Exchange Act and the Glass-Steagull Act shackled the whole banking industry for decades. Walter Wriston arrived at First National City Bank in the late forties and rapidly made a name for himself, especially after moving the bank into tanker financing with Aristotle Onassis. He tried to infuse the bank with new energy and took on government regulations every chance he got. He became the protégé of the impulsive and erratic, but quite brilliant Overseas Department Head, George Moore, who promoted Wriston to that position once he himself obtained the Presidency. Together Moore and Wriston, the 'Dynamic Duo', longed to lift banking in general to new heights of global expansion, and First National in particular to the exalted number one position.

This much Cedric gleaned from the reading material that his future fellow trainee had lent him. He could not know at the time, of course, that the two men would succeed beyond anyone's most visionary dreams, that by 1965, First National—later called Citibank to much wider renown—would boast a hundred and seventy-seven offices in fifty-eight countries in later decades, that Wriston would became the premier U.S. financier and instrumental in the expanded use of credit cards, the collapse of Bretton Woods and subsequent explosion of foreign exchange, the launching of Eurobonds and negotiable CDs, the installation of automated teller machines, that he would lead the recycling of petrodollars in the seventies, save New York City from bankruptcy, and fuel Third-World debt by proclaiming that "countries don't go bankrupt". Cedric could certainly not have guessed how this would affect his own career, nor the crucial role he would play in the period following Wriston's reign. Yet an image of this glittering and noisy future, still hazy and indescribable, appeared before him.

He could not say during that cold week of March '62 what the next three decades would hold, but three decades later he would look back and say that he was not entirely surprised. Wriston was such a man that he not only carved out his own destiny, but also that of an entire bank, transforming it into a mega-institution of finance.

Cedric returned to First National with a stoic acceptance of fate. Something inside him said that he couldn't come this far, be reduced to his last dollar, and *not* succeed. And succeed he did—Wriston walked in with a cup of coffee in one hand and Cedric's resume in the other. Without even shaking hands he said: "So, looks like you've been screwing around for the past two years!" Without batting a eyelash, Cedric responded: "Well, sir, I'd actually call it broadening my horizons..."

Wriston laughed, put down his coffee and shook hands with Cedric. "You're right! You're absolutely right! You can learn all about banking here, and you will if you have the intelligence, drive, and integrity, to educate yourself and be constantly dissatisfied with the status quo." He put an hand on Cedric's shoulder. "When would you like to start?"

Cedric turned out his pockets and pulled out a quarter. "Tomorrow would be great, if that's okay with you."

Wriston laughed boisterously. "This is something I won't soon forget! Well, you're a lucky man, Mr. Grant. Every new recruit has to follow a six-week training program. And there just happens to be one starting tomorrow at eight o'clock. Report to Lillian Garou on the lower level, and you're in business."

They shook hands, and Cedric managed a choked thank you. Executive Trainee in the Overseas Division of First National City Bank...An hour later, he was on the phone to his mother, Dean, and Russ Taylor Jr. and Sr.

◆   ◆   ◆

Five minutes after the trainee program started the following morning, Cedric almost jumped up and claimed false advertising. He wondered what he was doing at this round table of knights born and bred in the aristocracy of finance. He wanted to crawl back into whatever hole from which he'd emerged. The feeling of belonging to a group where alma maters and connected in-laws weighed nothing against hard work, ambition, dedication and goodwill, dissipated as each trainee spoke in turn about his illustrious background.

Lillian Garou was an elegant lady, old enough to be the mother to most of the mid- to late twenty-somethings gathered there that day, and she toured the table as if she were inculcating young society ladies on correct behavior and manners. Cedric jumped as he heard the fellow next to him stand and describe himself as Harold Maxwell the Second with a B.A. from Princeton and an M.B.A from Harvard, who spent summers with the Rothschilds in Paris, had completed an internship with Baring Brothers in London, spoke five languages and whose father was Chairman of some company that Cedric had never heard of but that everyone else seemed to know. Most of the twenty-two attendants of Lillian Group's trainee program had MBA's from top-notch schools and fathers on various important boards. When it was his turn, Cedric stood up, threw his shoulders back, and said: "Cedric Grant. University of Oregon. First Lieutenant Airborne Infantry."

A few days into his traineeship, Harry Overtoom, his former flatmate from Indianapolis during his time with American Can, called him up in New York to tell him that he was moving to the City, and suggested that they share an apartment together. The timing was perfect—Cedric was just getting ready to leave the hotel on Amsterdam Avenue, flush with the knowledge that he would soon be earning a salary (a pittance, true, at $4800 a year, but the prospects were good), and he felt that big fun-loving Harry would be the ideal roommate for his two-year traineeship in New York. Harry's wife and children were to stay in Chicago for a while longer and join him at the end of the summer or in late autumn. In the mean time, he and Cedric moved into an apartment on 64th street between First and York, where an interesting mix of Chinese laundry shops and rundown businesses were located. There was none of the hip appeal of the Village, nor the social prestige of the Upper East Side where one might expect a promising young banker to find his first apartment, but it suited Cedric just fine: unassuming, a little shabby, lively, and not pretentious. It still underlined how far he'd come from the bean fields of Portland, as well as the incongruity of his chosen path when considered against his overt, unassuming and unconventional personality.

After having learned from Lillian Garou the guts of branch banking—check writing, clearance, and racking, documentary and commercial letters of credit, traveler's checks, and use of the NCR 4200—Cedric officially entered the International Executive Training Program in early June. He was being primed for a posting abroad, and as such was sent to the only floor occupied by the International Division to begin his mandatory six months in the Letters of Credit department. Debits, credits, transfers, researching annual reports, checking the balances of foreign Central Banks, compiling credit lines and cash reserve requirements for branches around the world, soon became his daily fodder…Six months of slave labor, but Cedric never stopped smiling. He felt part of a large family, even though he caught his fair share of snide comments and glances from trainees in Domestic who handled the large accounts such as Chrysler and Ford, and considered International a quaint little enterprise that dealt with peanut farmers. Cedric didn't mind, on the contrary he felt unadulterated pride at belonging to what he considered the pioneering sector of the bank. He trusted Wriston—like everyone in the International Division had unbridled respect, even awe, for the man, and most expected him to be Chairman by the end of the decade.

Cedric adapted well to the fun of being a bachelor in New York. He was earning much less than at American Can, but enough to cover his basic needs—decent apartment, simple food, occasional dates, and sky-diving on weekends. Harry knew of Cedric's paratrooper past, and he himself had fallen in love with the sport while living in Chicago. Together they joined a club in Hopewell, New Jersey, and skydived almost every weekend.

They were soon joined on their trips by Katy Gammack, Griffin's secretary whom Cedric had befriended, and whose ebullient character and dry humor concurred with his own. A few months earlier, after a year of college, Katy had hopped on a Greyhound bus in her home-town of Des Moines, Iowa and, like so many others of her age, headed for New York hopeful that it would provide a life unimaginable in the Midwest. Right off the bus, she chatted with the loquacious taxi-driver, and when she mentioned that she had just arrived in the city and was looking for a job, the driver got all excited. "Ah, but my sister works for a bank! Maybe she can help you, yes, yes!" Within a week, Katy was offered a position as Griffin's secretary.

Katy wouldn't skydive but their outings allowed her to take her mind off her fiancé John Barner, another executive trainee whom she'd met during her first week at the bank and with whom she was starry-eyed in love, but whom Cedric had never met since John had had to interrupt his traineeship to complete an Officer Training Program with the Air Force reserves. John was a burly man with a temperament that bordered on the overbearing, but he was a gentleman in every way. He was born and bred in Athens, Georgia, and his experience in the South had lead him to take African Studies in graduate school. He was now driven by the desire to work in West Africa, "for the benefit of the Black Man" as he put it. Little could Cedric guess that the three would become close friends and that John and Katy would be in their own way, like Harry, instrumental in Cedric's choice of a wife.

One Thursday evening, with nothing better to do, Cedric and Harry went downtown to a party that Jane Conklin, a sky-diving buddy of theirs, was throwing for her biker boyfriend's birthday. Jane worked in the Manhattan offices of Young & Rubicam with Annette Hay, a young woman from Scarsdale, New York. She invited Annette to her party, and Annette, also having nothing better scheduled, decided to attend.

Cedric saw her leaning up against the jukebox. She was smoking a cigarette, looking not so much bored as bewildered and trying to hide it. Her hands waved about and caught his attention, and perhaps more, as he wondered if love at first sight were possible. No, simply intrigued, wasn't he? Enough to want to know more…Her eyes squinted as she puffed on her cigarette, and when she laughed she turned her neck delicately around. Her russet hair—surely not real, some form of failed coloring attempt—fell casually around her face until she removed the clasp, and then it reached down just past her shoulders. She conveyed an air of innocent assuredness, and a confidence in her position in the world that perhaps belied a deeper tragedy with which she had not yet quite come to terms. Cedric found himself walking up to her and asking her to dance.

Annette looked up at the powerfully built young man with the military crew-cut and horn-rimmed glasses, and gave a nod of assent. He smiled and she noticed the gap in his teeth and the drooping right eye, and she smiled back.

"You seem quite incongruous here," he said as they started dancing.

"You don't exactly strike me as the biker type yourself," she said.

"I sky-dive, that's how I know Jane…"

"And I work with her at Young and Rubicam," she said through a puff of smoke that made Cedric turn away. "Where Jane works."

She had been about to mention the fact that since she'd dumped her boyfriend the previous week (he wore white socks with black moccasins and refused to see the bad taste in that), she had had nothing planned for the evening…But this guy didn't need to know all that. What *she* wanted to know was why he danced so well: You can feel safe with such broad shoulders to clasp, she thought, but they shouldn't belong to such a good dancer.

"What do you do?" Annette asked him instead.

"I work for First National City Bank. International Division."

"Ah, a banker…Traveled much?"

"Some."

"Paris?" she asked.

"Ah, yes, Paris. You've been there?"

Annette smiled at a chance to surprise him. "I lived there for three years," she said with a winsome grin.

They finished dancing and sat down on the couch, and spoke desultorily for the next hour, mainly about their time in New York and their respective jobs, skirting around the issues of Paris and their backgrounds, as if they were playing at exchanging information while both knowing that there was much more to discover in the other, and holding back for later. When Harry came up to Cedric to tell him he was heading home, Cedric asked Annette if she wouldn't like to join them on their parachute meet that weekend in Pottstown, Pennsylvania.

Annette gave him a perplexed look. "I'll think about it. Certainly sounds like a different way to spend a weekend."

"Well then meet us in front of our apartment at six tomorrow evening."

"Maybe," she said lighting a cigarette and looking away.

"I'll call you tomorrow," Cedric said.

She raised her eyebrows, in surprise and lingering doubt, but she gave him her number at Young and Rubicam before leaving the party. She had nothing else crucial planned, nothing she couldn't cancel or postpone, and there was something crazy about driving to Pottstown with two guys she barely knew to watch them skydive.

When Cedric saw up her pull up in her old Ford convertible the following evening, he was overjoyed—Cedric rushed towards her and hugged her as if she were a long lost friend. He hadn't quite believed until that moment that she would actually come. He introduced her to Katy, and the two ended up chatting in the back seat all the way to Cedric and Harry's sky-diving club an hour later.

When they turned into the parking lot at nightfall, the car sputtered and stalled in a cloud of dust. It wouldn't start again after three attempts so they pushed it into a parking lot and stared at it for awhile. It was obvious they wouldn't be fixing it that night. There was only one bunk in the clubhouse, so the men agreed to sleep in the car. Jane arrived in her car the next morning, with her boyfriend Joe following on his motocycle. He took a look at Annette's Ford and told them that the tie rod had broken, but that it shouldn't be hard to replace. In the mean time, they all piled into Jane's car and took off after breakfast, with Cedric promising to find a new tie rod when they returned.

The two men did their jumps that afternoon—Cedric placed third coming within a foot and a half of the target, and Harry won in his category—while Katy showed Annette how to pack a parachute. That evening the four of them ate in a cheap diner where Annette was so put off by the food that she left her spaghetti meatballs untouched and smoked her way through the meal. On Sunday there was too much wind to jump. Annette and Cedric spent more time talking, discussions which continued on the drive home. He told her about his Oregon background, his love of travel, and recounted stories from his trip around the world; she told him about her youth in Scarsdale, and briefly touched upon her three years spent in Paris after her father's death in a car crash. The subject was happily interrupted when they stopped for gas just before reaching New York, and Cedric found a Bell helmet that the gas station attendant was selling for a good price. It was the Harley Davidson of helmets, he explained to the others, though he wasn't quite clear on where this fascination for helmets came from since he was far from a biker fan. But he hugged that helmet for the rest of the drive home, and Annette felt a surge of warmth every time she looked over and saw him grinning like a school boy.

The following weekend, Cedric rummaged through a junk yard, and found a Ford tie rod in excellent condition. He replaced the part on Annette's car and reached Scarsdale by Saturday evening. There he met Annette's mother, Jeannie Hay, and soon found himself invited to dinner. Jeannie talked incessantly, and Annette fluctuated between embarrassment and interest. When Annette mentioned that Cedric had traveled for two years, Jeannie launched into the story of her first fiancé, Michel Vieuchange, who had dreamed of being a literary adventurer like St. Exupéry, and who had planned an expedition to discover the forbidden city of Smara in Morocco. Jeannie had witnessed all his preparations, and in the Spring of 1929, Michel had set off into the desert dressed as a Berber woman…He found the city of Smara, but died upon his return, wasted by dysentery. "Oh, no! I have not had luck with men, I can say that!" Jeannie exclaimed with her lingering French accent as she cleared the table. "No, not much luck at all…" Cedric presumed she was referring also to her late husband but said nothing. He looked at Annette when her mother left the room, and she rolled her eyes as if to say that she'd heard it all before many times. "You mother seems to have lead a fascinating life," he said. "Not easy, but definitely fascinating…" Soon they both realized that Jeannie had been absent from the table for quite a while. They slipped outside.

After Cedric left, Annette remained on the porch for a long while, overwhelmed by the certainty that she had met the man she would marry.

◆   ◆   ◆

Jeannie met her husband John Hay a few years after Michel Vieuchange's death. She worked as secretary for his father, Marley Hay, a naval architect of Scottish origins, and a pioneer in submarine design. In 1939 they took advantage of a job offered to John in New York to escape the darkening clouds of war gathering over Europe. They soon adopted U.S. citizenship, and Annette was born on December 7, 1940. Their son, Gordon, was born three and a half years later. In 1951, John Hay—driving a VW Beetle with the engine in the rear—ran head on into a deer on his way home from a business trip, and was killed on impact. Left without the benefits of life insurance, disoriented and shattered by the death of the second man she'd ever loved, Jeannie moved back to France hoping to find solace in her home country. But after three years she realized that too much time had passed, that relations with her in-laws were somewhat tense, and that her children had trouble adapting to a foreign country at such a young age and bereft of a father. She returned to the States.

Annette eventually graduated from high school in Scarsdale, New York, and went on to Endicott College, but was unhappy there and left after a year to complete secretarial school. Just before her twentieth birthday she headed into the City and found work as an assistant to the Editorial Director of *Mademoiselle* magazine. Her boss was a domineering lady in her mid-forties with no sense of taste as far as Annette could see, after six months serving coffee to her boss's buddies, she found a new job at the advertising firm of Young and Rubicam. She started saving up to move to the City early 1963.

Cedric learned most of this through their lengthy evening phone calls that occurred several times a week. They went on one date—Tad's smoky steakhouse and a movie—but since Cedric was unwilling to drive to Scarsdale to see Annette, they never found another moment to meet up until she moved into the city. "You're simply G.U.—Geographically Unsuitable," he told Annette. "I'm not going to drive two hours roundtrip just for a goodnight kiss." Eventually even the frequency of their phone calls dwindled, and Annette began to wonder if she hadn't been mistaken in her thoughts of a future as Mrs. Cedric Grant.

Towards the end of the year, after almost eight months working for First National, Cedric found out that he had two weeks vacation due before the end of the year. He planned a trip through Central America in order to visit Bogotá, Panama City, Guatemala City, San Salvador,

Managua and Mexico City. He shared his plans with Jimmy Griffin, and was introduced him to the Senior Vice President of Latin America, who in turn cabled the Branch Managers of First National in the countries that Cedric was visiting and arranged for them to meet him at the airport and show him around. Cedric was flabbergasted, and felt very special—his loyalty to First National became solidly entrenched at this moment, a loyalty that would carry him through many difficult times later in his career when First National became the unwieldly and less caring behemoth called Citibank.

He returned to the States on New Year's Eve, and immediately called up Annette. Her greeting was glacial—he hadn't called in weeks, she had no idea he'd left on vacation, and he'd signed his only postcard from Guatemala 'COG', initials that held no meaning for her. But she didn't know him well enough to remain angry for very long, and two days later she was helping unpack in his new apartment (Harry Overtoom's wife had arrived from Chicago, and Cedric decided to relocate to a smaller apartment on East 46th street).

Since John Barner's return, Katy Gammack no longer accompanied Cedric on his sky-diving meets, and Harry's departure had deprived him of a jumping buddy. He soon convinced Annette to join him on Saturdays when he went sky-diving, and initiated her into the delicate art of parachute packing. One Saturday evening as she was folding his bright pink parachute, she said, "This is trust and love isn't it? I pack it wrong and you go plummeting to the ground!" Cedric smiled, pointed his finger, and said, "I like your sense of humor."

A month later, Katy Gammack and John Barner got engaged. They had learned of John's first overseas posting a week earlier, and he was set to leave by the end of June. Marriage seemed an obvious decision. John was excited and wouldn't stop talking about it—imagine, Liberia! Four years after the Independence of the Belgian Congo, and the continent was smoldering with the embers of colonization! There could be no more exciting time to head to Africa with so much to do!…

His enthusiasm was infectious—Cedric found himself more and more anxious to learn the location of his own foreign posting. He had asked to be sent anywhere, and he had meant it. First National had only a few branches in Europe with rare openings, and a trainee could wait years before being sent abroad if he requested a cushy post in Amsterdam, London, Paris, or Frankfurt. So when Jimmy Griffin walked up to his desk one afternoon in May, and asked him when he could be ready to leave for Monrovia, Liberia, Cedric threw down in his pen, jumped up, and said, "Tomorrow?" Jimmy laughed and said he would make it two weeks.

Cedric's initial excitement died down when he began to consider his relationship with Annette. They both knew that if she didn't join him, if he didn't marry her, then the relationship was doomed. "But it wouldn't work out anyway," he said jokingly to Annette. "You like your fancy diners and five-star hotels…I'm not saying you don't have a sense of adventure, but if I were to take a woman there, I think she would have to be the Peace Corps type!" Yet ending their relationship was also a reality they weren't yet ready to face. So they decided to postpone the outcome, and agreed that Annette would fly to Monrovia with Katy as soon as he and John were settled in. "We'll see how that works out. Maybe you'll hop back on the plane the day after you arrive!"

Cedric was wrong, however, about Annette's understanding of the situation. She knew that his reluctance to get engaged had little to do with Liberia and much more to do with his sense of independence. He had explained to her once his attraction to Schopenhauer's pessimistic outlook on life: everyone wallowed in misery and suffering, and it was difficult to be positive about anything; but he believed he had risen above it in a Nietzschean way, and if he was pessimistic about the world in general, he was optimistic about his own position within that world. Since he'd started working as a paper delivery boy at the age of ten, he had never counted on anyone's help—not for flying lessons, or college, or travels, or finding a job. When help came he greeted it warmly, but he firmly believed that he had created his own luck, and that ultimately he could only rely upon himself. What he didn't realize, or accept, was that this very sense of independence was inherently self-centered, and his reluctance to depend on others made him shun others' dependence on him. And marriage implied that one had to think for two.

5

George Moore became head of First National City Bank's Overseas Division in 1957. Stillman Rockefeller still solidly gripped the helm but he was already part of the slow-paced banking past, unaware that American financiers had shaken off the Depression blues and embraced globalism more warmly and much faster than American politicians. Together, Moore and Wriston formed a vision and planned a future that would carry the Bank through the latter half of the twentieth century. "Around 1960 we took a new position," Moore said when he retired. "We decided that we would not be merely a bank. We would become a financial service company. We would seek to perform every useful financial service, anywhere in the world, which we were permitted by law to perform and which we believed we could perform at a profit."[1] Though many of Moore's business decisions were not profitable, he and Wriston showed impressive foresight by positioning themselves globally. When they were respectively promoted to President and Overseas Division Head in 1960, they barreled ahead aggressively with the opening of branches around the world. Moore acted with childlike enthusiasm, like a chip-happy gambler throwing his bets around the roulette table. Several ventures eventually turned a profit, but the main gain was image: The Bank became a worldwide presence and the Overseas Division emerged as a five-star destination for hungry financiers.

Liberia certainly didn't feel to Cedric like a "five-star destination" as he at his desk on the second floor office of the two-story building on Randel St. that formed First National's headquarters and the *de facto* Central Bank of Liberia. He re-adjusted the rags around his wrists to

---

1.   Quote and information on Wriston and Citibank lifted from *Wriston* by Phillip Zweig

avoid the sweat dripping on the documents he was reading…Liberia was the asshole of the earth as far as international banking was concerned, far from the lofty South American or European postings, but the experience was not too far removed from what he'd expected, and to a certain degree from what he'd wanted. His experience in New York, and traveling around the European branches before arriving in Liberia, had imbued him with the sense of purpose that First National wished to instill in its employees. Even if he had trouble envisioning it as he sorted through the stack of checks on which he needed to sign off, he still felt deep inside that he was part of something much larger, something great. He had wanted experience and there was plenty of that in Liberia.

Cedric turned to the stack of checks, rubbed his eyes, and sighed. It was late morning, already hot and muggy, and he had trouble concentrating. It was time for a rainstorm. He felt like he was trapped in the udder of a cow that was just aching to be milked, though he knew that the frequent thunderstorms seldom offered release from the ubiquitous humidity. A shadow fell across his desk, and he turned to see one of his savings tellers, Jallah Prall, standing a few feet behind him, hands crossed in front of him. "Chief, Mr. Klingen sir wishes to see you."

If Cedric had ever formed an image of "The Big White Hunter", Klingen would be it: tall and powerful, shaped like a barrel, with distinct handsome features that shone through an abrasive personality. He pranced around the office as if he owned the place, which essentially he did. He expected everyone to be in awe of him, and generally they were. A self-made man from New Jersey (if lingering in Liberia at forty-six could be considered "making it", Cedric mused), he had lifted himself socially by marrying a woman of education and wealth. Fat, obnoxious, cold and cruel, she seemed the perfect mate. Their two children—a five-year old boy and a three-year-old daughter—gave them the appearance of a typical harmonious American expatriate family. Only it was an appearance reflected in Alice in Wonderland's looking glass: instead of being kind and friendly and healthy and full of shiny white smiles, they were grim and strange and aloof and full of dark energy.

Klingen had served in the Army during World War II, joined the bank after the War and had been sent to Bombay, where he contracted tuberculosis before being posted in Japan. The account of his time there was murky, filled with rumors of borderline deals with business officials. Klingen certainly did not seem concerned with what New York might think of the way he ran the bank in Liberia as long as he was turning a profit, and New York didn't seem to care, not only because they looked primarily at profit, but also because most local staff were probably unable to locate Liberia on a map. Cedric wasn't sure how much he could trust Klingen personally, but there was something about the man that he respected professionally—Klingen was the only branch manager in Liberia to invite junior Black officers to attend meetings, and generally he gave good advice on the job.

Cedric entered his boss's office to learn that he had to fly up that afternoon to the FNCB in Nimba, in the northwestern corner of Liberia near the Guinea border, and hand over to the branch manager, Larry Osbourne, the usual cases of cash to cover the LAMCO payroll. It was a Liberian-American-Swedish iron-mining consortium that had been awarded a concession over the reserves in Nimba, and an important client of the bank in the region. After lunch, Cedric drove an hour and a half to the Robertsfield International airport in Harbel sixty miles away, along a death-defying single-lane road through savanna and rubber tree plantations with asphalt so cracked by tree roots and weeds that the car would almost jump off the road at every turn.

The pilot met Cedric at the airstrip and they took off immediately because of a thunderstorm that threatened to delay the flight indefinitely. They managed to reach Nimba, but the pilot told Cedric that he was turning around and heading out while he still could. Cedric understood and figured he'd find his own way back to Monrovia soon enough. He knew that he couldn't wait till the storm abated: at that time of the year, it could last for days. Larry Osbourne suggested that he hop on one of the LAMCO freight trains heading to Buchanan. Isolated deep in the awesome rain forest, cut off from the coastal infrastructure in Buchanan, and far from any major transportation link, LAMCO had built a 170-mile railroad from Mount Nimba through Grand Bassa county all the way to Buchanan to expedite their shipments of ore. Freight trains rattled south round the clock, through the rain forest all the way to the coast.

Some time around two o'clock in the morning, Cedric embarked on one of these trains, carrying two suitcases filled with worn currency that Larry had given him to take back to Monrovia so that it could be mutilated. Larry had urged him to take along two pistols as a precaution. It was a long, uncomfortable and muggy five-hour trip until the freight train pulled into Buchanan just as the sun was rising. Cedric hopped off onto a deserted railway platform. The heat had remained constant all night, and Cedric could smell his own body heat rising from his clammy shirt. He couldn't find a single taxi at the station, so he tramped into Buchanan to find one. The pistols were stuck down his pants, one in front, the other behind, and he had to stop every two hundred yards or so to re-adjust them so that they wouldn't keep digging into his back and thighs. He found a driver sleeping in his car outside a closed shop and woke him up. The man agreed to drive him the hundred and thirty miles to Harbel to pick up his car, but after only a few miles they were prevented from crossing the Saint John River: the ferry across the bay was out of service.

Cedric turned uncomprehendingly to the driver. "July 26, sir. Independence Day. Everything, it is closed." Cedric sighed and paid the driver. He had forgotten. Now he remembered why he had been annoyed the previous morning when Klingen had asked him to make this trip, beyond the fact that he would be leaving a stack of work behind. He breathed in deeply and tried to ignore the mosquitoes and flies, and the tendrils of mugginess that wrapped themselves snuggly around him. Finally he found a man willing to take him across in a dug-out canoe, and he felt fortunate to see a taxi idling on the other side of the river. The driver became quickly aware of Cedric's plight and turned it to his advantage to charge an exorbitant fee. Cedric didn't have the strength to haggle; he finally arrived home at the bank compound at eight o'clock that evening.

The compound—reserved for the white expat officers of the bank exclusively—consisted of fourteen acres of sprawling green and brown grasslands within a concentration of ironwood and mahogany trees. Seven furnished bungalows with high colonial style ceilings, marble floors, spacious rooms and large bay windows, were set out in a circle, in the middle of which perched the General Manager's house on top of a knoll. It was located six miles from Monrovia on the Farmington River, at the end of the potholed asphalt coastal road that headed north. They had access to a private beach surrounded by palm trees two miles away where they would lounge on weekends and organize barbecues. Cedric shared a bungalow with John Barner, and as the most recent arrival he was in charge of supervising the staff—gardeners, maids, houseboys—that worked within the compound, as well as organizing the weekend parties, and starting the generator when an electrical blackout occurred.

As Cedric settled on the sprawling terrace, his houseboy Charlie bought him a whisky soda and a telegram. Charlie was a native Liberian of the Kpelle tribe with impeccable Western manners. He's seen too many British colonial films, Cedric thought the first time he set eyes on this small gangly man in his early forties, dressed in white shorts, white sneakers, tall white socks and a white V-neck slipover sweater. His hair was cut somewhere in between a crew-cut and an afro, and he seemed to glide around the house in uncanny silence. Charlie never showed anger, joy, impatience. He was more exemplary than the most reserved British butler, and he second-guessed John and Cedric's every wish.

"Good news, sir?" he asked Cedric in a monotone voice.

"I think so," Cedric answered slowly. It was from Eva, confirming her wish to come to Liberia. *Good for October when Katy there stop would be nice to have company stop miss you stop Eva.*

Cedric had left New York at the end of June 1963, and for ten days he visited First National City Bank's European branches in London, Paris, Frankfurt, and the new one that had just opened in Amsterdam. Africa and Europe came under the same regional division within the overseas department, and Cedric got the chance to meet briefly with the people with whom he would be doing business. After this veneer of business travel, he had a week to do some personal traveling before he was expected in Liberia.

He remembered the story of Jeannie's fiancé, Michel Vieuchange, who in 1929 had paid with his life to chase his dream of discovering the forbidden city of Smara in the Rio del Oro region of Morocco, and who had headed off into the Sahara desert dressed as a Berber woman to try and find this city that had never been contemplated by Western eyes. Now that Smara was now open to tourism, Cedric decided to make that his destination. He proceeded to Las Palmas in the Grand Canaries, and joined a group of hotel guests making a day trip to El Ahoun. On the DC-3 flight from the Canaries to North Africa, he sat next to an attractive and outspoken Swedish girl in her twenties named Eva, who was traveling with her parents. He aborted his trip to Smara and spent the day visiting El Ahoun with Eva and her parents. He asked her out to dinner that evening, but she claimed to have plans already. Their return flight was delayed for so long, however, that when they finally arrived back in Las Palmas at one o'clock in the morning, there was no-one was waiting for her.

She and Cedric spent the next five days together, and the two became so smitten with one another that they agreed Eva would come visit him in Liberia a few months later. They continued to write, and Cedric began to envision a future with her. When John mentioned that he was flying Katy to Liberia in October, Cedric immediately cabled Eva to come at the same time, and finally—and yes, with trepidation—wrote to Annette to break the news to her.

John and Cedric picked up the two women in Harbel, and almost immediately things went awry. While Katy bubbled with excitement, Eva could not manage to adapt to the strangeness of Liberia. At the end of her stay, she and Cedric knew it was over: Eva refused to ever come back and live in that hell hole. Katy flew back to New York with the good news, but Annette had tried to put the whole thing behind her and was dating a banker with Morgan Guarantee named Howard. "I can't just wait till the boy figures out what he wants," she told her friend.

When Katy and John returned to Liberia as a married couple in early 1964, Cedric moved into a smaller bungalow on the compound and took Charlie with him, while the Barners' acquired the services of a new houseboy named George, with whom Katy would entertain a tenuous relationship over snakes. Green mambas, black mambas, Gaboon vipers, cobras—whatever the shape, length, name or however much poisonous, Katy squealed, and despite George's lackadaisical removal of them, she never got used to them. Every morning and every evening she made sure that her supply of anthrax serum was still in the refrigerator.

One evening over dinner, Cedric was unaccustomedly quiet. When Katy asked him what was eating him, he said: "I see you two and I think that Annette *would* enjoy herself here. Like you Katy."

"Cable her, Rick. Tell her to meet you somewhere and propose," John said. "Ah, I dunno, do something!"

And Cedric did. He arranged for a two-week leave at the end of March, and cabled Annette to meet him in Paris, with plane ticket to follow. A month later he flew to Timbuktu via Bamako, Mali. He finally landed in Le Bourget military airport on his birthday, March 20, and took a bus to Orly to meet Annette.

There, among the diesel fumes, standing behind the bus before boarding, Cedric proposed. And she said yes.

Dear Mrs. Hay,

I would much prefer that Annette and I were in New York to discuss our engagement and wedding plans with you. Since lack of time prevents me from returning to New York, I must communicate with you by letter. I hope that our engagement does not come as a surprise or a shock.

Unfortunately the only time that I can obtain a week's leave will be in late April or late May. Any other time will place too much work on the other five Americans at the bank and create unnecessary shifting of departments. I also would like Annette to be settled in Monrovia before the "rainy season" begins. I apologize that this doesn't give you much time to prepare for the wedding.

I now realize that I should have married Annette before I left the United States last July. Due to the lack of information and the wrong information, I had absolutely no idea about life in West Africa. I had doubts about Annette's ability to adjust to the climate, food, natives and living conditions. I believe that everything that occurred after I left New York was a reaction to "running away" from her. Now I know about West Africa and I know that Annette will adjust and will like it there with me. I love Annette and will do my best to make her as happy as possible.

Sincerely,

Cedric

Despite the relative lack of time, the wedding went off well. A connected socialite friend of Jeannie's arranged for the post-wedding party to take place at the Colony Club on Park Avenue. Around five o'clock in the evening, bride and groom changed into casual attire more appropriate for traveling. They took a limousine to the airport and flew to Lisbon—not for a honeymoon, but on their way to Liberia, where they arrived on Sunday afternoon.

Katy and John met them at the airport in Harbel and drove them back to the compound. The four then headed to the beach for a barbecue and a dip in the ocean. Instead, they found a bloated and crab-riddled corpse washed up on the shore. Annette turned on her heels and headed back to the compound.

"Welcome to Liberia," Cedric said.

◆   ◆   ◆

They lived in a large house facing north with a shaded patio. The front door opened onto a living room cum dining room with marble floors, dark furniture, gold curtains and blue walls, with a bay window facing south and three facing west. There were two bedrooms off to the side, separated by a common bathroom, with white and turquoise tiles and no tub. At the back of the house were the pantry and a big kitchen that stretched along the whole northern wall of the house. After her confined quarters in Manhattan, Annette was overjoyed.

She felt like she hadn't slept at all when she drowsily noticed light seeping in through the bedroom window. She almost believed she could drift off to sleep again when the sound of music reached her ears. She raised her head and slipped out of bed. She searched for her slippers and robe, and realized that even at this early hour it was warm enough to do without, so she stumbled out of the bedroom and collapsed on a chair at the kitchen table where Cedric was digging into a plate of eggs and fiddling with his tie.

"Could you turn off the goddamn music!" she said.

"I always listen to music in the morning," Cedric began. But he stood up and went to shut it off.

"So, you want breakfast?" Annette said in a voice that expressed her desire to do anything but get up from the chair and start messing around with pots and pans. Or even just a coffee maker.

"Don't worry about it, Charlie can handle it…"

As if on cue, Charlie appeared next to Annette. His sudden silent presence almost managed to startle her fully awake. "How many eggs, Missy?"

She mumbled.

"I'm sorry, but I couldn't hear you Missy," said Charlie.

"Two eggs, Charlie!" she cried out. "And don't forget the coffee!" She looked around for her cigarettes and realized they were back in the bedroom.

"By the way, don't worry about the dishes, Charlie will take care of everything," Cedric said. What's left for me to do? Annette thought, though the growing realization that she would be able to cook and not clean up afterwards appealed to her.

Ten minutes later she started toying with her eggs, and Cedric was heading out the door. He gave her a kiss. "I'll see you around seven or eight. Oh, and by the way," he added with a smile, "don't feel obliged to get up in the morning. A drowsy good morning kiss before I head out the door will be just fine." Annette set about unpacking her suit-cases, and wrote down all the things she was missing and that she needed to have sent from New York. Then she wrote a long letter to her mother, describing the discovery of the corpse on the beach, and how the Liberian police showed up that evening asking accusatory questions until Rick and John were able to convince them that since the crabs were dining on the poor guy's innards, it was most likely that he was some fisherman who had unfortunately drowned and washed up to shore after a few days at sea, rather than a victim of their homi-cidal tendencies.

Katy dropped by that evening after work. Annette mentioned all the things she was missing and how she hoped that her mother would get around to sending her stuff ASAP.

"It's not the complete jungle here, you know Annette. Monrovia has plenty of stores. Very American, you should be able to find a lot of things you need."

"Yes, but I hate to spend money on stuff we already have…Well, maybe for an emergency. But we really can't do much entertaining until our shipment gets here!"

She and Katy both looked at each other then burst out laughing and said together: "Married life!" Annette launched into an account of the morning episode with Rick's music and Charlie's eggs.

"Oh, you should feel lucky! John *expects* me to sit at the breakfast table. Whether or not he'll actually engage in conversation is another matter…The first morning I was here, I was so eager to be the good career wife that I laid out his clothes, even put the belt in the belt loops, went to help George make the breakfast—so, so pleased with myself—and I brought John's breakfast to the table, and he said, 'you put my belt in backwards!' At least Rick's more laid back about the whole thing."

Soon the rainy season descended upon Liberia, bringing violent thunderstorms and long stretches of downpours. Even a blue sunny day could turn dark within minutes, to clear up a few hours later for an intermittent period of sunshine. Annette spent time sewing curtains with the help of the German wife of one of the other bank officers, writing letters, and lolling on the beach when the weather allowed it. Without a telephone or radio in the house, and very limited access to newspapers, there was very little to remind her of the time. As she wrote several times to her mother, the only thing she was quite sure about was the year. She was obliged to repeat this often in three letters of apology to placate her sensitive mother after she forgot to send a card for Mother's Day.

In July 1964, she found a temporary afternoon job working for the Manager of the Ducor Intercontinental Hotel in Monrovia. Cedric felt some financial pressure lift, as the added costs of paying back Jeannie for the wedding and setting up the house—not to mention the hefty food bills—had been preying on him for several months. On weekends and intermittent weekdays, Annette, Cedric, Katy and John would get together for bridge.

Annette's office at the Ducor provided her with a fantastic view of the bay and port. She loved the sight of the city after a heavy rainfall, as the colors of the ocean intensified and the city seemed cleansed. Look-ing back, Annette realized that these were the high times of her life in Liberia, when she was still able to tell her mother that she and Rick were in good health and enjoying themselves, and mean it. When she could handle the rains and high cost of living, the frequent, though temporary, electrical shortages, or the snakes that infested the compound. She could bear Klingen's ribaldry when, for instance, he qualified her *boeuf bourguignon* as "glorified stew" the first time he was invited for dinner. She loved mingling with the international crowd present in Liberia through the Firestone company, FNCB, Chase Manhattan, and Pan American, and was thrilled to host her first party at their house on the compound, while Katy pointed out those members of the Embassy that were—according to Rick and John—most certainly CIA. "Liberia is the most important strategic US base in Africa!" she emphasized.

Yes, these were the high times in West Africa.

Dear Mother,

Well, well…Monrovia is quite different from what I expected. Colonial style houses and more modern buildings. Quite spread out with certainly enough convenience stores. It's when you get out a few miles that things get rough. The American presence is strong here, or at least the influence brought over by the freed American slaves, who in turn—from what I understand—colonized the Native Africans. The American-Liberians are still in all the important economic and political posts, while education and possibilities remains slim for the Natives. A dual class system where both classes are Black. After all the social tension in the States over racial issues, it seems a strange almost ludicrous situation, and certainly difficult to understand for the moment. But perhaps that in itself is a racist view: to think that just because they are all Blacks that they should think the same way. Goes to show that color plays a real backdrop to culture. First National City Bank employs many natives and you should see some of the letters Rick gets! Apparently one of his cashiers told him a while back that he had to skip town for a few weeks because the village witch doctor had placed a curse on him and his head was splitting in two. He's been gone for two months!…

I really like it here—although I find myself faced with quite a bit of responsibility. This house really needs a thorough spring cleaning and overhaul. Well, not so much overhaul as simply needs STUFF—we don't even have curtains! However, everything is made so much easier because I have a houseboy and a laundry boy. I do most of the cooking and planning of meals, but Charlie serves and does the dishes. As Katy says, one day we're going to regret the luxury of that!

The weather has been beautiful for the last few days. I think we're entering what they call here the "mid-drys". Just wish I could take advantage of it and go to the beach. Unfortunately I must look at it through my big bay window. I really love the rainy season...It is so cool and breezy, and surprisingly we aren't having half as much rain as I expected; then, on the other hand, I was told that this was a very mild season and most unusual. How lucky can you get! However, we did have a storm two nights ago which tore down our little orchid tree in the back yard.

All is very well...

For Cedric, however, life was not so light-hearted. He felt estranged from the New York headquarters, and subject to the whims and fancies of an overbearing boss. The running of business seemed out of kilter here in Monrovia, and subject to jungle regulations. As the country's Central Bank, First National City Bank played an important, but sometimes controversial, role in Liberia's twisted economic policy. It was a hands-off behavior common to all banks, and which has defined banking since the Swiss made such a venerable institution of it. Cedric understood this most vividly when he accompanied John Barner to deliver a half a million dollars withdrawn from the Government account by the President of Liberia, William V.S. Tubman, for spending cash on his upcoming trip to Europe.

Fortunately, Cedric benefited from the presence of a "mentor", the Chief Accountant Kerry Hemming, who took him under his wing and showed him all the intricacies of branch banking. Although Kerry would be transferred to Amsterdam after Cedric's first year in Liberia, and eventually leave the bank altogether for Chase Manhattan, he would be become a lifelong friend. Very early on he explained to Cedric that there were three types of expatriate businessmen in an outpost such as Liberia. Those, usually in a position of authority, who considered the exotic and foreign location an excuse to dismiss traditional codes of conduct and run business as profitably as they could, first for themselves and then for the company. Then there were those, usually in a subaltern position, who believed that they were there to follow orders and not question the way business was run. And finally there were those, whether in positions of authority or not, who believed that it was precisely because they found themselves so far from company headquarters and in such a different culture, that rules and regulations should be adhered to implacably and enforced rigorously, so as to avoid breakdown. Kerry and Cedric tried to place themselves in that third category, but Klingen didn't always make it easy.

As compound manager, and as the most Junior expat officer in the bank, Cedric was often handed the most mundane tasks. One Saturday morning in mid-August, he was asked to stock up at the Aboujoudi & Azar supermarket on over three hundred dollars worth of hamburger meat, hot dogs, buns, and beer, for an informal American-style barbeque that Klingen was throwing to celebrate the opening of the Harbel branch of FNCB. The necessity of a branch close to the rubber plantations and Firestone headquarters had become essential for Firestone; the party, however, was just a pretext.

When Cedric came across the bill while processing accounts in the General Ledger, he found it to be almost a thousand dollars. Checking it more closely he realized that the items listed entirely different from those he had bought: lobster, champagne, caviar, smoked salmon…He went to see Barner and found him quite nonchalant about the whole affair. "I don't like it any more than you do, but what can we do?"

"Misappropriation of funds?" Cedric asked. "I don't understand."

Barner shrugged. "Klingen triple-invoices all the parties. That way he stocks up on food at bank expense. What are you going to do—expose him? Just post it to the sundry account as a business promotion, and let it be. New York doesn't particularly care, it's like a reward for working in such a shithole." Cedric considered the already large benefits they accrued for working a hardship post—higher salary, three month leave every two years, housing and odd expenses…But he said nothing and nodded. "Don't worry about it, we should start preparing for the Senior VP's visit in two weeks." Jack Goodrich—head of the Europe/Africa/Middle East department of the Overseas Division—was planning a tour of the branches under his supervision, and Cedric knew that Klingen wanted to pull all the stops to impress him: meeting with President Tubman, followed by a large cocktail party with all the bank officers, Liberian societal bigwigs, and foreign company representatives.

Cedric finished processing the General Ledger, then called his most trusted savings teller, Jallah Prall. "I want you to keep this somewhere safe," he said, handing him the receipt he had received from Aboujoudi I Azar. You never know when we might need it."

Goodrich's visit later that same month started out badly. Klingen sent a car to pick him up at the airport, but since the plane was delayed several hours, the chauffeur drove around showing off the car. Goodrich and his wife finally flew into Harbel at midnight, but halfway back to Monrovia the car ran out of gas. They didn't reach the capital until six in the morning, and Klingen had scheduled Goodrich's meeting with President Tubman for seven o'clock. The party that evening was also an embarrassment. Bank officers' wives were attributed menial tasks, such as babysitting Klingen's kids. To show how far ahead of his time he was and how well he treated the Liberians, Klingen had all the Black officers mingling with the crowd while the American expat officers tended bar or, in Cedric's case, valet parked the cars of the four hundred guests that attended the party.

Klingen's plan to impress the Senior VP backfired, however: when Goodrich found Cedric in the parking lot, he took him aside. "Rick—if I was in your shoes, I would resign. But please don't. I'll deal with this when I get back to New York."

He kept his word. A few months later, bank auditors arrived in Liberia and smelled the subterfuges. Various employees dropped hints, and Jallah passed on the documents that Cedric had quietly stowed away for this very occasion. The auditors also discovered that Klingen was running a personal overdraft with the bank by transferring all his money to New York, writing checks against an empty account, and not paying back either principal or interest. By the end of 1964 he was gone from Liberia, and Cedric heard later that even Wriston disowned him. "That guy will never rise above Assistant VP," he said.

Before the extent of his machinations came out, however, Klingen tried to remove the danger that Cedric represented by simply sending him to Harbel when the manager of the newly instated branch fell severely ill and was forced to quit the bank. Even though he was wary of the reasons for this dubious promotion, Cedric was thrilled to get the chance to manage a branch. He and Annette debated whether only he should move, since she enjoyed her job in Monrovia and Katy's proximity, or whether they should both move together. Eventually they chose the second option—Cedric found the commute daunting, and Annette soon learned that John had been promoted to manage the Nimba branch, so Katy would no longer be nearby anyway. She wasn't thrilled about leaving her job now that she felt settled in, but she was hopeful that she might find something in Harbel to keep her busy. They moved in mid-September 1964 and found a house for $450 a month near the Robertsfield International Airport and the Institute of Tropical Medicine.

◆   ◆   ◆

The Harmatan season arrived in February, bringing very dry and pleasant temperatures in the low eighties, but the constant desert winds mirrored the oppressive inactivity of Annette's life, and made her unable to enjoy the best weather of the year. She sat outside on their porch in Harbel and felt like a fish in a bowl observed by the natives. When the heat and humidity returned, she found solace in their bed-room, the only air-conditioned room of the house. There were few major companies in Harbel and no-one was hiring an expat's wife. All of Annette's alternate plans to fill the seamless days with painting and sewing shattered with the parched brittleness of boredom and the total lack of any kind of mental stimulation. Her only avenue of escape was a young couple whom they'd met in Harbel, Linda and Ted Pearson, who comforted Annette by making her realize that she wasn't the only one whose motivation for productivity and creativity was sapped by the insipid tropical atmosphere.

Ted, lanky and effete and resembling a young Montgomery Clift, worked for the Farrel Lines shipping company, while Linda did volunteer work at the Research Center near Harbel. On weekends they would invite Annette and Cedric to go water-skiing. But then Mondays would arrive and the doldrums would return. Without a car, Annette was practically isolated, surrounded by native villages, with only myriad bugs and snakes to keep her company. Their house was so close to the airport that she had to peel herself off the ceiling when the first planes woke her up at 9am. To kill time, she began playing bridge with some the Pan American and Firestone wives that lived close by, but these ladies in their forties had given up any hope of a more exciting life, and would start on their gin and tonics before noon. When their husbands returned home at five o'clock, they were completely drunk. Soon Annette's routine gelled into waking up at noon, reading Ian Fleming novels until two, then cooking until six o'clock when Cedric would return home to a gourmet meal. Once a month, she would stay up till three in the morning surrounded by stacks of paper and a bottle of white wine, to help her husband with the end-of-month reports, processing customer statements, and Firestone and Pan American payroll records.

That spring, Marjorie lost her job at the Bureau of Immigration, and Cedric soon found himself supporting his mother. On top of everything else, Annette found herself strapped for cash, a situation for which she was unprepared and of which she was not very accepting. She was barely twenty-four, and after one month in Harbel she felt that she was throwing away the best years of her life.

During these long dismal months Annette kept up a certain pretense, so as to not worry her husband and mother with additional concerns over a situation that she considered temporary. She even managed to quit smoking for a while, and convinced Rick to take her on a trip north to Voinjama and Zorzor, veritable bush country filled with missionaries, Peace Corps volunteers and Lebanese traders. They ventured into Sierra Leone to visit the local market, only a twenty minute drive from the border along a treacherous, creviced and rutted road. But what uplifted Annette's spirits the most was the news of their impending home leave in September. Cedric was entitled to three months, and this was to be their honeymoon: a trip through the Middle East, India, Australia, the South Seas, and finally the United States.

For a few weeks in March, Annette remained busy preparing for an imminent succession of VIP visits, notably the new General Manager, Walter Jennings, and the Vice President in charge of Africa, Warren Wheeler. Annette was enthused with the new Manager and his wife. He was in his early forties, tall and thin, with wispy dark hair that barely covered the bald patch near the back top of his head; spindly round spectacles completed his gawky yet friendly appearance. His wife, Vanessa, was in her early thirties but looked ten years older. Slim, almost thin, she always appeared nervous, constantly wringing a handkerchief in her left hand. Her handshake was clammy and her gaze unfocused, but a ubiquitous smile lit up her face, and Annette was immediately charmed. Or perhaps it was just a reaction of pure relief after Mr. and Mrs. Klingen.

When the frequency of cocktail parties dropped off as the Jennings settled in, Annette fell into a virtual stupor—waking at noon, reading James Bond, spending the afternoon in the kitchen, waiting for her husband to return...Cedric finally realized that his wife wasn't quite herself when he returned home one evening to find her in tears and Charlie fired. She went on about how arrogant and impolite he was, and didn't care about anything she said, and when he had asked for a raise she had told him to leave. That Annette felt the need to assert her-self so harshly meant that she did not feel entirely in control, Cedric surmised, and the fact that she was in tears meant that somehow she knew it.

He defused the situation by suggesting a trip to Nimba to visit Katy and John in June. It was such a welcome breath of fresh air for Annette that a month later she was asking to go again. Cedric's workload had increased even more, however, since his home leave was in three months, and Jennings had told him that he would most likely be expected back in Monrovia after that. Annette was overjoyed, and Cedric certainly wasn't saddened by the news himself, but it meant that he had to put things in order and train his deputy Jallah Prall to take his place as manager of the Harbel branch, and he could hardly afford to take off a full weekend. Finally, he arranged for Linda to drive with Annette to Nimba for a five-day trip, and managed to stave off temporarily what Annette didn't recognize, and Cedric didn't want to recognize, as the beginnings of a full-blown depression.

Dear Mother,

...The rainy season has just about started and soon it will rain every day—but that means we're just that much closer to leaving—Oh! Rick just received the news that he had gotten a $1300 dollar raise which could not have come at a more opportune time for the trip—we're so happy! But the weather here is getting very oppressive and I'm feeling rather de-ener-gized.

As you know, Linda and I visited the Barners in Nimba two weeks ago. Rick was too busy to go, but Ted was able to join us for the weekend. It was so nice to get away from here and into a different atmosphere for a while, although I did miss Rick—it was our first separation! Katy and John took us to the top of Mount Nimba where the iron ore mines are located—it was most interesting. I'm not so sure I like their house which is tiny and too much in the center of everything—there is no privacy. The bank rents the house for them from LAMCO and it's on this large settlement with rows and rows of houses which are all on different level of terrain according to your position. The Swedish are apparently very class conscious!

Like Harbel, there isn't much in the way of activities up there, so we did a far amount of bridge-playing and drinking. Katy is such a riot, so much laughter and fun, and we exchanged cynical jokes on our jungle life here. John managed to sober us up, however, with a trip to the Ganta mission which is a leper colony. We bought a few interesting carvings, some of which I'll be bringing home with me. It's a startling sight for western eyes...Reminds of Biblical scenes, Jesus curing the lepers, you know...I would like to know a little more about the illness because it's rather shameful tip-toeing around these people not knowing whether you can get close or not.

And then of course we called you! I could tell by the sound of your voice that you were terribly surprised. We'd just heard over the radio that we could call the States so we took advantage of it. It's just too incredible because here we have no phone and have no connections between Harbel and Monrovia. I couldn't even call Rick from Nimba to tell him that Linda and I would be late coming home. I'm sorry I missed Gordy, however. I hardly recognized him in the pictures you sent with his long hair—it is so becoming and makes him look his age if not a bit older. Tell him congrats for getting into his graduate program at Maryland. Masters in Social Work? Next thing you know, he'll be joining us in Liberia with the Peace Corps!

As you can well guess, I'm so glad to be moving back to Monrovia—and absolutely ecstatic about our trip to Europe, Middle East and Asia. And of course back to New York for a few weeks. Can't wait to see you!...

The Grants finally left West Africa early October 1965. Rick did not reveal the whole trip to Annette, but only let her know what the next destination would be when they arrived at the airport. The itinerary held its promise: Lagos, Nigeria; Addas Abbaba, Ethiopia; Athens, Greece; Tel Aviv, Israel. Their concepts of tourism, however, diverged drastically. Rick was up early, ready to visit all the sights in a day, while Annette wanted to enjoy her cup of coffee and cigarette on the balcony and enjoy the view. By the time they reached Tel Aviv, she was exhausted, and the second night in the hotel, she threw up several times on the steps leading up to their room, her stomach ravaged from the various ethnic foods that Rick insisted they try.

After that he cut her some slack. From Tel Aviv they made their way to Tehran where they got stuck for over week because of the Indo-

Pakistani war. Eventually they caught a KLM flight to New Delhi and on to Bangkok. From there Rick pounced an adventurous surprise on Annette as she discovered that their next destination was Saigon. They only stayed one night: Annette struck up a conversation with a young and traumatized GI while they were waiting on the tarmac for their luggage, and when she asked him why his hand was shaking so violently, he answered, "Last week, a mortar shell killed five men here." Annette promptly grabbed Rick and forced him to book them on the next flight out, wherever it went. Fortunately it was for Hong Kong and Rick's itinerary was not even perturbed. They remained there several days with a bank colleague named Peter Wodtke, and Rick was back in Annette's good graces as she had the chance to literally shop till she dropped. By the time they reached Sydney, Annette's feet were so blistered and sore that she could no longer wear shoes. But the 22-day cruise to Tahiti enabled her to rest and recuperate. From there, they flew to Los Angeles to visit Cedric's father, and they finally arrived in New York end of November.

Jeannie asked her daughter how she was faring in Monrovia, but Annette sensed that her mother didn't want to hear anything too grim. "It can be tough, lonely sometimes. But it's an adventure, and I'm having fun. I'm looking forward to leaving though!" Annette brushed off her mother's general lack of interest, and chalked it up to the fact that she had received so many letters and knew all about her life there. It was not as easy for her to explain away her friends' lack of interest, however. Some would ask her a few questions, and as her answers dragged on, she noticed that their attention drifted rapidly; others didn't even want to know, and expected her to re-integrate their social life as if she'd never left. Rick was there to cushion her disillusion. "People are either jealous or can't relate," he said. "You can't win. Just goes to show you that the only things worth doing are those you can never tell a soul about."

Their lives were so different from everyone around them, they realized so evidently during their stay in New York. Cedric's father actually understood the best—Otto knew all about displacement from his years at sea. He simply asked his son if he enjoyed his work, and was satisfied with the positive response. "If you can get up every Monday morning and not dread going to work, well it's almost as if you weren't working," he'd said.

Cedric wasn't actually surprised, therefore, when Annette decided to return to Liberia before Christmas. After three weeks, she was tired of New York and anxious to resume what had become her life. They would be back in Monrovia, and the Barners were also likely to move back from Nimba very soon. Annette was almost happy to go home. It felt odd using that word for Monrovia, but that was the truth now. Unfortunately, she wouldn't feel that way for long, as Liberia decided to wring her emotions dry before allowing her and Cedric leave for good.

6

After his stellar clean-up work in Harbel, Cedric was handed the messiest department in the Monrovia branch upon his return to Liberia. He arrived at seven in the morning and pulled twelve hour work days, and Annette was left to her own devices, without even a home to attend to, prostrate in the aftermath of culture and reverse culture shocks. While the house they were suppose to occupy was having a bedroom added, Annette and Cedric stayed with the Osbournes, another Bank couple who were away on home leave, and Annette was suffused with a very disagreeable and uncomfortable feeling of not belonging.

The Grants' house was still not ready when the Osbournes returned in January, and so—as Annette wrote to her mother—they went out of the proverbial frying pan into the fire by moving into a spare bedroom in the Jennings' house. Whatever empathy Annette may have felt towards them upon their arrival evaporated completely within the first few days of experiencing the new General Manager's aloof disregard for his staff's predicament and his obvious disinterest in Liberian affairs, all masked by a boisterous congeniality that she found more wearisome than Klingen's brassy vulgarity. To make matters worse, she could find no respite in his absence, constantly confronted with his pill-popping wife Vanessa, whose swings from depressive catharsis to frantic yet unproductive activity left Annette feeling exhausted.

None of this helped to overcome her own destabilized and fragile mental state. The cultural desert she experienced in Harbel had been followed by a whirlwind of exposure on their world trip. She felt very little connection with her former life in New York, and her two-year absence from the States had shielded her from the full germination of issues such as peace and love and war and demonstrations and hippies and flower-power and racial tensions and Vietnam and the Beatles…She had found the picture of her brother in long hair amusing and becoming, nothing more; and she was startled to find so many men with similar hair-dos and shaggy outfits roaming the streets of New York.

At the age of thirty-one, Cedric with his crew-cut and horn-rimmed glasses belonged to an entirely different generation. Indeed, his political views were quite in opposition to her brother's, as she witnessed during a rather loud argument one evening after dinner, where Cedric came very close to accusing Gordon of being non-patriotic. Cedric could understand Jeannie's fears as a mother of seeing her only son march off to a war in a country that very few Americans could place on a world map, but he could not understand that this kid would voluntarily wish to shy away from his duty as a U.S. citizen. He advised him to join the officer training corps to avoid being drafted as cannon fodder, whereas Gordon denigrated the whole concept of fighting in Vietnam: it had nothing to do with protecting the United States, so why should he feel bad about not wanting to go there? When Cedric suggested he join ROTC, Gordon responded that he didn't want to cut his hair. Cedric walked out of the room and away from the argument, incensed at such a ridiculous statement. Living so far from the United States, he could not grasp the horrific nature of the Southeast Asian conflict. He could not understand what an anathema it was for a university graduate student to voluntarily join the ROTC in 1966. Gordon didn't need a way to avoid being drafted as cannon fodder; he wanted a way out of the draft itself.

When Annette was once again thrown into a semi-state of forced hibernation upon her return to Liberia, all of these preoccupations and concerns were shunted into oblivion. She soon slipped into a depression that quickly became noticeable to everyone, with the possible and probable exception of Walt Jennings. Vanessa seemed almost happy to have a companion in misery and tried to encouraged to her to take Valium. "Makes everything just *so* much easier to bear!" Annette refused. She could not stand the increased sense of displacement, and because of this the Valium seemed to increase her moroseness rather than assuage it. Furthermore, a timid but shrill voice inside said that she did not want to end up a neurotic yoyo like Vanessa for the rest of her life, deprived of ego and dependant on pills.

When they were finally able to move into their house in mid-February, her state worsened instead of improving. Cedric would return home to find only a few more clothes unpacked, but little more—no curtains across the windows, the kitchen in disarray, the bed sheets unmade, and sometimes Annette still in her nightgown. He immediately gave up asking her what she did with her days, when he was confronted with a screaming litany of accusations and self-deprecation. His days at work lengthened.

Annette hid most of this from her mother, but for someone able to read through the lines of her listlessness, her imminent breakdown would have seemed evident. Jeannie only knew that her daughter was not terribly happy and she attributed most of that to Liberia. When the Grants finally found the services of an efficient houseboy, Cedric promptly invited the Barners down from Nimba for the weekend. Ted and Linda also joined them from Harbel, and the Osbournes from the Monrovia compound, so it turned out to be quite a festive dinner party. Katy, however, was alarmed at the state in which she found Annette. She was shocked to see that her friend had lost interest in almost everything around her. "It all seems so terribly without meaning," Annette said. "I would feel like Sisyphus except I don't even need to roll the boulder up the hill to feel the absurdity of it all."

Katy confronted Cedric with her usual tact immediately after dinner. "Are you aware that she is heading for a nervous breakdown, if not already in one!"

"I know, I know, but I don't *know* what to do," Cedric sighed. "I'm working fourteen hour days, dealing with a stack of letters from employees requesting five dollars advances for a wife to finish her studies, or to put food on their kids' table, or telling me that they have to leave for a few months because the witch doctor put a curse on them, and they have to find a stronger witch doctor to remove it. I just don't know what to do."

A few weeks after the dinner party, a cash shipment from Monrovia to Nimba went missing, mysteriously replaced by boxes of women's Kotex packages. The Police were called in, and the Barners' and the Grants' houses were raided immediately, while John and Cedric were held on suspicion. They tried to explain that the boxes must have been switched by an employee of the Liberian National Airways who had observed FNCB's modus operandi over the past several months. Using his experience with American Can, Cedric tried to convince the Police that they could probably track down the culprit using the Kotex serial numbers and find out which local store had received the shipment and who had placed the order. His suggestion was received coldly and the Police never inquired.

For the first time in his career, Cedric found himself on shaky ground. He was never directly blamed for the loss of $75,000 since he had followed protocol to the letter, but he was afraid that a stigma of irresponsibility would nevertheless taint his reputation.

Three weeks later an employee of the Liberian postal service told the Police that his brother-in-law was spending surprisingly large amounts of cash on his girlfriend and he wondered where all the money was coming from. The Police raided the man's house but found nothing to incriminate him. Frustrated, they resorted to a tribal method of interrogation called the Sassywood test: the local witchdoctor would a heat a knife until the tip was white hot and then place it upon the tongue of the accused. If his tongue remained unscathed, he was innocent; if it blistered, he was guilty.

The scientific explanation was that a guilty man's tongue would go dry from fear, and blister, while an innocent man's tongue would remain moist and therefore protected. Cedric knew, however, that if the Police had chosen to carry out such an interrogation on him after raiding his own house, his tongue would most likely have dried up from fear alone. As it was, the postal employee's brother-in-law confessed before the Sassywood trial could even take place, and Cedric's name was cleared.

He, Annette and the Barners celebrated that same night. But when Annette asked a few days later what had happened to the missing cash shipment, Cedric could no longer ignore that his wife was in the throes of a severe nervous breakdown. He made an appointment to see the doctor the very next day and bought Annette a dog, a beautiful Alsatian named Sacha.

After a few months of vitamin B shots (to cure what had been diagnosed as anemia), and with Sacha growing in leaps and bounds, Annette's spirits began to lift. She harnessed enough energy to find work as a secretary in an architectural firm, and being active was the key to her recovery. By the end of spring, Annette was her ebullient and energetic self once again, and she decided to follow in her mother's early footsteps: she tried out for and obtained a part in *The Tender Trap*, a play that was being produced by a group of expat' thespians named "the Monrovia Players".

Annette's improved morale had such a positive effect on Cedric that by the middle of summer he was suddenly moved by the urge to grab his old Army duffel bag and head off into the unknown…One evening as he and Annette were entertaining the Osbournes, the conversation drifted to Ric's former travels, and how he still regretted not having followed through on the plans hatched in Paris to travel across West Africa by jeep. This in turn lead to the story of Jeannie's erstwhile fiancé and brother of Gordon's godfather, Michel Vieuchange. Rick was telling the Pearsons how Michel had indeed found the city of Smara, but died of dysentery on his way back, and that his travel notes had subsequently been published by his brother, Jean, gaining no small measure of fame. These travel tales resulted in encouraging a rather inebriated Larry Osbourne to propose that he and Cedric cross the Sahara desert from South to North by Land Rover. Cedric had had something rather more solitary in mind, but the adventurous prospect of driving across the Sahara—an endeavor which he knew would be not just foolish but potentially fatal to attempt alone—was simply too alluring. He immediately began to formulate plans.

Dear Mother,

…and Liberian National Airways flew the rugby team (including wives) to Freetown for a match against Sierra Leone. We really had a wonderful time—Freetown itself is much older than Monrovia, and the center of town is not as nice, but the surroundings are much nicer. They have stretches and stretches of beautiful beaches with coves and lagoons for water skiing and most of the houses are all set up in the hills overlooking the harbor (apparently it is the third largest natural harbor in the world). There is more in Monrovia in the way of restaurants and nightclubs, but the Casino in Freetown which is located about seven miles from the town along the beach is very plush. We had lunch with a very nice Sierra Leone couple—both born there but having a mixture of many races. He was a local dentist. I believe that in ten years this place could be quite a tourist attraction, along the same line as Abidjan in the Ivory Coast is now. As much as I might be branded for saying this, but such things as infrastructure (or lack thereof) show the absence of Colonial rule. The English and the French did accomplish quite a bit. And if you consider that 95% of Liberians have suffered, and suffer still, under the quasi-colonial rule of the 5% of Black American-Liberians, well…I'm not going to defend the abuses of Colonial rule, but if the world is moving closer together, and Africa is inevitably opening up to the Western world—tragically or not is not for me to say—then those countries who benefited from the infrastructures set up by the French and the English are in a better position to succeed.

Anyway, speaking of tyrannical rule—the annual Presidential Ball happened last week! It is apparently the biggest even on the Liberian Calendar, except for the Inauguration Ball which is only once every four years. We had a very good time, but I was really disappointed in that I expected a State Affair to be a bit more chic—this one came off like something out of a college Prom! Before hand a group of us—Ric and I, the Barners, the Osbournes, the Bradleys another bank couple, and young couple from Mobil Oil—congregated at the Bradleys' house where all the men got dressed. So funny!, no one knew how to tie a bow tie properly! It was howling…I must say Rick looked very dapper in his tails and very handsome.

The tables were set up in rows, seating about ten people at each table covered with plain white table cloths. The room was very long in a "L" shape with a dais at the end before the elbow of the L where the President sat, the Tribal Chiefs and high-level government officials, and off to the side the various Ambassadors...The President arrived only a half an hour late, and as he came in, the band played the Liberian National Anthem and of course everyone stood up. Then there was the Grand March, which the President and his daughter-in-law led, followed by the government officials, ambassadors, managers of large companies, and then anyone else who wanted to join in the March. We just sat on the sidelines and watched—it was fun and we had a chance to see the outfits, some of them quite funny, with men in coats and tails but no shoes, the women in flowing robes and turbans—what a potpourri of outfits. The Grand March started off to the tune of "Bridge over the River Kwa"" and lasted for nearly a half hour with the band playing various dance tunes. Drinks were passed around any old how in bottles, and if one wanted to be sure to have a full glass at all times, we had to tip the waiters who were decked out in soiled white uniforms looking as if they had slept in their clothes for days...We left the Ball at about two am as the music was starting to get very monotonous, and went with a few Bank people to the Ducor Hotel where a second smaller Ball was going on. We only stayed there forty-five minutes as the band there had stopped playing, and we all ended up at a small nightclub, "The Key Club", where we spent the rest of the evening. All in all it was worth going to once, and I am glad we had that chance to see it...

◆　　◆　　◆

While Annette flourished in her new role as an amateur theatre actress in *The Tender Trap*, and in her job at the architectural firm, Cedric spent most of his spare time reviewing plans to cross the Sahara. He and Larry convened every two weekends to discuss logistics—they planned to take a well-traveled trail road of three thousand miles from Niamey to Tangiers ('well-traveled' being a relative term, since the car could break down along the way and leave them stranded for days until another soul showed up), that used to be controlled by the French and that was still *relatively* safe. They purchased an old Land Rover with a new engine, hiring the services of a mechanical engineer from Black-wood-Hodge to make sure it would survive the trip with minimal foreseeable problems. Then they would make their way by boat to Algeria and on to Paris to meet their wives.

One morning early September, Cedric was sitting at his desk in the corner of the second floor of the Bank building in Monrovia, suffering under a hot tin roof with his ubiquitous wet rags wrapped around his wrists to avoid sweat from pouring onto the documents he was revising. The air-conditioning had broken down for the third time that month, and Cedric only bore the heat by telling himself that it was ideal preparation for the Sahara crossing. His face was flushed, his heart raced and his head pounded: Cedric started to wonder if he wasn't suffering from something more serious than heat and humidity. Suddenly his whole chest constricted, as if caught between two pounding jackhammers. His vision clouded over, and he wondered in disbelief as he slumped to the floor how he could possibly be having a heart attack at the age of thirty-two.

When he awoke, he still had trouble breathing, his head felt as light and stretched as a hot air balloon, his body was racked with fever, and towering above him was a form of spotted moon wearing a wig, which turned out to be his wife's face once his eyes managed to focus.

"We didn't drink *that* much last night, did we?"

Annette told him that he was suffering from the combined afflictions of positive malaria and hepatitis, a potent mix that would put him out of work for several weeks. Work? Cedric mused. What about the Sahara? Oh, yes, the Sahara too, Annette said. No way.

Within a few days Cedric was feeling, if not quite sprite, certainly well enough to realize that he was thoroughly bored. He found himself in the Firestone hospital in Harbel, which meant that Annette could visit him only one or twice a week, plus weekends. He managed to strike up some intriguing conversations with the attending physician, Frau Krölein who freely admitted to having worked as a doctor in the SS Panzer division on the Eastern front during the Second World War.

Cedric wasn't sure whether to feel frightened or reassured by her medical expertise.

This may have had some bearing on his decision to borrow the five huge volumes of Churchill's history of World War II from the hospital library. The books managed to keep him occupied and sedated during his convalescence, quite a feat for a man who hadn't set foot in a hospital since his plane crash in Oregon. After Churchill he turned to reading the classics, perusing philosophy, brushing up on his German and Italian…By the end of the third week, however, he was feeling restless, cranky, and anxious to get home to his wife, and to a job which he felt simply could stand such a prolonged absence, especially after he learned of the collapse of the Intra Bank in Lebanon. Everyday the newspapers dwelled on the manipulation of fiscal affairs by corrupt politicians, and the ever-growing repercussions on the banking world throughout the Middle East. Cedric felt much more defeated, however, by the shelved plans for the Sahara trip—the Osbournes were scheduled to leave Liberia before the end of the year, and he feared that the trip would never take place.

Better news awaited him upon his return to work in mid-October: a new trainee was due to arrive in a few weeks with the Senior VP and head of the Middle East-Africa (MEA) division, Jack Goodrich, to replace Cedric in Monrovia. "You can start thinking about departure," Jennings told him. "You'll be heading to New York first for six months to take a Senior Credit training course." This was to prepare him for a substantial promotion to Credit Officer; the actual location of his future overseas posting, however, had not yet been determined.

If Annette dreamed of Frankfurt or London, she was sorely disappointed. As Goodrich's altered title indicated, Europe and MEA had been split into two separate divisions. Annette tried to maintain a flicker of hope that they would still be sent somewhere decent like Morocco, but she refrained from badgering Jack Goodrich the moment he walked through the door at the dinner party held in his honor.

Cedric and Niles, the new recruit, sympathized immediately. Cedric reviewed aspects of the job and the more fascinating facets of Liberia, while Niles told him how he'd hopped on a motorcycle with his wife Claire after graduate school, and traveled all the way from Arizona to New York sleeping under the stars before starting his traineeship at Citibank. When he had showed Goodrich his shamefully low moving expenses, the Senior VP had quintupled it out of principle. Hearing this, Cedric put a friendly arm around Niles's shoulder and asked: "Niles? Ever thought of crossing the Sahara by jeep? You're just the person I've been waiting for…I was supposed to go earlier this Fall, but I came down with malaria and hepatitis. But I think you would make the perfect travel companion." Niles agreed immediately.

Galvanized by renewed possibility of such an adventure, Cedric hopscotched through the dinner party crowd to find Jack Goodrich and good-naturedly ask him in a boisterous voice: "So Jack, what language do I learn next? Where am I heading?"

Jack swiveled around and answered point blank: "Ah well Rick, you'd better learn Arabic: you're going to Jeddah, Saudi Arabia!"

There was a loud pitched scream that sent Sacha scampering off into the compound grounds with her tail between her legs: Annette, who'd been charmingly entertaining her husband's boss, pitched forward and almost fainted. She ran into the kitchen and remained there crying for the rest of the evening.

She managed not to dwell on Cedric's next assignment over the next few months. In any event she was quite unable to, as if her mind refused to allow her to consider a situation about which she knew very little. Instead, she told herself that she would be spending six months in New York, and began to make plans—work perhaps, or return to school—she would have very little chance of pursuing any kind of career in Saudi Arabia.

Cedric's second home leave was due several months before the Grants were scheduled to leave for New York. They planned a "European Trip" and in December, he and Annette flew to Italy where they met up with Harry Overtoom, who was on vacation with his wife and children. Together they visited Rome and Milan, then Cedric and Annette continued on to Athens, Beirut (where they met up with Ted and Linda still on their home leave from Farell Lines), Damascus, and Petra where they celebrated Annette's 26ᵗʰ birthday.

The four of us rented a car and driver and drove to Ba'albeck and Biblos (supposedly the oldest city in the world), and Crack des Chevaliers (a fantastic fortress where we were the only tourists). Liked Beirut very much—the climate is certainly very enticing. During the spring you can go skiing—as good as the French or Swiss Alps—and come back to the city—just over an hour's drive—and go swimming! The beaches are gorgeous.

Then we moved on to Damascus where we toured the famous bazaar—every bit as smelly and fascinating as it is supposed to be. Linda's and my tongue were hanging out at the sight of all the yummies. Unfortunately space and finances would not permit us to indulge our fancies to any great extent. I do definitely want to return to Damascus (perhaps while in Saudi Arabia, ah!) if only to purchase one of those beautiful round copper and brass tables. The materials also are out of this world. For my twenty-sixth birthday, Rick, Ted, and Linda got me enough material to make an evening dress out of magnificent Damascus brocade. I shan't attempt to make it myself, but would rather wait until we get back to New York.

Then we continued our trip to Jerash, now a dead city, where we had lunch and explored the ruins. Then down to the Dead Sea where we stopped briefly before going onto Jerusalem where we spent the night. The next morning we left early for Petra—an ancient Nabatean city carved out of the rock, and lost to the Western world until a Swiss explorer discovered it at the turn of the century. To reach it, we had to abandon the car about a mile away and take horses and guides. It was a full day horseback riding and we returned to Jerusalem very tired but terribly excited. That was December 7ᵗʰ—a birthday I shall certainly never forget.

Merry Christmas!

Upon their return to Liberia they learned that John had received his transfer notice to Johannesburg. Annette found it ironic that John Barner—the good ole Southern boy championing the rights of Negroes—would be confronted with racism in all its horrific splendor in South Africa. She devilishly enjoyed hearing John try to defend the fact that he would be working for a White government that upheld an oppressive and institutionalized Apartheid that made the United States' eroding segregationist laws seem highly emancipatory. To celebrate their respective departures—though they were not due for another few months, and though they all knew that the separation would be a sad and tearful affair indeed—Annette and Katy decided upon a series of reciprocal weekend dinners.

Late one Friday afternoon, Annette arrived home from work and shopping to prepare for the evening only to find that a virtual hurricane had blown through the house—curtains shredded, wall-to-wall rug in the living room pulled back half way, and couch innards exposed. She knew that Sacha was in heat, but could not believe that she was responsible for such a disaster. When she saw her pet tearing around the house in visible pain, however, foaming at the mouth, she reconsidered. She let Sacha out of the house, but despite her maniac tearing around the grounds, the dog never strayed far from the house. Cedric arrived an hour later with John, and Annette greeted them in tears. She could see through the bay windows that Sacha had gone completely mad and was in excruciating pain. She insisted on accompanying them to the vet. During the trip, Sacha kept jumping from the front to the back of the car, and occasionally put her mouth on Annette's arm, as if to calm the pain, but never bit down.

The vet, an congenial and rotund British gentleman who looked like he should have gone into retirement a few decades earlier, diagnosed bronchitis and handed Annette a vial of pills to give Sacha three times a day. Annette glared at him and insisted that bronchitis would not lead a dog to tear a house apart. The vet was willing to check for rabies, but admitted that the clinic did not have the necessary equipment to run conclusive tests. After some debate, Cedric and Annette agreed to have Sacha put out of her misery.

What hurt almost as much as losing Sacha, was not knowing what had happened. Because the Alsatian had remained unaggressive, rabies seemed unlikely, especially since she had received all the inoculations. The only other possibility was that she had been poisoned—the brain was inflamed and the throat congested—possibly by the locals who, for some reason, had never been able to approach Sacha without her barking and nipping at their heels. They suspected that glass had been ground into her food, but Annette would always remain uncertain. Whatever the reason, her desire to leave Liberia had been strongly reinforced.

By May 1967, Cedric had wrapped up his work, and Annette had packed and crated all of their possessions. They were allowed another three months travel before returning to New York, and Cedric decided this time to go by ship, all the way from Marseilles, France, to Yokohama, Japan. They threw a farewell party, though they knew at least they would be seeing the Barners again before Saudi Arabia. John wasn't slated to be transferred until the end of the year, and Cedric had definite plans with Niles Hemboldt to cross the Sahara after his training course in New York and before his transfer to Saudi Arabia in early 1968. Niles had assured him that he would take care of all the logistics while Rick was in New York.

◆   ◆   ◆

The same month Cedric returned to New York, Stillman Rockefeller retired. George Moore was named Chairman of the FNCB and Walter Wriston became President, despite facing the rockiest period of his career when a speculating trader in Brussels caused that branch to post an eight million dollar loss. Rockefeller went even further and, wary of Moore's impetuous and erratic governing style, he amended bank bylaws to give the President, rather than the Chairman, final authority on bank policy. Wriston effectively became Chief Executive Officer of FNCB.

Ambitious and innovative, he set out quickly impose his own style of management, and hired a similarly-minded old hand from Latin America, Al Costanzo, to head the Overseas Division. Together they embarked on a mission to expand contacts with foreign heads-of-state, and increase the number of foreign national officers to rid the division of its colonial culture where District VPs ruled like tribal kings. Wriston recognized that he did not want FNCB to view itself merely as bank, but rather as a technology-based financial institution that would perform any financial service anywhere in the world. To do so, Wriston knew the bank needed a complete structural overhaul, one that would be implemented during the first few years of his reign, and completed by the early seventies. But concurrent with propelling FNCB to the pinnacle of world finance, it would also provoke a radical shift in banking mentalities, from congenial and family-oriented, to confrontational and profit-oriented.

Between June 1967 and January 1968, Cedric took lessons in Arabic language, history and culture, and attended the Senior Credit Analysis course at First National City Bank's new headquarters at 399 Park Avenue. It was a tough course that relied on practical case studies, and was designed to allow junior officers targeted for positions as overseas branch managers to learn how to analyze and present complex credit proposals. It gave the Bank a certain security in raising the signing authority limits for these officers and, in the case of loan requirements that surpassed their limits, taught them to present a rigorous and standardized credit proposal. The course was run like a boot camp by Jack Heilshorn, a tall burly ex-Navy officer in his early forties.

In October, Cedric met the head of the MEA division, as well as his new boss Carlton Stewart, to hear the details of his assignment in Jeddah. The man had a ferocious intelligence that was unfortunately matched by a heartless disposition. Jack Goodrich, who had been transferred to South Africa as Country Head—and as Barner's immediate superior—liked to joke that Stewart could make even a reptile's blood freeze. "He's very likely to put you in a compromising position, and then drop you when the heat is on," he told Cedric. "And you've been away so you don't know much about the battery of consultants that have been filling these hallways. There's definitely a changing of the guard. Wriston is a tough and ambitious man, and wants to put his stamp on City Bank history. I've got a feeling the friendly family atmosphere that we've been used to is going to go out the window as they run for profits. Got this smart techie guy named John Reed in Operations trying to reorganize the back office. From what I hear, he pushes his staff so hard that half are in the process of getting a divorce, the other half are candidates for an early cardiac arrest…And Stewart fits right in with a smart cutthroat mentality like Reed's."

In his assessment of Cedric's future work, Stewart made clear his dire outlook of the business situation in the Middle East due to the effects of the June '67 Arab-Israeli war. "A lot of loans have gone bad over there," he said. "Still, we expect you to help the branch make budget. There's a new policy in place here—we're aiming for profit now. You'll be working for a guy named Cliff Cooper, and in a year or so, if things go well, you should be taking over from him as branch manager. Other than that, you'll be expected to submit quarterly reports to the Regional Head, Peter Wodtke, who's based in Beirut." Cedric had met Wodtke during his trip with Annette to Hong Kong, and had liked him immediately: a real gentleman, competent, elegant and erudite, but without an ounce of snobbism about him (or at least nothing that couldn't be put down to British eccentricity). After Klingen and Jennings, it would be a relief.

Before he dismissed Cedric, Stewart called in another personality, whom he introduced as the CIA Director of Operations for the Middle East. The guy seemed unassuming—tall, lanky, and constantly fiddling with his spectacles and running a hand over his bald patch. Cedric was surprised to be introduced to the CIA, but not entirely shocked. He knew by know that bankers at his level in South America collaborated with the CIA to some degree. Carlton Stewart explained: "There's a war going on in Yemen, and it's not much of a secret that we're helping Saudi Arabia in its support of the royalists. You'll be handling the CIA account down there. Money will be coming in, and every so often there'll be withdrawals. Other than that, you won't have any contact. You might be expected to make reports on the different construction projects financed by FNCB in the regaion, but all you have to do is make copies of the reports you submit to Wodtke. You'll meet Ambassador Hermann Eilts when you're there, and he'll introduce you to the CIA liaison. In general you won't have many dealings with them, nothing much more than business, but it's in your job description."

Annette kept herself busy during those months in New York, auditing design classes at Hunter College, and taking Arabic language courses. Neither she nor Cedric were particularly fazed by the gatherings in the Village, the race riots or the war protests taking place across the country. They had fallen quite out of touch with US politics while in Liberia, and since they were leaving for Saudi Arabia in a few months, they felt a sense of displacement and incomprehension that translated into disinterest. Their implication with the Vietnam imbroglio was limited to Annette's concern for her brother Gordon. Cedric still felt that Gordy should enlist in an officer training program: without a television in New York, he and Annette were not subjected to the dinner-time spectacle of body bags on prime time television.

◆   ◆   ◆

In January 1968, the Grants flew back to Monrovia. Cedric and Niles headed out across the Sahara, while Annette stayed with Claire, Niles's wife, on the bank compound. She found it pleasant, if strange, to back in Liberia as a visitor, as she wrote to her mother.

The scene right now is on the beach, the hot sun beating down on my lily white body. The weather since our arrival has been really gorgeous. I'm *leaving on February 9th for Paris, where I will meet up with Rick and we will head to Jeddah. I'm actually looking forward to that now, a new adventure…In the mean time, I have lots of time to relax here. The compound has changed with so many new people, and it is a funny feeling being back. There was a definite time lapse and a "just visiting" feeling. Vanessa Jennings has had a baby, and she is adorable.*

Rick and Niles were joined by a third boyscout, Jim Kammort, who traveled as far as Niamey, Niger, with them. He returned on Saturday and told us all about the first part of the Sahara trip. Sounds as if they were having a marvelous time. They even went to a game reserve park in Dahomey (between Togo and Nigeria), and arrived in Niamey right on schedule. Just had minor repairs to make on the Land Rover before starting off on the longest and hardest part of the Safari. From Agades to Algers, it will be strictly camping out…If all goes well, we should be meeting in Paris on the 11th.

Jim just finished a "tour of duty" in the Jeddah branch, so he was able to brief Rick about the area, the people, and the branch manager Cliff Cooper, who sounds like a lackadaisical character, but a good man. I have also, of course, been asking him many questions, and he's made me feel so much better about everything. He said there's not much in the way of entertainment, but that the social life is plentiful, with embassy and client parties, and the like.

The Land Rover used by Niles and Cedric had been modified to carry three weeks of food supplies and 110 gallons of water and gasoline across 5000 miles of African roads, tracks and desert. Cedric had taken care of the visa requirements and automobile papers, while Niles and Claire, being in Liberia, had organized the food and medical kit, and supervised work on the jeep. After all this organization, the trip itself seemed almost anticlimactic, but the excitement returned quickly after two days in the African bush. After Niamey, they headed to Zinder, Niger; after that, it was the long stretch of desert, and Cedric and Niles were pumped full of adrenaline.

They followed camel tracks and pushed on through the soft sand, getting stuck only once on their second day. Of more concern was their fourth tire blow-out within a few days of leaving Zinder: with only five more spares and over a thousand miles until the next supply point at Ain-Salah, they had reason to be anxious. The track soon became easier, however, and their concern dwindled among the majestic décor and the ubiquitous Blue People, the Taureg tribesmen of the Sahara.

Agades was our favorite city, Niles later wrote in an article for Citibank Magazine. *The heavy air throbbed with the sound of drums. Tauregs raced through the streets on white camels raising dust that turned golden in the afternoon sun. We spent the afternoon searching first in vain for tires and then more successfully for native silver jewelry. If for no other reason, Agades is exotic because of its location. It is 200 miles from the next town and 700 miles from the nearest city. Except for several gas stations and an occasional truck, there are few concessions to the 20th Century. Camel caravans share almost equally with desert trucks the task of bringing in supplies.*

Beyond Agades, they drove through 600 miles of trackless desert, with disparate water holes along the way. They were soon engulfed by the starched blue sky, the heaving silence of the desert, the grandeur of endless sand and stark stones that become almost overpowering. They realized later that the desert was not something that could be truly savored as they traveled through it. But its presence would be fill their dreams and inhabit their almost trance-like movements for weeks after their return to civilization.

They passed through two wells before reaching the Niger-Algerian border, where formalities delayed them for more than a day. The stretch would prove to be the most difficult of the crossing. Once in Tamanrassett, Algeria, their major worries of tire, gas and water supplies would be behind them (they had carried 30 gallons of water and 82 gallons of gasoline to ensure the long stretch from In-Guezzam to Tamanrassett). Their increasing fascination with the splattered sunsets that colored the horizon like grenadine syrup tinged with ink, would soon be overshadowed by a new enemy: miserably cold nights when high winds caused temperatures to close to freezing.

Anxiety briefly returned when, after the 435-mile crossing from Tamanrasset to Ain-Salah, they were unable to find more spare tires for the Land Rover. They refused to let their spirits dampen, however, and they bolstered their confidence with the knowledge that it was only 255 miles to El Golea, after which the roads were supposedly paved. And they had yet to blow a fifth tire.

About one hour north of Ain-Salah we climbed an escarpment to the Tademait Plateau. This 120-mile-wide maddeningly level plateau will forever be our most uncomfortable memory of the trip. The surface is a mixture of small sharp stones with the finest, most irritating dust imaginable. Before descending the other side of the plateau, we spent six agonizing hours on it without seeing a single living thing, not even a blade of grass. We had to close the Land Rover up tight in 90-degree heat to keep the red dust out, but even then it infiltrated our steaming vehicle, choking us, settling as red mud on our sweat-soaked clothes and caking our faces and forearms. When we stopped, the fiery choking clouds swirled around us and drove us immediately back into the Land Rover. The sun and motor combined to heat the vehicle to such a point that we could not even touch the dashboard. This, with the engine noise—all the greater with the windows closed—drove us almost mad and reduced our conversation to short bursts of profanity.

They experienced life as it might have been for the mercenaries of the French Foreign Legion when the finally reached the northern end of the Tademait, and camped out at Fort Miribel. Shortly after sunrise they came across another Land Rover "parked" on the side of the road. They accosted the two men that flagged them down, and after a few halting exchanges in various languages, found out that the men were Russian and their only spare tire had been shredded by the sharp stones. Niles and Rick willingly offered them one of their own, *with elaborate references to peace among nations and the brotherhood of man,* wrote Niles. *Although the desert continued for nearly 300 miles after El Golea, and the danger of a breakdown far from help still existed the trip was finished. It was astonishing how quickly it was all over. We awoke one morning still in the Algerian desert and the next night we were in Europe. Cedric left the next day and flew to Paris to collect his wife and went on to Austria to go skiing. I set off for Amsterdam to meet my wife and son. As I drove north along the Costa del Sol, I thought back over the events since Monrovia and realized that already it was impossible to recall all the little details. Spain, which on my last visit had been so foreign, felt like home. The next stop would be Amsterdam and I would see my family and old friends. I settled back for a long drive and thought of how I would spend the rest of my vacation.*

Cedric's attraction to the desert, the Sahara in particular, had only just begun. And now, Saudi Arabia lay ahead to offer indolence and charm, and provide Cedric with the foundation of his success at Citibank.

4:55:44
SEIKO

1985 FINISH N
Rudin Family MANUFACTURERS Ⓗ
HANOVER
ROAD R

1985 New York Marathon

بسم الله الرحمن الرحيم

Alwaleed Bin Talal Bin Abdulaziz Alsaud

FAX # 00 41 22-280-683

                                                    February 25, 1991

Mr. Cedric O. Grant
Vice President
Citibank N.A.
Geneva
Switzerland

Dear Mr. Grant,

This is to authorise you to transfer from my account the sum of US$ 590,000,000 (U S Dollars Five Hundred Ninety Million) to Citicorp, New York, on Thursday, 28 February 1991.

You are requested to coordinate with Mr. Paul Collins on the procedures to be followed for that transfer. This transfer will be effective upon the receipt of the certificate of ownership of the preferred issue by our lawyers, Hogan and Harston, in Washington.

Regards,

Al Waleed Bin Talal Bin Abdulaziz Al Saud

Note : The original of this fax will follow by mail.

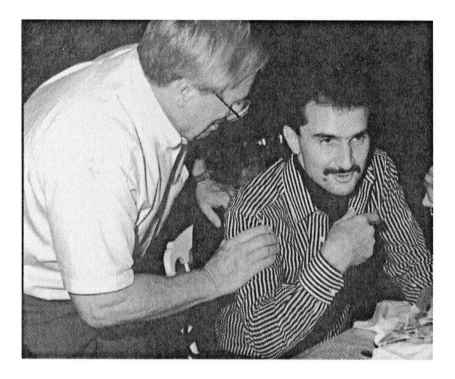

April 15, 1994

Mr. Cedric O. Grant
Vice President
Citicorp Investment Bank
16, Quai General-Guisan
P.O.Box 162
CH-1211 Geneva 3, Switzerland

Dear Rick:

Many thanks for your nice letter of March 28. I always remember the day you walked into the Overseas Division and we had a conversation that resulted in your hiring. It was a great day for the bank as you have made such an outstanding contribution over the years. The other time I remember very clearly was when I had an audience with the King of Saudi Arabia which lasted over an hour, and as I was finally leaving the King's translator snuck up to me and said "give my best to Rick Grant", which was just another indication of how you have taken care of the customers over the years.

All the best.

Sincerely yours,

7

o o o o o o o o o o o o o o o o o o o o o o o o o o o o o o

"I summon my blue-eyed slaves anytime it pleases me. I command the Americans to send me their bravest soldiers to die for me. Anytime I clap my hands a stupid genie called the American ambassador appears to do my bidding. When the Americans die in my service their bodies are frozen in metal boxes by the US Embassy and American airplanes carry them away, as if they never existed. Truly, America is my favorite slave."

—King Fahd Bin Abdul-Aziz, Jeddah 1993

◆   ◆   ◆

Annette waited a full week before making her first excursion into the odoriferous world of the Jeddah souk. She ventured out dressed in sandals and a white long-sleeved cotton robe, and made a half-hearted attempt to cover her head with a multi-colored New York Village scarf. Within fifteen minutes she suddenly felt a sharp pain on her ankles, and turned to see an angry-looking old bearded man rapping her heels. She promptly withdrew and scurried home to safety. She had just been introduced to a member of the Mutawa, the Religious Police that enforces public morality, especially women's dress codes.

She would not venture out again for another two weeks, until she had acquired a dark caftan and a companion in the person of Ulla Grammar, the wife of one of Cedric's colleagues, who helped Annette get acquainted with the Saudi mentality. Her second excursion completely dispelled her fears of appearing in public. Their scavenge hunt was a notable success: Annette purchased an old Baroque table and acquired an armoire for an equivalent of $77, made in India from ornately carved oak, with Saudi swords engraved on the top; Ulla was happy to purchase spices, and a rug at a price that would today be considered theft—the Bedouins had not yet clued into to Westerners' acute keenness for such items which they carelessly unfolded on the desert sands, under their tents, when settling down for a rest.

Domestic chores took some getting used to in a country that had only just begun to enter the modern age. Since there was no hot water heater in the kitchen, Annette had to boil water every time she did the dishes; and since the sink had no stopper plug, she risked flooding the kitchen and adjacent bathroom every time she threw more than a bucketful of water down the drain. The stove worked haphazardly, the wringer-washer broke the first time she used it, portions of the wall would crumble when she pulled a plug from the socket...

She remained unfazed, until the kitchen was invaded by a huge cockroach a few hours before she was due to serve dinner to Rick's Middle East Regional Head, Peter Wodtke. She pulled out a can of insect repellent and challenged the cockroach to a duel. Not only did it not curl up, flip over and die, but it was suddenly joined by a hundred members of its extended family. Annette beat a hasty retreat, closed the door, sat down on the porch with an Agatha Christie, and promptly forgot about the whole affair. "Welcome to Saudi Arabia," she told herself cynically.

When Cedric returned a few hours later with Peter Wodtke, she apologized with a slightly manic smile that there was no dinner. After a brief visit to the kitchen, Cedric and his boss agreed that they should dine out, and Wodtke introduced them to one of the few restaurants in Jeddah. Annette had liked him when they'd met in Hong Kong; she adored him now.

Wodtke immediately confronted Cedric with the difficulties of his job. The Suez Canal was closed and the country was suffocating. Down at the docks, the ships were idling: no shipping, no commerce, no money. Loans had been extended to people with good credit, but many were unable to pay back at the moment. He did not expect Cedric to generate a lot of business, but he would be required to do an extensive "clean-up" job. On the flipside, there were some good prospects. Saudi Arabia was using its oil revenues to modernize the country: Siemens was building a sewage treatment plant and Hutehägerfeld was laying down the sewage pipe lines; the Japanese were in charge of a desalinization plant; Hochtief, another German firm, was building a military cantonment at Khamis Mushayt near the Yemenite border; and a US firm, Airway Engineering, was primed to sign a contract to build a large international airport outside of Jeddah. Many of these corporations were FNCB clients and Cedric would be in charge of their accounts. Wodtke expected quarterly reports on their progress, and advised Cedric to get out of Jeddah, visit the clients, make contacts with the Saudis, learn the geography.

The port town of Jeddah, with a population of about 300,000, was primarily contained within the crumbling old city walls. Multi-storied Turkish-style houses decorated with wood carvings and latticework lined the streets. Beyond that was the desert, the Great Nafud, which extended north in sloping ridges, a hundred meters high, divided by flats. This region of Saudi Arabia was desolate and hostile: since the Israeli occupation of the Golan Heights, the only economic viability of the region, the Trans-Arab pipeline, had all but shut down. Stretching along the southern frontier of Saudi Arabia was the daunting *Rub al-Khali*, the "Empty Quarter", the largest quartz sand desert in the world and one of the most forbidding, with hard-packed sand and salt flats from which sand dunes rose as high as three hundred meters, sometimes forming ridges up to thirty miles long. And then there was the *Dahna*, which formed a great arc from the Nafud westward to join the Rub al-Khali.

East of Jeddah was the holy city of Mecca; several hundred miles north was the second holiest Moslem city: Medina. Linking Jeddah and Mecca was the first road built by King Abdul Aziz to facilitate passage for the pilgrims during the annual Hajj. It was dubbed "the Jesus Christ bypass" by foreigners: forbidden to non-Moslems, Mecca is home to the Kaba, a dark, rectangular, stone structure that stands in the middle of the Haram Mosque, and that was built, according to the Koran, by Adam himself. Along with Taif, the summer residence of the Saudi royal family, located at six thousand feet in the mountains east of Mecca, these cities formed the economic hub of the Hijaz (western) region.

The capital Riyadh was situated in the eastern region of Central Arabia, called the Nedj, from where the royal Saud family originated, and was slowly evolving from a post-World War II mud-brick city to a modern drab-looking concrete capital. Between Riyadh and the Persian Gulf was the Eastern Province, the economic powerhouse of the country where the famed Dammam no. 7 hit oil in 1938, giving its name to the capital of the region, and home to the country's petrochemical industry. Appropriately enough, Aramco located its headquarters in Dhahran, just south of Dammam, for proximity to the a hundred and twenty mile long Ghawar oil field, and to the oil rigs off the coast of Bahrain.

Muhammad ibn Saud, ruler of the Saud family, and Muhammad ibn Abd al-Wahhab were both born around 1704, in the Nedj region. By 1744, al-Wahhab's preaching formed the basis of the puritanical revival movement based on the very strict Islamic doctrine of *Tawhid* which was firmly rooted in Sunni Islamic law. Expelled from his native town, Shaykh ('teacher") Muhammad was invited to stay by the local Amir of the nearby town of Dariya, Muhammad ibn Saud, and converted his host to wahhabism. By the time Amir Muhammad ibn Saud died in 1765 most of the Nedj had come under his rule, but the family was unable to retain its dominance in the region, and the Saudi state collapsed over the next 150 years.

The modern history of Saudi Arabia began with the birth of the twentieth century, and unfolded like a swashbuckling epic. In 1901 a member of the deposed royal family, Abdul Aziz ibn Abdur Rahman, an imposing man well over six feet tall, with a commanding presence, set out from Kuwait where he had been living in exile, to regain the family's former domains. In 1902, with only 200 followers, Abdul Aziz captured Riyadh, expelled the Rashidi dynasty, and proclaimed himself ruler of the Nedj. During subsequent years he recovered and consolidated the outlying provinces of the kingdom, defeating Turkish attempts to subjugate him. Having restored the House of Saud as a ruling dynasty, Abdul Aziz became known as Ibn Saud.

Realizing the strength and power of religion, Ibn Saud instituted the formation of Wahhabi colonies, known as Ikhwan ("Brethren") throughout the territory under his control. The first Ikhwan settlement was made in 1912, and about a hundred more were established over the next fifteen years, bringing Wahhabi doctrines to scattered communities in remote desert areas. Ibn Saud later relied on these colonies to form a centralized organization and gain power over the various tribes that ruled the region. By the outbreak of World War I, Ibn Saud reigned over central Arabia, including the Hasa coast of the Persian Gulf. In March 1924, Ibn Saud marched on the Hijaz to claim Mecca and Medina. After a campaign of only a few months against the Ottoman Empire, he forced Caliph Hussein to abdicate. He eventually drove Hussein's eldest son Ali out Jeddah a year later, and became King of the Hijaz in January 1926. Finally, on 23 September 1932, Abdul Aziz ibn Saud formed the Kingdom of Saudi Arabia by joining the Hijaz and the Nedj regions. Then he began the slow process of bringing his country into the twentieth century.

His attempts were hindered by the country's extreme poverty. It was not until after World War II that oil revenues grew enough to enable King Abdul Aziz to implement his plans. He died in 1953 and was succeed by his eldest surviving son, Saud, who would later be forced to relinquish his position as King after bringing the country to the brink of bankruptcy. The official explanation was that he was unable to cope with the country's rapid growth and increasing wealth. A more accurate picture was the rampant corruption that his reign supported, a situation exposed by Prince Talal bin Abdul Aziz, the favorite son of King Abdul Aziz's favorite wife Munayir, when he traveled to Egypt in 1960 to denounce King Saud's regime. He also lent his support to Nasser's desire to unit Arab countries under the banner of his United Arab Republic, which provoked the wrath of the Kingdom, and Talal—who would play a crucial role in Cedric's career three decades later—was thereafter banned from getting involved in any form of Saudi politics.

In 1964, Crown Prince Faisal became King, and set about putting the countries affairs in order. He pushed for greater control of the oil concessions and continued the implementation of his father's policies for modernization. He was in no rush to import alien Western political institutions, and seemed to gauge quite accurately just how far and how fast he could nudge his people toward modernity. He was able to counter the oppositions made by ultraconservatives in his government based on religious grounds, due to his extensive grasp of Islamic law. When the Grants moved to Saudi Arabia in early 1968, they could already sense the profound social and economic reforms that were about to follow.

◆   ◆   ◆

Avenues for diversion in Jeddah itself were slim. There was barely a restaurant in town to enjoy a change of scenery, only two or three dismal hotels, and movie theatres were banned. Cedric and Annette joined the weekly Monday night duplicate bridge sessions at the Raytheon complex, but otherwise their nightlife revolved around private Saudi or Embassy parties. But their social life was hectic nonetheless, made up primarily of parties. The Saudi week began on a Saturday, since the "weekend" started Thursday afternoon and the Islamic day of rest was Friday. Cedric would go into work from about 7.30am to 2.30pm, return home to eat and nap for an hour and a half, then return to the office until 8pm. After that there was usually a dinner party to go to, although dinner wouldn't be served until after midnight, and guests wouldn't return home until almost two in the morning. It took the Grants a while to get used to this new schedule, and to the various ways of computing time in Saudia Arabia. There was Standard Time, or GMT plus three, which the Westerners used; then there was Sun Time, for prayers, used by local and foreign businesses and which varied from Standard Time by fifteen to twenty minutes; finally there was Arabic Time, which could vary by as much as nine hours. There were rumors circulating that King Faisal would issue an edict putting Saudi Arabia on the same time wave as the rest of the world, though undoubtedly Sun Time would always endure.

Their first party to meet members of the community took place at the end of their first week in Jeddah around the bank compound pool. A few Saudis were present with foreign wives (Saudi wives were virtually never seen at mixed gatherings), but the guests consisted primarily of various expatriate groups from the US Embassy, Raytheon, Saudi Arabian Airlines (run by TWA), and a few other small companies. This in turn, led to other embassy parties, and invitations for bridge at the Raytheon complex, a large fenced-in compound near the Red Sea, about a twenty-minute drive from Jeddah, and where about a hundred families lived. The strict no-alcohol policy at these parties was almost never enforced, even at the homes of Saudi businessmen and high-ranking government officials. Status and power conferred immense privileges in Saudi Arabia. News of dissolute behavior abroad by members of the royal family were quickly repressed and never made their way into the local press. The police generally ignored foreign consumption as long as it was done behind "closed doors" and not thrown in their faces. Foreign nationals could procure a wide selection of spirits and liqueurs, quite easily from Lebanese and Arabic bootleggers at $15 a bottle. If in Liberia it was the most junior officer's duty to be in charge of the compound, in Saudi Arabia it was his duty to provide FNCB staff with black market alcohol.

There was another method for acquiring alcohol, which the Grants' embraced with gusto: making their own wine. Cedric visited a local chemical plant and bought a ten-gallon glass carboy used to contain sulfuric acid. Then he obtained a bottle capper and caps from the Pepsi plant. Finally, at the Lebanese-run market in town, he would buy twelve bottles of non-pasteurized white and red grape juice, which he would mix with thirty-six bottles of water and yeast, and add five to ten pounds of sugar, depending on whether they wanted dry, semi-dry or sweet wine. The carboy was plugged with an S-shaped glass tube wrapped in Kotex, and topped with wax after an air trap had been placed to let out the gas. Cedric would then allow the mix to ferment for about ten days until the wine was ready. Finally it was bottled and capped, and put away to age for two to three months. Or two to three days if urgently needed.

The British and Germans had perfected a triple-distillation process of grain to produce a type of moonshine called Siddiqi (Arabic for "my friend") which vaguely resembled gin, and which they sold at $15 a gallon, when they had any left over from their personal consumption. Though they sometimes mixed it with tonic or Seven-Up, Annette and Cedric preferred to refrain, since its potency could reach as high as 180 proof.

On their second weekend in Saudi Arabia, Ulla and John Grammar drove the Grants' to a regular Saudi and expat weekend hangout: the Creek, an inlet off the Red Sea, ten miles north of Jeddah. All the wealthy Saudis had secondary residences there, beautiful villas overlooking the bay where their boats were moored. For the expats, a series of wooden cubical shacks had been built at the point of the creek, where they could stow their stuff while they went swimming, snorkeling, diving, or water-skiing. Each family had their own bathhouse consisting of one room and a toilet, sometimes a shower and a small utility kitchenette; if they were lucky, a camp bed or two. Cedric and Annette chose a place at the mouth of the creek, ideal for snorkeling since water-skiers avoided it, and Annette immediately felt at home. She paddled around for hours, exploring caverns, color formations and a multitude of variegated and intriguing-looking fish.

Dear Mother,

The weather continues to be balmy and delightful—a softening of the heat to come when Spring ends. The sky has been buzzing with jets from all over the world for a while now, bringing Moslems to their holy land for the Hajj. I happen to be quite aware of the noise as our house must be close to the landing and take-off pattern. In any event the airport is right in town! The Hajj is the annual pilgrimage to Mecca. Season lasts up to two months as the pilgrims travel great distances at great expense and financial sacrifice, and want to take advantage of their visit to see Medina also. The Hajj itself lasts four days, during which time we are told that the pilgrims (close to a quarter million!) perform ritual prayers and cleansing at specified sites in and around the holy city of Mecca. A very interesting time. The airport and port are jammed full of pilgrims, and so is the city, though the Coopers told us that they quickly get bussed out to camp near Mecca.

The bank, as everything else, will be shut down for seven days during the Id festivities afterwards. The town is as alive as can be, but we will probably take a vacation with the Grammers, since it will be no fun for us women. We've purchased a new 1968 Chevy Impala with air-conditioning which we should have in a few days time, and the bank will provide a driver for each family which will simplify matters enormously since women cannot drive here. That should enable us to get out of town.

Speaking Arabic, or at least a cursory knowledge of it, is almost a must if one is to get along properly in the souk which sells everything from soups to nuts, and is a fascinating experience of myriad smells—incense, spices, and others not quite so pleasant! Everything is far more primitive than Monrovia, however, and as a woman one does feel repressed as even the veiled ones on the street are sparsely seen. Shopping isn't easy: no pork of any sort which eliminates ham and bacon, but we're better off for it I suppose. One can obtain lamb fresh, and beef fillets that have to be marinated for a long time but are then quite edible. The fresh vegetables are more plentiful, but must first be washed thoroughly, first in Tide then in a disinfectant—they are apparently fertilized in human excrement!

We're still waiting for our shipment which was supposed to have been here on Thursday. Apparently it is being held up pending a letter from the Ministry of Information saying that the contents of the crate which contained books has been scrutinized and is okay to release—such red tape—it's worse than Liberia. I heard that some Saudi national was executed for trying to "smuggle" in a Bible! It's an odd feeling in a country filled with elegant, intelligent, educated and westernized Arabs to hear of such barbaric treatment. To execute someone for murder or rape, or even cut off hands in case of theft, is one thing—that is their law, and I must say that one feels extremely safe here. But the executions are public! I managed to discuss this with the US Ambassador here, Hermann Eilts, and he said that every once in a while the US government asks him to inquire with the Saudi government (i.e. the King) as to the steps taken towards democratization, political reform, and human rights. Apparently King Faisal answered him: "Would the United States really want the Kingdom to be turned into another Berkeley campus?" I must say, he had quite a sense of repartee.

Speaking of anti-Vietnam riots, we are anxious to hear what Gordon's plans are now that he has graduated. It's a real dilemma. Have read about the government refusing deferment to graduate students so this is no outlet. I wonder if the best solution would not be to enlist? If he is drafted, he is sure to be sent to Vietnam—it looks bad either way.

At the beginning of April, the weather began to cool off. The Grants were invited to the house of Omar Saggaff, a tall and gallant man who could trace his lineage all the way back to the Prophet Mohammed, an honor which conferred on him more status and nobility than his position as Minister of Foreign Affairs. He lived in a small palace on the outskirts of Jeddah, and his estate, replete with Olympic swimming pool and stables for his thoroughbred horses, spread into the desert like a huge splash of green paint, dotted with palm and fruit trees. He had heard of the Grants' arrival through one of the Raytheon representatives, and decided to invite them to one of his dinner parties.

The evening kicked off around nine o'clock and for several hours people drank cocktails and engaged in poker and bridge games. A sumptuous buffet-style dinner was served around one o'clock in the morning, after which everyone would head home. Annette and Cedric became regular weekly guests and met a number of fascinating characters, among whom Hassan Yassein. He was a Yale educated young man, a few years younger than Cedric, son of a former Syrian advisor to King Abdul al Aziz. He worked for his cousin, Adnan Khashoggi, a notorious billionaire and the biggest arms merchant in the Middle East. Though he would later introduce Cedric to Adnan Khashoggi,

Cedric would have little chance to attract business from the man because FNCB policy would hardly support it. As far as he could see, Khashoggi's business in 1968 seemed perfectly legal and above board, but he required lines of credit that went well beyond Cedric's signing authority. "Banks here work on the pretty safe assumption," Yassein told Cedric, "that Adnan can and will pay back any loan that he takes out. But big US banks require collateral, background checks, and proof of solvency. That is your problem in the States: no trust! We here are people of honor. Our word is binding. Remember that!"

As hectic as their social life may have been, Cedric and Annette had trouble keeping up with world events. Annette learned of Bobby Kennedy's assassination from the teletype at the U.S. embassy: the Saudi press, radio and television were strictly censored; in fact, Saudi religious leaders had long considered TV as an instrument of the devil. King Faisal had managed to circumvent their opposition by requiring the Koran to be read mornings and evenings at prime time. Annette tried to keep up to date with the upcoming US elections—Kennedy, Nixon, McCarthy—as best she could through letters received from her mother and Gordon, who now considered joining the Peace Corps or Vista if he managed to avoid the Vietnam draft.

Jeannie sent her daughter a silver baby spoon for mother's day in May and the reference was not lost on Annette. Though the Grants had decided not to have a child in the tropics, they were now debating the issue. After all, Beirut was not far away and had excellent medical facilities. Cedric would not remain in Saudi Arabia forever and besides, they could not continue to consider forever their location a hindrance to having children, since Cedric's career would most likely never provide an ideally stable situation for raising kids.

At work, Cedric primarily managed loans that creditable businessmen had trouble paying back because of the economic situation. Top on his list were the Zahids, a large and influential family in Jeddah, and the largest importers for GM Motors in Saudi Arabia. After the Suez canal was closed, car sales dwindled to almost nothing. Furthermore,

Cedric found out, not only had the Zahids taken out loans from other banks against similar collateral used with FNCB, they had also been using long-term loans for short-term ventures that had gone sour in the wake of the Arab-Israeli war. They were now on the verge of bankruptcy. After several meetings in Beirut, Cedric finally convinced Wodtke to give them some breathing space by obtaining legal titles to their property in the Eastern Province, and using it as collateral against loan repayments. The economic situation was already looking brighter, and Cedric figured that they would eventually be able to pay up. It was an exhausting and trying process, however, since no foreign bank had ever obtained a legally binding pledge of Saudi property. Matters were not made any easier by the fact that the lawyer hired by FNCB to handle the negotiations happened to be related to the Zahids (a piece of useful trivia of which Cedric was not aware at the time), and helped them stave off the process for six months. The situation would not be resolved until Cedric moved to Riyadh, over a year later. He ended up making the ten-hour drive to Dammam six times in four months, until, having run out of excuses, the Zahids finally caved in and cut a deal whereby FNCB obtained control of their property, but without authority to sell, until the Zahids repaid their loan.

Cedric quickly realized that banking in Saudi Arabia was remarkably different than in Liberia—more sophisticated and involving much more money. Like anywhere, contacts were important, but in Saudi Arabia, with its heavy insistence on family ties, they were crucial. One of his first assignments for his assistant Mahmoud Jawdat was to approach all the secretaries and assistants of top level dignitaries and Saudi businessmen, and offer them triple interest on their savings if they placed them with First National City Bank. He wanted to canvass everyone he could, up to and including Anwar Ali, Governor of the Saudi Arabian Monetary Agency, or SAMA—the Saudi equivalent of the Federal Reserve, but controlled by the government. "Want to get them on our side," he explained to the burly Saudi. "You never know when we might need access to their bosses."

Mahmoud Jawdat had started out as an assistant accountant, and had slowly made his way up the ranks. Cedric recognized not only his many useful connections but also his hard work and ambitious drive, and the two would soon become inseparable. Jawdat's father had been a Turkish-Kurd lieutenant in the Ottoman army during World War I. He'd then fought against Abdul al Aziz when Aziz ousted the Ottomans from the Hijaz. Abdul al Aziz found Jawdat's father to be so brave that he asked him to form his National Guard; Jawdat was so taken in by Aziz's charismatic personality and heroic quest to unite the Arabian peninsula that he agreed. He was eventually elevated to the rank of General, and could be found at the King's side at all times. Mahmoud therefore had access to many members of the royal family and the Saudi elite, and though this would become more important when he followed Cedric to Riyadh as his Assistant Manager, there was already a wealth of information with which he could provide his friend and boss in Jeddah. One important tidbit that would pay off less than a year later was the knowledge that Anwar Ali, Governor of SAMA was writing a book on Islamic history. Though Cedric had only met him once at a US Embassy party, he decided to send him all the books he could find on the subject, with a small note of appreciation.

On the first day of Spring, and the day after his thirty-fourth birthday, Cedric received a call from Nicolas Abud, the obese and sweaty Lebanese personal assistant to the black sheep of the royal family, Prince Talal ibn Aziz. He requested an immediate withdrawal of $50,000 in traveler's checks since his Highness was leaving the country that very afternoon. Cedric could hear the urgency in his voice, and could almost see him wringing his fat hands and dabbing his brow on the other end of the line. The Jeddah branch manager, Cliff Cooper, advised Cedric against it. "He knows we need more notification than that, and he won't pull the account if we refuse. He's just not dependable."

Cedric decided to set up the traveler's checks for Prince Talal any-way. He was willing to run the risk as a favor to Nicolas Abud, whose ties with Talal enabled him to open a good many doors in the country. Early in the afternoon he drove over to the Prince's mansion where he found him in ensconced in a bridge game. Talal had inherited his father's good looks, additionally spiced by his mother's delicate fea-tures, and appeared decidedly regal in his flowing blue and white thobe and black headdress. He was born in 1931, and therefore close in age to Cedric; but Cedric sensed that large, if indefinable gulf that lay between them. An American kid from Oregon, a Saudi Prince from another world…Cedric waited an hour, and heard Abud tell the Prince several times that his flight was leaving. On the third occasion, Talal erupted: "You know very well that the plane will wait. They don't care about the other passengers, I'm the only one who counts. Now leave me alone!" Eventually he accepted to sign the checks, and Cedric left him to finish his bridge.

When he returned to his office, Mahmoud confronted him with an accounting headache that often occurred in Saudi Arabia: Many of the bank's clients initially refused to receive interest on their deposits, or *riba*, considered usury and banned by Islamic law; in return, the bank would not charge commission for service fees on issuing letters of credit for Saudi businessmen involved in import-export. But the bank nevertheless set up a "shadow balance" which computed the difference between the interest that would have been paid and the commission fees that would have been charged. Generally, the bank kept reserves to cover this balance if it came out in the client's favor, but unfortunately they did so too infrequently. Jawdat had just been asked by one of their clients, Ibrahim Arab, to "receive payment for services rendered to the bank", in other words the balance of the interest payments due to him. Cedric asked Mahmoud Jawdat to pull up the account, and together they studied their options. Arab was a major Saudi importer, primarily of rice from Japan. Cedric's predecessor, Bill Roberts, had opened a current account so that Arab would not receive interest on capital and would not be charged commission. The "shadow balance", however, came out largely in Ibrahim's favor, and the bank had not set aside any cash reserves to cover the amount Ibrahim requested as his *riba* payment. If the bank paid Arab the full amount owed him, it would burn up their quarterly profits, and they would not make budget. The best Cedric could do was triple Arab's interest over the next four months: the bank would be able to pay up without posting a loss. But he had to stall Ibrahim until the bank could set aside the sum to which he was entitled.

A week later, Cedric and Mahmoud paid a visit to their client, half an hour before the first call to mid-morning prayer. For fifteen minutes tea was served and courtesies were exchanged; as required by Arab etiquette, one never gets down to business immediately. When they sensed that their client was about to tackle the matter at hand, Mahmoud turned to him and said: "Ah, Mr. Ibrahim, did you know that Mr. Grant has been reading the Koran?" Ibrahim, a deeply religious man, could not let this slip by without a reaction. "Indeed? Would you care to recite a *Hadith*?" Cedric acquiesced, and Arab was so impressed with this Westerner's budding knowledge of the divine sayings of the Prophet that he called in members of his staff to hear Cedric repeat them. Before he could even finish, Ibrahim was called off to prayer, and Cedric and Mahmoud were saved for another month.

For three months, they were able to keep him at bay by always arriving at the same time, and having Cedric declaim newly learned passages of the Koran. On the fourth month, they scheduled a more appropriate time, and Cedric proudly presented Ibrahim with a check in the amount owed to him by the bank.

◆   ◆   ◆

In early September, Cedric flew down to Khamis Mushayt, only sixty miles from the Yemenite border, to visit the military cantonment that was being built by Hochtief and financed by FNCB. His primary job was to prepare his quarterly report to Wodtke; but he also brought along a camera and film, since he was to submit a copy of the report to the Embassy's Military Attaché and the CIA liaison officer. He arrived at Khamis Mushayt on a Thursday afternoon, visited the site, snapped some pictures, took some notes, met with the Project Manager, the Personnel Officer, and finally the Treasurer, Otto Rieben. The Hochtief compound was a sprawling array of pre-fab shacks that closely resembled the LAMCO compound in Nimba—functional and soulless. That evening, Otto invited Cedric to their weekly weekend party. Each guest was greeted at the door with a tall glass of Siddiqi, and would not be allowed in until he'd downed the full contents. "We have a whole shack dedicated to distilling this stuff!" Otto exclaimed merrily. Very shortly Cedric's memory of the party became rather hazy, though he did remember enjoying the banter between guests that was usually absent from the more formal Saudi or Embassy parties. He enjoyed it at least until sometime after midnight a few men started singing old Wehrmacht tunes…

Cedric arrived back in Jeddah on Saturday, still smarting from the night's revelry. His new Chief Accountant, George Haddad, gave him no time to recover, and showed him the photocopy of the bank compound's exorbitant utility bill for the month of August. "Ahmed Shams submitted this for payment, but it makes no sense. There are only three houses on that compound, and on average it's about fifteen Riyals a month for each house. This bill shouldn't be higher than fifty or so." Yet the bill was ten times that amount.

Ahmed Shams was the "fix-it guy". He dealt with all the tiresome and time-consuming bureaucratic red-tape for the bank: permits, drivers' licenses, utility bills, etc. He also performed the occasional bribe, logged under "cost of clearance." Every foreign company had one, needed one, but Shams was a particularly unappealing individual—sniveling, obsequious, and constantly whining about how difficult his job was. In 1968, Jeddah only had four international phone lines, and one of the operators happened to be Shams's cousin. When an FNCB officer urgently required to make an international call, Shams would arrange it with his cousin for four hundred dollars a minute. This was not entirely uncommon, but Cedric knew Shams was getting a kick-back, and he wouldn't put it past him to tinker with a utility bill, that had never been closely examined until now, in order to pad his savings account.

"Could it be a mistake by the utility company?" Cedric asked.

"Could be…" George said dubiously.

"Why don't you go back and check all the other bills. Water, gas, anything. See if there are any other discrepancies, and if you can, find out how he did it. I don't want to confront him right away. He's a greasy little bastard, but he does get the job done."

Two months later, George Haddad entered Cedric's office with a ream of papers and announced the bad news: "It's Ahmed Shams: he's as guilty as sin on these utility bills. Must be. From what I can make out, he's been photocopying the original statements and adding a dot." Cedric whistled. A dot in Arabic is equivalent to a zero: Shams was charging the Bank 500 Riyals for a 50 Riyal bill and pocketing the difference. Haddad estimated that Shams had swindled the bank for over two hundred thousand dollars over several years.

"He's fired."

Mahmoud Jawdat intervened with a discreet cough. "Ah Cedric, I would strongly suggest a higher degree of diplomacy: Shams's brother is head of the al-Mabahithal al Aama, the General Investigation Bureau, the Secret Police. I hate to imagine his revenge if you accused him outright of theft…What you could do is show him the discrepancy in the last bill and ask him to check with the utility company to see if they've made a mistake. He'll know he won't be able to, but he can't know for sure that you're accusing him of embezzlement. But hopefully he'll understand and have the sense to quit with his honor 'intact'."

Cedric called Shams into his office, and the man immediately started whining and professing his innocence. Finally Ahmed said he would check with the utility company but doubted that anything would come of it. His parting glance chilled Cedric's blood, and made him doubt the wisdom and sanity of his decision.

The Police came knocking on his door at seven o'clock the next morning and hauled him down to the station for questioning about his Chief Accountant.

After their previous accountant had quit, Cedric and Cliff had decided to break with the tradition of hiring British accountants searching to escape high taxes and bad weather in their homeland for a few years. Instead, they decided to hire an efficient and punctilious Lebanese, George Haddad, from the Beirut branch. Unfortunately, after four months at the bank, Haddad still had no work permit. The police told Cedric that his Chief Accountant had been working illegally on a tourist visa and was going to be deported back to Lebanon. There was not much he could do to save Haddad's job, but at least he didn't face the same fate as the two Ethiopian assistants whom Haddad had hired to help him inquire about Shams's phony utility bills, and who had had their houses ransacked and been severely beaten. Cedric wrote a five-page deposition stating that he was solely responsible for Haddad's illegal work situation and would cover all the deportation expenses. The police seemed somewhat subdued, and Cedric vaguely relieved. Five minutes after leaving the station, he cabled the details to Peter Wodtke, and quickly arranged to have George Haddad hired back by the FNCB branch in Beirut.

For several days, Cedric expected to be arrested by the police on false grounds and be deported, or worse. He immediately went to see Ambassador Eilts to explain: "In case anything happens to me, I want you to know beforehand so that you can intervene," he said. It would take several weeks before Cedric's fear and anxiety ebbed. A month after the police had come to Cedric's house, Shams walked into his office and told him that the utility company had lost the records. Therefore he couldn't prove anything, he said, but since he disliked the aura of suspicion floating around him, he had decided to quit FNCB and accept a job with the United States Geological Survey. Cedric wondered what he would do if the Survey called him for a reference, but fortunately they never did.

Cedric was making good progress on the clean-up job that Wodtke had outlined for him. Business was picking up again, loans were being paid back, and he had high hopes of soon making some concrete profits for the bank, especially with a project that had already made some "easy money" and that promised to rake in some substantial benefits.

When Cedric had first arrived in Saudi Arabia, the government had asked for bids from major construction companies to build the new Jeddah airport designed by Airway Engineering. U.S. Ambassador Hermann Eilts contacted Cedric and suggested that FNCB finance the bid bonds—monetary guarantees equivalent to 2% of the total budget that had to be submitted to the Saudi government at the same time as the bid proposals—for those construction companies that were competing for the project. Cedric knew that if he issued the bid bond for the winning team, chances were high that he would be asked to handle the financing of the project, and that would mean several million dollars profit for the bank. Eilts put him in touch with Airway Engineering, and the firm contacted him each time a construction company picked up a bid package for the airport. Six European consortiums and one Japanese were in the running, and over the course one month, as Eilts had predicted and thanks to FNCB's strong international representation, Cedric was able to acquire five of them as clients. The proposals hovered around three hundred million dollars: charging a $100,000 service fee per consortium for issuing a simple guarantee that the Saudi government would be paid 2% of the total budget if the winning company retracted, Cedric made the bank an easy half a million dollars in a few weeks.

In the Fall of 1968, the Saudi government announced that the US-Greek consortium Archiroden had submitted the lowest bid for the airport construction and would be handed the project—for some reason, however, the consortium had misread the tender documents and miscalculated the 2% bond value which Cedric had issued. Essentially, their bond was undervalued by a half a million dollars and the Saudi Finance Minister had given them two hours to come up with an additional bond covering that amount, or the project would be passed on to the British consortium as the second-lowest bidder, one which FNCB had not financed.

"I understand if you can't do it," Eilts told Cedric in an emergency meeting, though his pleading voice indicated otherwise. What he really meant was that he hoped Cedric would put his career on the line by issuing an additional $500'000 line of credit that was far beyond his or even Cooper's signing authority. Since it was Saturday, Cedric did not even have the option of calling New York for advice.

Considering the circumstances, Cedric reached his decision quickly. Archiroden was already present in Saudi Arabia as FNCB clients, since they were handling the construction of the new berths in the Jeddah harbor, and he was convinced that their excellent reputation and positive track record with FNCB would convince New York that he had made the right decision in drafting up the extra half-million dollar bond. Nevertheless, he wrote a four-page memo to Wodtke, outlining his reasons for breaching his signing level authority, with the rueful smile of a man about to jump across an abyss that might turn out to be just a little too large. He forwarded a copy of his memo to New York, and eventually it reached all the way up to Al Constanzo, Head of the Overseas division and Wriston's right-hand man. Cedric was called to Beirut to defend his position, but when he arrived, he found out that the furor had not only subsided, but that Al Constanzo had found the project so appealing that he wanted FNCB to be actively involved in the project. Far from being reprimanded, Cedric returned to Jeddah with the authorization to approach the Finance Minister committing the bank to a hundred million dollar loan—and a firm indication that he would be promoted to Branch Manager upon Cliff Cooper's departure early 1969.

The story could end there, except for a final ironic twist of fate. When Cedric went to see the Minister several months after the bid disclosure, he found out that King Faisal had canceled the project. What actually happened, Cedric later discovered, was that certain members of the royal family had been a little slow on the uptake, and had not had time to position themselves to make big money off the project by buying land and setting up development projects. The airport would finally be built some fifteen years later for a hugely inflated budget of fourteen billion dollars.

◆   ◆   ◆

The Grants moved into the Cooper's house in March 1969 just as the Hajj went into full swing, and renovations kept Annette busy well into April. After being handed the reins of the Jeddah branch, Cedric found his job as Manager to be actually easier than in the months preceding Cliff's departure. With no-one to hinder, directly or indirectly, his decision-making process—he only saw Bob Grant, the man who'd replaced Peter Wodtke as Regional Head, once a quarter at budget meetings in Beirut—Cedric moved along quickly. He was allowed the comfort of defining a management style, which he would retain for the rest of his career, and that lent itself more to delegating authority and responsibility rather than micromanaging everything himself.

There was one hiccup early in his tenure, when the branch found itself threatened with closure by SAMA because of under-capitalization. Saudi Arabia required a fifteen-to-one capital-to-deposits ratio; according to this law and with a capitalization of $230 million, FNCB should have shown proof for invested capital of fifteen million dollars. Their capital had not been increased in years, however, and in 1969 it amounted to only one million. He was required to remit $14 million within one week or Omar Bahjined, SAMA's deputy governor, would close the branch. Naturally, he was worried about the financial consequences of avoiding such an outcome: If New York wired the money within a week, FNCB Jeddah would be paying 5% interest on a $14 million loan that would sit with SAMA for several months until the capitalization increase was officially processed, and earn no money. Cedric faced an effective loss for his Jeddah operations of over two million dollars. Afraid that his career would not recover from such a blow, Cedric asked to call on SAMA governor Anwar Ali; he had done several favors for him in the past, and Cedric hoped that he would find a "mutually satisfactory solution" for them both.

Ali's secretary had been one of those allured by Jawdat's offer to triple their interest on savings. Cedric had therefore little trouble gaining access to Ali to explain his situation. Anwar Ali was a Pakistani who had been hired by King Faisal to help put the Saudi economy back on track after King Saud's dismissal, and he was on secondment from the International Monetary Fund. He was so effective that every year Faisal finagled his continuance, and Ali would eventually remain Governor of SAMA for sixteen years. He was well disposed towards Cedric for having cleared up FNCB debts to SAMA on exchange rate variances for certificates of deposit in the amount of $130,000, and for having sent him so many books on Islamic history.

He greeted Cedric amiably. "What can I do for you?" he asked. When Cedric explained, Ali verbally dismissed four potential months of red tape, and authorized FNCB to increase its capitalization to fifteen million dollars, Cedric was effectively able to loan the money from New York and invest it in high-yield Saudi government bonds, without waiting for further approval from SAMA.

"I would also like to discuss the issue of the Saudization of foreign banks," Ali then added. "I have met with King Faisal and he would like to move to a limited and private form of nationalization whereby Saudi investors would acquire 60% of bank shares." This was an attempt to spur internal investment possibilities. In exchange, the banks would no longer be restricted to two branches, would have their choice of staff and board of directors, not to mention the chance to expand anywhere in the kingdom. "I would hope that FNCB will pave the way, and make it easier to convince other banks to take a step that will ultimately prove inevitable. For the moment it remains a choice, however, but if you do so now, FNCB will be amply rewarded."

Cedric showed his support for the project in a memo to Beirut and New York. He not only tried to point out that many developing countries were taking the route of nationalization, and indeed this was not truly nationalization, but national privatization—hence the term 'Saudization'. Furthermore, he pointed out, FNCB would get their top pick of founding shareholders, high-rolling businessmen who would boost business through their myriad contacts. He wrote that in the long run, FNCB would be set to make more money with a 40% stake in expanded business than a hundred percent in their current state. The affair reached all the way to Wriston, and was flatly refused: "If FNCB takes the initiative on this project, we will look amenable, indeed favorable, to nationalization. We cannot afford that," he said. Cedric returned to Ali with the news and shared in his disappointment. "I honestly think it would have been the way to go."

As Ali had predicted, the Saudization process moved ahead anyway, and in the mid-seventies FNCB would be the last bank in Saudi Arabia to be saudized. Even maintaining full share of the profits during the oil price spike of '73 and '74 would hardly be to FNCB's advantage, since most of the revenues immediately left the country as massive loans to Latin America, fueling the petrodollar recycling machine initiated by Walter Wriston himself.

◆   ◆   ◆

Concurrent with Cedric's promotion to Jeddah branch manager came the news that he would soon be a father.

Since the medical facilities were far superior in Lebanon than in Saudi Arabia, Annette left for Beirut when she was eight months pregnant to settle into an apartment and await her mother's arrival. Jeannie arrived later that month precisely on the due date. But the baby was late, and Cedric found himself holed up in a small apartment in Croydon Manor with his mother-in-law for four days. Jeannie was in terrifically high spirits, happy as only the mother of a young man who has just escaped being drafted for the Vietnam War in 1969 can be.

Gordon had spent a year as a Vista Volunteer in North Georgia where he learned tough lessons in patience among a proud and independent local populace that often accused the volunteers of "inviting in all the niggers and having drinking parties with whisky and beer". But when his assignment was over mid-1969, he had been unable to avoid his draft notice. Jeannie had desperately called on all the people she knew and whose possible influence on the outcome of Gordy's assignation ranged from nil to slim. Yet it paid off: Dr. Jean Vieuchange, Gordon's godfather, worked as a researcher with the Institut Pasteur in Paris. As such, he knew several doctors involved in research in the United States, many of whom sporadically worked for the government, primarily to evaluate the physical aptitudes of Vietnam draftees and their ability to serve. When Gordon was called in for his medical visit, the doctor discovered that he had a congenital back disease that made him ineligible for military service—an issue of flat disks between the third and fifth, and the eight and ninth vertebrae. This affliction was so common among young men his age, however, that it was usually no cause for dismissal. Jean Vieuchange notwithstanding, Gordon would always think of this doctor as the man who saved his life.

To wile away the time in Beirut, Jeannie engaged Cedric in four days of storytelling, unaware that she had already spent many hours in Scarsdale telling her son-in-law how she had met Jean and his brother Michel, who'd died in the dissident region of the Rio del Oro, Morocco, at the age of twenty-six. This in turn led her to recount the events of her childhood: the German bombings of Paris during World War I, her anticlerical father who thwarted her theatrical ambitions, her swallow-like mother who sang so beautifully and who colluded in her daughter's visits to her lover, and about her engagement at the age of nineteen to a beguiled Count Ribert, which she later broke off because of her affair with a married man named Rodolphe de Baillen-court, an eager proponent of women's liberation.

As fascinated as Cedric may have been, his patience was beginning to wear thin by the end of the fourth day—September 2. Not only was he anxious that his daughter—he and Annette had agreed on the name *Nicole*—was now five days late in appearing, but his mother-in-law's biography had barely retraced her teens. Since she was now sixty-three years old, Cedric was afraid that at that rate her storytelling would take them well into the middle of the next decade. He was therefore almost relieved to get a call from Mahmoud Jawdat telling him that his pres-ence in Jeddah was urgently requested for two days. After checking with the doctors, Cedric decided to make the trip, and be back by the 4th, by which date the doctors would urge Nicole out of the womb whether she liked it or not. The chances were still quite high, however, that he would miss his first child's birth, and the relief he felt at leaving his mother-in-law was replaced by an anxiety that never ebbed during the time of his stay in Jeddah.

The reason for Jawdat's call was the impromptu visit by a duo of dapper bankers from Switzerland, Jean-Pierre Cuoni and Peter Stoneborough, who had visions of grandeur and prestige. They had convinced a few people in New York that FNCB Switzerland should have its own Private Bank sector, that indeed it was the future of bank-ing in Switzerland: big money with low capital…The old corporate hands who dealt with monsters like Nestlé smiled benevolently and gave them some office space. Carlton Stewart, Cedric's stone-cold boss in New York, not only lent them his support, but suggested they tour the branches in his division to explain the nature of private banking, and acquire contacts and clients in the Middle East.

Jawdat had drafted a list of top wealthy businessmen in Jeddah. Cedric arrived at the bank few hours before Cuoni and Stoneborough, and the four of them went out for dinner to get acquainted. The fol-lowing morning, they called an officers' meeting, after which they went through Jawdat's list of wealthy clients. At each meeting, Cuoni would adjust his three-piece Italian-tailored suit, squint his beady bespectacled eyes, wipe the early bald patch near the back his head, and tell Cedric that he could not join the meeting.

Cedric said, "I arrange for you to meet the wealthiest businessmen in the area, and as branch manager you're telling me I can't join you?"

Cuoni forced a wan and woeful smile, and claimed private banking secrecy as an excuse. "The client must feel that whatever is discussed with Peter and myself is absolutely confidential," he said.

Over the course of the following month, Cedric and Jawdat would come to realize that Cuoni had had no qualms about soliciting clients away from their branch. In doing so, he provoked an exodus of fifteen million dollars in Riyals of deposits from Jeddah. Cedric not only lost the net interest on these deposits (totaling some three quarters of a million dollars a year), but he suddenly found himself short of local currency. So many people were investing their oil-derived capital outside the country at double the interest rates that Cedric was forced to borrow Eurodollars at a loss through the branch's line of credit in New York. Unfortunately it was the kind of practice that was becoming endemic in a First National City Bank under Wriston that was by now completely focused on achieving 15% annual growth.

Cedric returned to Beirut on the midday of the Fourth. He arrived at Croydon Manor to find a note stuck to the refrigerator door telling him that Annette had left for the hospital that morning. His heart racing, but confident that he had several hours ahead of him, Cedric put a six-pack of beer in the freezer, took a long shower, settled on the balcony for a few beers, and trundled off to the hospital where he arrived at 4.30pm.

Annette was already in the delivery room. Apparently her waters had broken very soon after she had gone into labor, and she found herself virtually running down the street to the hospital, with her mother gasping for breath behind her and carrying her night bag. Nicole was born shortly thereafter at around five in the afternoon. At seven o'clock the next morning, Cedric had her birth certificate signed by the attending physician, arranged for a photographer to meet him at seven thirty, and had his daughter's picture taken. He picked up the photos an hour later and arrived at the US Embassy at 9am to have Nicole's passport made. At eleven o'clock he visited the Lebanese Foreign Department with photos, passport, birth certificate and parents' passports, and obtained an exit visa for his nineteen-hour old daughter; then he went to the Saudi Embassy for an entry visa. At two o'clock in the afternoon, he dropped off passport and visas with Annette, and at 5pm he was on the plane to Jeddah. Annette, Jeannie and Nicole flew back four days later. In the plane, they ran into Omar Saggaff and were invited to join his small entourage in the first class cabin. Jeannie was completely smitten by this elegant and refined gentleman, and would remember every detail of the plane ride even thirty years later. ("Such a polite man! He reminded me so much of the *courteoisie* among Parisian men in the thirties!") When they arrived in Jeddah, Saggaff rushed them through customs and arranged for his driver to take them home in his limousine, where a surprised but relieved Cedric was preparing to leave for the airport to pick them up. At the age of five days, Nicole had already flown between two countries, been spoken to in Lebanese, Arabic, English and French, and had been cuddled by the Saudi Minister of Foreign Affairs, a direct descendant of the Prophet Mohammed. Fortunately unaware of these events, however, she would not spend the rest of her life tying to live up to this illustrious debut.

◆   ◆   ◆

In January 1970, Annette and Cedric traveled to London for a three-day conference uniting most of the senor staff of the Overseas Division, renamed the "International Banking Group", or IBG, under the McKinsey reorganization. During one of the recesses, Cedric found himself passing Intourist, the Soviet travel agency on Regent Street. Ever since his trip to Moscow and Leningrad in 1960, Cedric had cherished the desire to travel on the Trans-Siberian Railway. He entered the Intourist office without much hope and asked them what it would take. "A valid passport, four photos, a fixed itinerary, and cash for the ticket," the travel agent said. "That's it?!" Cedric responded, and signed up immediately. Annette sighed, but graciously accepted. They decided that he would return to Jeddah while she flew to New York, where he would meet her a month later after the trip. Since John and Katy Barner had also scheduled their home leave at the same time, Cedric asked John if he wouldn't mind joining him on the trip, and John eagerly agreed.

After spending a week respectively in Jeddah and Port Elizabeth, Cedric and John met up in Beirut then flew to Moscow. They spent a few days there before boarding the train—relatively modern carriages with first-class accommodations (for John and Cedric) that owed more to Soviet-style austerity than Dr. Zhivago-like romanticism. Nevertheless, they were both happy as clams, and for the first four days of the trip, Cedric cashed in all his food coupons for caviar—breakfast, lunch and dinner. The train ride itself lasted ten days, with stops in two of Russia's oldest cities, Yaroslavl and Krasnoyarsk, as well as Ekaterinburg, Irkutsk, Ulan Ude, Khabarovsk and Nakhodka. Each time they were greeted by two friendly and pretty female representatives of Intourist who made sure the pair didn't stray too far out of town. From Nakhodka, they took a Soviet motorship to Yokohama and flew to Anchorage, where they called their respective wives to let them know they'd arrived safely, and to share their ineffable enthusiasm. Finally they parted—John to Des Moines, Iowa, and Cedric to New York. A week later, Cedric and Annette flew to Italy to spend the remaining three weeks of their home leave skiing in Cervinia.

They arrived back in Jeddah at the end of March still bubbling with ideas of further manageable travel adventures. Cedric was greeted by his Regional Head, Bob Grant, and informed of his imminent transfer to Riyadh.

Foreign banks were only allowed to operate two branches in Saudi Arabia. Because of the business provided by the pilgrims during the Hajj, most foreign banks were concentrated in Jeddah. As the last foreign bank to open in 1956, FNCB had the fortunate opportunity to open their second branch in Riyadh. At the time it was a mud-brick town of no importance, but when King Faisal moved the Government Ministries to the capital and opened it to western business, the city suddenly became a very attractive place to be, and FNCB the envy of other banks as the only western presence in the capital.

By 1970, the Saudi oil pumping stations were more active than ever and business in the country had not only picked up but was booming. The European economies continued to expand and required increasing quantities of fuel, while the United States was making the transition from exporter to net importer of oil. When Head Office in New York decided to make Cedric Country Head of Saudi Arabia, it made perfect sense for him to relocate Riyadh to ensure better cohesion between the two branches.

Annette's positive attitude towards their move could not disguise the fact that they both found Riyadh to be the proverbial dumps. They found pleasant isolation in the compound, but the evolution of the capital from post-World War Two hovel to modern pre-fab concrete city had been effected with little apparent urban planning. The bank offices were located in a brand-new marble building on Batha street, but a wide open sewer ran the length of Main Street in front of the FNCB branch, and on the other side of the building was a stretch of desert land littered with monoliths—the unmarked graves of Saudis practicing the teachings of Shaykh Muhammad ibn Abd al-Wahhab who had decried the veneration of holy men's tombs common in the eighteenth century. When the building compressor broke down during an electrical shortage at the beginning of Cedric's tenure as Country Head, bank employees were obliged to keep the windows open all day long, and if the wind happened to blow in from the west, they were inundated with the stink of the garbage floating by the building; if the wind blew in from the east, they received the dust of the graveyard.

Jawdat relocated with Cedric, and together they drafted a list of the top one hundred people in Riyadh whom they felt he should contact. Cedric knew that he shouldn't wait for a specific reason to call on them: he told Jawdat to take him to any event at which he should be seen, and every night there was somewhere to go, like the funeral of some wealthy merchant at which top businessmen and members of the royal family would be present. At times like these, Cedric would often be the only Westerner, and he soon became part of an elite circle.

Despite the environmental unpleasantness of his first few months, Cedric's time in Riyadh marked a golden period of success, when work was far more often pleasure than pain and he knew that he could not be happier doing anything else, the moment at which he reaped the dividends of his Liberian toils. He enjoyed the country, the people, the business, and business was booming. The world oil glut was ending, Saudi Arabia was the top exporter among OPEC countries, foreign businesses were moving in, FNCB was getting much of the business, and Cedric was achieving a respected stature within the Middle East division.

Ministers and members of the Royal Family were sending their children overseas to be educated, and were preparing a new generation of westernized Saudis to take over the economy and the government. It remained, however, an exclusively male-oriented society, and beyond the stringent controls on women's behavior, Annette found herself excluded from many of the luncheons and parties to which her husband was invited. But she remained happy in Saudi Arabia. She was making new friends, notably a woman who made spectacular coral jewelry, Doreen; she went horseback riding; the varied international community provided a stimulating social life; and of course, there was Nicole. By June the baby was pulling herself up in her crib and standing for short periods of time, then began scooting around in her walker. She began mumbling her first words, *dada*, *mama* and *na-na*.

With her blonde hair and blue eyes, she assumed—according to her mother—Cedric's "overall appearance": high forehead, eyes close together, and a cute chubby nose. Cedric bought an 8mm camera so that Annette could catch Nicole's progress on film.

In November, Cedric traveled to the Yemen with David Ransom, an employee of the US Embassy who had been forced to leave the country, and who was now returning to see what he could salvage of his time there. Civil war had broken out in September 1962, at the death of the Imam, head of the Royal Family in the Yemen. Backed by Nasser's United Arab Republic, the Yemen Arab Republic was proclaimed, and it was recognized by the Cold War superpowers by early 1963. Fighting would continue until 1969, however, as Republican and Royalist forces were respectively backed by the USSR and Saudi military supplies (with covert CIA backing). Nasser also stepped up his support, and by 1967 Egyptian forces in the Yemen numbered eighty thousand. Their withdrawal in January 1968 bolstered the Royalists who soon threatened to take over the Republican capital of Sanaa.

When David Ransom left the U.S. Embassy for Jeddah, the royalist military effort was in decline. The Saudi Arabian government diminished its aid, and in March 1970 Yemenite Premier Muhsin al-Aini and his foreign minister met privately with Saudi officials during the Islamic foreign ministers' conference in Jeddah. A peace agreement was apparently signed; in any case Saudi Arabia opened diplomatic relations with the Y.A.R. in July 1970. The situation having cooled off, David Ransom wished to return that November to clarify U.S. interests which had been turned over to foreign embassies still operating there, and perhaps to see if there was anything left to salvage. He asked Cedric to join him, and Cedric was more than happy to oblige. They arrived in Sanaa on one of the first flights from Saudi Arabia that were allowed into the country, and found the town in a primitive state of unbelievable ruin. The dry hilly landscape surrounding the capital was littered with burned-out tanks, armored cars, and half-tracks. Men lounged on the sidewalks in a semi-stupor from ghat and whisky. In the mornings, before the ghat crop was available, the Yemenites lined up outside the embassies to obtain visas to work abroad. All that David found in his former apartment riddled with bullet holes were a few strewn photographs and a Marine hat from his military days.

Soon after his return to Riyadh, Cedric and Annette went on Christmas vacation to Morocco, visiting the Osbournes in Casablanca. It so happened that Kurt was touring Europe in between jobs, and the three of them spent two weeks visiting Marrakech, Rabat and Fez together, thrilling Kurt with his fifteen-month old niece. While Kurt slummed at the local hostels, Annette and Cedric slept at rather more upstanding accommodations, particularly in Fez—a breathtaking hotel in the heart of the ancient city, a reconverted palace with most of the original mosaic, stained-glass windows, and carved plaster work intact, at the bottom of a steep and narrow cobblestone path, in what Annette described as the Garden of Eden.

While on vacation, Annette realized she was pregnant again. But any happiness they felt was quickly overshadowed, upon their return, by the news from Bob Grant that Cedric was be re-located to Lagos, Nigeria, within the year.

Any glamorous thoughts he may have had of high-stakes banking were now crushed between the lines of the letter from his boss. He tried to rationalize that he was a simple kid from Oregon after all, that his future was not with the Harvard-educated global bankers of this world, but that he could carve out his niche in Africa and the Middle East, in the "backwaters" of international banking…Annette took much longer to adjust. She did not break down in tears, but she fumed with anger for several weeks. It was perhaps because her mother was so much more devastated than they were, that Annette was able to embrace the destiny of Cedric's career with so much stoicism. In defending their move to her mother, she was able to accept it.

Carlton Stewart is not the type of man who gives people a choice. If he needs a man somewhere, he wants that person to be flexible and expects him to accept. One cannot play games with the Bank, and Cedric knew this when he signed on. Other reasons for our acceptance could be laid out as followed: (1) We had expected to spend another eighteen months to two years in Riyadh, so that a change coming at this time, especially this assignment to open a branch in a developing and oil-rich country is just a gain in Rick's career. (2) Rick feels that his job here has been completed and that staying longer would only involve problems regarding expansion programs he doesn't agree with. (3) Most important is the work he will be doing in Lagos—he has been picked, according to Bob Grant, because of his ability to mold a team, his excellent background and reputation in branch banking, and his knowledge of all facets of operations. I don't think that with Stewart, the fact that Rick has an adventuresome spirit counts for much. And Stewart might be a pretty tough nut, but Rick does respect him, and feels he has some good ideas, though his personnel policy might stink. (5) For heaven's sake get an up-to-date encyclopedia! We don't know much about Nigeria, but we did spend thirty-six hours in Lagos and had a brief tour of the city. It is a BIG city, very modern, and I think the British have left a lot of nice social amenities behind. There is apparently a lot of foreign investment and business, and from his Liberia days Rick found that the Nigerians working in the bank were the most intelligent, the most cultured and the nicest, with the best sense of humor.

The first and last two points were most certainly true (though Cedric would temper the last with a long exposé on Nigerian corruption). The third point about his work in Lagos being a gain was partially hopefully thinking—while it could be true, Cedric felt somewhat reserved, though he kept his reservations to himself. He also allowed Annette to believe that he had completed his work in Saudi Arabia, even though that felt very far from the truth. In fact, he had not even begun to capitalize on the contacts he'd made. He enjoyed the people and his work there, and had barely spent six months in the capital.

Cedric eventually sussed out the true combination of events that led to his being chosen for the post. Stewart had been sticking his neck out with regards to Nigeria—it was an important place to be and, despite the difficulties of opening a branch there (the first person to sift through the preliminary work quit the bank within a month), Stewart claimed to everyone that FNCB would soon be a hallmark in Lagos. The new profit-oriented and cutthroat mentality that was beginning to emerge within the Bank meant that this kind of talk did not go unnoticed. Stewart found himself sinking more and more money into the project, and he knew that he would need to show for it soon to those who thought it was a lost cause, notably Ed Palmer, Executive Vice President, head of the Senior Policy Committee, and third member of the ruling triumvirate of the bank that included the president and the chairman.

Stewart needed someone fast. He called Cooper into his office and asked him who had experience with developing countries, opening a branch, and would be willing (i.e. stupid enough) to go to Lagos. Cooper suggested that Rick Grant in Riyadh would more than likely accept. With the feeling that his banking career was in a rut and headed for a dead end, Cedric began to prepare for his departure scheduled immediately after the Middle Eastern visit of FNCB President Bill Spencer.

◆   ◆   ◆

Spencer's tour was planned to culminate with a meeting with King Faisal. Since the King's schedule kept changing, however, Spencer's visit was consistently postponed. And since Cedric was expected to greet the President, his departure for Nigeria was equally postponed.

By end of February 1971, Annette began showing unusual signs of fatigue. Cedric briefly feared a relapse into the depression that had gripped her in Liberia, but that soon gave way to fears that the pregnancy was not going well. Annette remained unconcerned but did agree to return early to New York, leaving Cedric to deal with the packing and shipping, and with Spencer's visit, now scheduled for the end of March. She arrived in New York on the verge of collapse. Her only thought was to sleep for three days straight once she reached her mother's apartment, but Jeannie took one look at her daughter's off-yellow coloring and immediately rushed her to the doctor. Annette was diagnosed with hepatitis, and since she was pregnant, the doctor wanted her hospitalized immediately. Ensued a battery of blood and liver tests and gynecological exams that made her feel like a lab rat—or worse, when an arrogant intern approached her bed, took one look at her, and said: "Bah! Garden-variety hepatitis!" Annette was to remind him of this statement when she ran into him six weeks later, still bedridden. A nurse soon made her feel somewhat better, however, by telling her that just down the hall, Johnny Carson was also being treated for hepatitis…

The doctors were stymied: Annette was suffering from severe hepatitis as well as anemia, and was not reacting to traditional treatment. As a last resort, they began cortisone injections, despite the fears of how that might damage the fetus. Annette cabled her doctor in Beirut to ask his opinion as to whether or not she should consider an abortion. He wrote back, saying that if the cortisone were to have a negative effect, chances are she would abort naturally. She did not, and the issue soon became moot as she moved well into her second trimester.

Cedric's visit at the end of April 1971 was shrouded in doubt and anxiety. His wife had to remain hospitalized for an indeterminate period of time. There was a high risk that his second child would be born handicapped, and between the added costs of a private room for Annette (because of the fear of contagion), and live-in help for Nicole, his savings were dwindling rapidly. The prospects of commuting—however temporarily—to Lagos only deepened his anguish when he returned to Riyadh to act as tour guide to the President of FNCB and prepare his own departure from a country he had learned to love despite its severity, and its odd mixture of modernity and medieval mentalities.

He could never have imagined the President's visit going off so poorly. Cedric's sullen state was completely outmatched by Spencer's irascible temper, and from the moment the President missed his flight connection in Dhahran and was forced to wait an hour going through customs for a second time, his trip went from bad to worse.

It was informal bank policy at the time for a Senior Official of the bank to stay with the top-level official of the country he was visiting. It was with some anxiety, therefore, that Cedric arrived home with Spencer and his wife in tow, only to find the guest room flooded because the cheap hot water heaters had blown their gaskets. His maid had called in some friends to help mop up the mess, but Spencer was shocked by the state of the room in which he and his wife would be sleeping. By evening, Spencer's room was livable again, but in the mean time, Cedric's kitchen stove stopped working while dinner was being prepared for the local staff, delaying the meal (and hence Spencer's bedtime) by more than an hour. Then in the middle of the night the air-conditioning stopped working, and Spencer was kept awake until dawn by a horde of stray dogs barking, a sound that had, until then, been mercifully covered by the air-conditioner. Cedric awoke early that morning to find his President huddled over the kitchen, grumbling loudly: "Didn't even want to be here. I should be in Kenya on a goddamn safari trip that cost me a fortune." Little had Cedric known that the repeated postponement of Spencer's visit to Saudi Arabia had caused him to miss out on a hunting trip—and for a tough Westerner from Colorado, that amounted to heresy.

It wouldn't be the only thing of which Cedric was unaware. After a morning budget presentation, during which Spencer promptly fell asleep for two hours and snored loudly, Cedric had organized a Bedouin-style lunch with top Arab businessmen. They removed to a desert location just outside Riyadh, and sat cross-legged under an open-ended tent for an hour and a half—an excruciatingly long period of time for Spencer who suffered from a bad back, and who tried to shift the pain around every thirty seconds while blowing the flies off his food at every mouthful. The following day, Cedric accompanied him to meet the King, and while they waited an hour for Faisal to appear,

Spencer once again nodded off while one of the King's top advisors was talking to him. It would take Cedric his few remaining weeks in Riyadh to repair the damage...

A week after Spencer's departure, Cedric received a wrathful cable from Wriston himself telling him that if he ever treated a President of the bank that shoddily again, he would be fired immediately. He swallowed the bitter pill of irony, and prepared his departure.

Cedric's brief trip to Lagos before returning to New York did not bode well. The bank lawyers at Irving & Bonner laid out to him the precise difficulty in obtaining a commercial license in Nigeria: The government didn't want one. They would be happy to grant a merchant banking license, but not a commercial one. Try as he might to impress upon Carlton Stewart the Wriston logic of getting a corner stone in the country—better a merchant bank that none at all—Cedric's boss wouldn't hear of it: he had promised Ed Palmer a commercial bank in Lagos, and a commercial bank he would deliver. So Cedric began the fruitless and uninspired odyssey of commuting once a month to Lagos, alleviated only by evening and weekend MBA courses at Columbia University.

Shortly after their second child, Eric, was born on August 12, 1971—apparently healthy against many expectations—the doctors had told Annette that she could not return to live in a tropical climate. Her immune system was extremely fragile, and any further exposure to tropical diseases would place her health in danger. Cedric broke the news to Stewart who showed little sympathy: "Well, you go then and leave her behind. Commute back from time to time. Bank will pay. It'll be a year, eighteen months, time for her to recover..." This was taking dedication a little to far, Cedric figured. Without even bothering to consult Annette, he flatly refused. Stewart sighed. "Oh, well, then...Keep commuting until I bring someone else in. Just get that goddamn branch open—Ed Palmer is preparing a tour of Sub-Saharan

Africa that includes opening branches in Pretoria, Kinshasa and of course Lagos!"

The enmity between Carlton Stewart and the Executive Vice President was palpable, and instead of explaining to Palmer the difficulties they were having in Nigeria, Stewart had simply told him, "Sure, you'll open a branch there." It pacified Palmer, but made Cedric feel like fat in a frying pan. The trip was two months away, but Stewart wanted everything settled. He told Cedric: "Palmer will arrive from Kinshasa at four in the afternoon, and leaves at noon the next day. I want television reporters present at his arrival, then he'll be flown by helicopter over the city to the Federal Palace to meet with the top people there for dinner; and the next morning he'll meet with President Yakubu Gowon to cut the ribbon and officially open the branch." Cedric said nothing and left for Lagos the following week.

Cedric decided to tackle the issues one by one, and set aside for a moment the problem, reiterated by the bank lawyer, that the Nigerian government would not approve the articles of incorporation necessary to set up a commercial bank; not in the conceivable future and certainly not in two months.

The other issues also fell through the cracks one by one. Cedric could not have reporters present at Palmer's arrival expecting him to open a branch, and then find out from the Minister of Finance that the project had not been approved. It would be a media disaster. It would be equally impossible to fly Palmer by helicopter over the city: the Biafra civil war had ended barely a year before, and only the military was allowed to fly over Lagos. At four in the afternoon, it would take three hours in rush-hour traffic to drive Palmer to the Federal Palace, a prospect Cedric would not even contemplate. Furthermore, several embassy officials (Canadian, British, US, and French—Cedric did his homework)assured him that it was highly unlikely that many people would show up at such a dinner party. They would all say yes, and then desist, leading to an organizational nightmare. And finally, as evidence of the forces conspiring against him, Cedric discovered that President

Yakubu Gowon consistently worked until five in the morning and didn't get up till past noon—a breakfast meeting and ribbon cutting with Palmer was out of the question.

Cedric looked at the bright side: it was so obvious that Palmer's visit would be a disaster that Stewart would have to drop the whole thing. He didn't realize, however, how deep a hole his boss had dug himself with this idea of a branch in Nigeria. When he confronted him back in New York with the results of his preliminary attempts to prepare for the EVP's visit, Stewart turned red. "I don't care how you do it, just do it! Get your ass back there, rent an office, hire staff, and fake the whole fucking thing!" Cedric didn't know whether to laugh or cry, and he had a sudden sense of distorted reality. But it was real enough, and he knew he was facing the ethical Rubicon of his career. It took him twenty-four hours to decide, but he realized that he would not cross it. He would plan for Palmer's visit, but would hide nothing from him when he arrived, let the chips fall where they may.

The least he could do was prepare for the actual visit as best he could. Having learned from the Spencer fiasco in Riyadh, he went to see Palmer's secretary with a list of twenty questions: does he have allergies? a bad back? pet peeves? does he like to tour or rest by the pool? what are his likes and dislikes? what are his wife's? would he like flowers and champagne, or does he like things simple? Etc. Cedric had planned to see the secretary while Palmer was in a meeting to avoid running in to him, but fate had other plans: Palmer's meeting was cancelled, and in the middle of Cedric's eighth question, he walked out and passed right behind him. His secretary called out: "Oh, Mr. Palmer! This is Cedric Grant. He's asking me some questions relative to your visit to Lagos." Cedric felt his blood seep into the company carpet. Palmer called him into to his office and asked if the branch in Lagos would be ready to open for his visit.

"Well, actually, the Nigerian government doesn't seem to want to grant a commercial banking license…"

Palmer hit the roof, and to Cedric's dismay and shock, he promptly called up Stewart: "Carlton?! Grant's up here in my office telling me we don't have a goddamn banking license in Lagos? It that true? You *lied* to me?!"

Palmer canceled his trip, and for him the affair was over. He remained oblivious to the difficult situation in which he'd placed Cedric by calling Stewart's bluff so bluntly. Indeed, Stewart called Cedric into his office and told him he was finished in his division. "You can keep that piddling marketing desk job, but I swear I won't find you another job in my division…You can kiss your career in IBG goodbye…"

Cedric returned desperately to his classes at Columbia and to his Marketing Director desk job that amounted to little more than a title, and waited for the axe to fall. There were no solid grounds for dismissal, and he could not afford to leave the bank. But the situation could only last for so long before someone realized that he did not in fact have much of a job. The first three months of 1972 were the most painful of Cedric's career, relegated to bank oblivion with hospital bills to pay back, and a wife and two children to support.

8

Nixon's decision to float the dollar in 1971 heralded the end of the Bretton-Woods agreement that had held world currency markets together in the post-World War II era, a decision that Wriston would later qualify in an Op-Ed article of the *Wall Street Journal*, November 12, 1985, as "a key step in the emergence of a global information standard." Sometime thereafter, representatives of the Group of Ten (the US, the UK, Canada, France, West Germany, Italy, the Netherlands, Belgium, Sweden and Japan) met at the Smithsonian Institution and agreed to realign their currencies at newly determined rates. The dollar was devalued against gold, while the other currencies appreciated against the dollar by nearly ten percent. The Smithsonian Agreement turned out to be only a temporary solution to the international currency crisis, and was doomed to failure. No gold or world money backed the major currencies, and the United States continued to be plagued with price and money inflation, and an increasingly huge balance of payments deficit. In February 1973, a second devaluation of the dollar was announced, and West Germany, France, Switzerland and other hard currency countries could no longer afford to buy dollars to prop up the currency. Inevitably, Japan and the EEC countries decided to let their currencies float.

Against this seemingly bleak financial backdrop, FNCB Chairman Walter Wriston seemed unnervingly buoyant. Inflation was helping him meet his yearly profit earnings growth target of fifteen percent, and floating exchange rates squared with his own extreme free market outlook. Indeed, floating rates would lead to new rules in foreign exchange trading, a game that Citibank would master to become the biggest forex trader in the world, raking in hundreds of millions of dollars in profit throughout the seventies.

Wriston's troubles lay closer to home than the Vietnam War and the US economic debacle, as the fallout from the McKinsey reorganization to matrix management left the IBG with a host of problems in dealing with international customers, as country heads and the domestic corporate group openly and subversively came to blows over multinational clients. Phillip Zweig recounts in his expansive review of Wriston's life and career that "multinational customers were often treated just as shabbily as the $150-a-week waitress trying to force the FNCB back-office bureaucracy to correct a five dollar error on her checking account". Serving such customers demanded much more than an information system, Wriston realized, and in 1973, he decided to set up the World Corporation Group, a multinational unit that wrested control of four hundred big companies from the international and domestic corporate banking groups to better serve their interests. This was not initially a popular move, but after great turmoil and under the leadership of Tom Theobald—one of a select few that many considered had the potential to be the next FNCB Chairman—the WCG was soon regarded as one of the bank's more successful restructurings, and its development would influence most of America's largest banks.

Following a similar train of thought—after Ed Palmer had reported on a distinct lack of special services for High Net Worth Individuals on his world trip in early 1971—head of IMG Al Constanzo decided to create a division specialized in handling wealthy individuals on an international scale. FNCB had the largest global network of all U.S. banks, but service and coordination remained haphazard. Costanzo asked former Corporate Planner Robbie Meyjes to spearhead what would become the International Investments Services Division, integrated with the Private Banking Group, and later renamed PAMG, or Private Asset Management Group, in 1972.

Meyjes constituted a small group of "founding members": Peter Sperling, his personal secretary, Doris Cohen, and representatives for Latin America, Asia, and Europe. The division became officially active on January 2, 1972, but Robbie Meyjes was still worried about the Middle East and Africa region (MEA). Carlton Stewart put forward Cedric's name as someone who was available since he could no longer go to Nigeria. Robbie Meyjes was an intelligent, energetic, and well-spoken man in his early forties who impressed Cedric immediately. Born in Holland in 1932, Robbie's family was forced to escape to England when Nazi Germany overran Europe. He later studied at the Sorbonne in Paris, and received an MBA from Harvard. He joined FNCB in the early sixties as Wriston's overseas planner. In September 1971, he left Corporate Planning to head the nascent IISD and begin coordinating FNCB's minimal private banking activities around the world. Over breakfast at the Four Seasons Robbie told Cedric a little of his background, then of the IISD and the work which would be expected of him within the Private Bank. A bemused Cedric listened with growing interest to the job description that Robbie Meyjes was giving him, and realized that his career was now back on track, and in a much more inspiring environment.

He would integrate IISD as MEA Marketing Director, with the primary objective to solicit wealthy individuals in that region to invest with FNCB, primarily in time deposits in London, in fiduciary placements in Switzerland, and in real estate. The group needed someone who enjoyed traveling and working with people, and who needed and wanted to get away from the desk. This was no pencil-pushing and number-crunching job, and Cedric knew immediately that it would be ideal for him. To compound this sensation of a dream job looming on the horizon, and in direct opposition to the general mood of profit centeritis that ruled the bank since the McKinsey reorganization of recent years, Robbie Meyjes told him that he didn't expect money to come pouring in right away. "MIS-style management won't work here. As you know, High Net Worth Individuals aren't just assets, and profits and progress in the IISD depend largely on client relations which can't be quantified. So your primary concern is to network and build a contact base. For the first few years I don't want even to see you! You'll be judged on miles flown and money spent," he emphasized this with a warm smile. Cedric felt like a kid who had just been given free rein in a candy store.

The last element they discussed was the location of his headquarters. Meyjes had singled out London or Beirut as being the most convenient, with a preference for London. Cedric concurred, adding that not only did the volatile political situation make Beirut an unpalatable option, but he knew from experience that clients from the Arabian Peninsula held London in very high esteem. Cedric wrapped up his work during the months of April and May, and ended his studies at Columbia Business School. In June he officially joined the IISD group, met Serge Arujo, the South American representative, and Jean-Pierre Cuoni, the European representative. He was then sent to the Bahamas to learn about the mutual fund business, and it was here that he discovered the potential of establishing Private Investment Companies, or PICs, for wealthy clients

In the large complex of FNCB's London operation, Cedric was small fry. He was given office space within the London International Banking Service, or LIBS, an investment service for non-UK resident accounts opened London, and he was virtually scrambling around for chairs, phones, notepads and pens. LIBS was a dying operation filled with about fifteen unenthusiastic deadbeats at the end of their career tether, and would quickly be absorbed by the IISD to deal mainly with logging time deposit orders that Cedric placed with them for his Middle Eastern clients.

In September 1972, Robbie and Cedric made their first joint trip to Bahrain, Dubai, Jeddah and Riyadh to call on potential clients, and for Cedric to introduce Robbie to the contacts he had made while living in Saudi Arabia. Robbie encouraged Cedric to continue his fruitful association with Mahmoud Jawdat, and authorized his establishment as the Private Bank representative in Riyadh.

Cedric was away from England at least sixty percent of the time, courting clients, and visiting branch managers to sollicit potential clients. He also went to all bank and non-bank investment conferences where he could network, especially MEA corporate meetings in Athens, Bahrain and Paris. He listed the sixty-eight countries for which he was responsable, and established those he would prioritize, the most important being countries where there was big money (oil and mineral resources) and no exchange controls, the least important were those with few natural resources and high currency restrictions. Africa held little current interest, aside from copper-rich Zaire which Cedric did not wish to touch because of the Mobutu regime, so he focused his attention on the Arabian Peninsula.

It's a steal, he wrote to Dean, his mother, and Kurt, after a few months in London. *Simply put, I'm being paid to have fun!* Even the appointment of his former nemesis Carlton Stewart as UK Country Head could not affect his happy state of mind.

◆   ◆   ◆

When the Suez Canal closed in the wake of the Arab-Israeli war in June 1967, Saudi Arabia attempted a first oil embargo which failed due to the persistent, even if declining, oil glut. The tanker shortage subsequent to the war, however, placed a premium on Libyan oil, and Libya responded by imposing a price increase. In September 1967, a group of Libyan army officers under the leadership of Colonel Muammar al-Qaddafi seized power, and soon thereafter obtained a twenty percent increase in oil and tax revenues from oil concessions, which encouraged other OPEC countries to issue similar demands. Qaddafi also initiated the nationalization of the oil concessions. Mirroring Libya's efforts, the Saudi government's "Saudization" process enabled the country to acquire a greater portion of shares in their concessions, even full ownership, through the scheme developed by the Saudi petroleum minister, Ahmad Zaki Yamani.

On September 13, 1973, four Israeli fighter jets were accused of violating Syrian airspace. In retaliation, President Hafez al-Assad ordered a contingent of MiG fighters to intercept the Israelis who requested backup. The ensuing dogfight allowed Syria to convince President Sadat of Egypt to join in preparations of an attack on Israel. War broke out on October 6. Wary of the United States, King Faisal of Saudi Arabia warned that he would not hesitate to use oil as political leverage to offset one-sided US support for Israel, which he said allowed Israel to resist conceding Palestinian self-rule. President Nixon personally assured King Faisal that the US would remain objective and strive for a cease-fire—and then returned to the United States and asked Congress for $2.2 billion in military aid to Israel.

The Saudi monarch considered the request a gross betrayal of US concerns for the Arab cause and peace in the Middle East. He united OPEC in instituting a stringent oil embargo that would completely cut off supplies to the United States and the Netherlands (the most outspoken defenders of Israel), and initiated a cutback in production to ensure that the US and the Netherlands could not import from non-embargoed countries, who would otherwise simply purchase more from OPEC as an offset. To convince Aramco owners (representing four of the Seven Sisters) to gear their international supply network to deny Arab oil to the Americans and the Dutch, Faisal threatened to cut off Saudi oil supplies completely.

If the initial price increase of 17% was well justified economically—US wage and price controls, as well as devaluation of the dollar, had led to the doubling of world commodity prices and a decline of real oil prices—the 130% increase of December 1973 was purely political. The embargo lasted until March 1974 and was highly successful, meeting with surprise and outrage in the United States. As billions of dollars of ready cash poured into Saudi bank accounts, the fear that Arabs would dominate the world economy began to rise.

Wriston, however, remained yet again unfazed. Loyal to free market variables, he declared that the oil cartel, like any cartel, was doomed to fail. He did recognize, however, that the huge surge in Arab wealth was a destabilizing menace to the world economy, and he quickly worked on how to recycle the billions of dollars of foreign exchange amassed by the Arabian Peninsula. As President Gerald Ford would later say: "I suspect [Wriston] was a calming influence on the whole situation. He wasn't as panicky as some financiers were." And as Phillip Zweig writes: "Important as it was to Wriston to retain total control of Citibank's own Mideast gusher, that would become something of a sideshow to the main event. As billions of dollars poured into these Sheikdoms, the world's oil-consuming nations, particularly the less-developed ones, were faced with the daunting task of how to pay their skyrocketing oil import bills; the producers faced the problem of how to spend the windfall. No-one was more ready and willing to show the world how to do it than Wriston."

In 1972, in one of the numerous attempts to legally circumvent the restrictions imposed by the Glass-Steagull act on banking operations and ease into investment banking, FNCB set up a London-based Merchant Bank operation named Citicorp International Bank Limited, or CIBL, which would allow them to dabble in loan syndications, private placements, foreign exchange trading, government bond underwriting, corporate financing, and mergers and acquisitions. Former Country Head of France, John Fogarty—a smart and ambitious Harvard graduate who had been the youngest Resident Vice President in FNCB history—was named head of CIBL.

When Wriston started casting his eyes south to Latin America as the major recipient of petrodollars, CIBL grew from a small operation of five to "a juggernaut with an army of syndicators. Led by CIBL, Citibank—and to a lesser extent Bank of America, Morgan Stanley, and Chase Manhattan—drove the recycling machine. CIBL gave rise to a generation of bankers who spent more time in the first-class cabins of Boeing 747s than they did at home in New York and London" (Phillip Zweig). It was a lending frenzy, and bankers worldwide believed that they would soon be making billions off loans to resources-rich and fund-hungry Argentina, Brazil, Mexico, Venezuela…By 1975, CIBL served as manager or co-manager for sixty-six syndicated international credits amounting to more than $6.6 billion. Cedric would later say, his disregard and dislike of Fogarty's haughty management style not-withstanding, that "FNCB was grabbing money with the right hand and throwing out with the left. We felt in the eighties that those responsible for the overly speculative loans to developing nations had pissed away all the money we'd brought in."

The aggregate Arab surplus soon peaked at $170 billion, and much of this was funneled into third-world loans. There were problems, however, that were not addressed at the time and that would lead to the government defaults of the late seventies and into the eighties. But bankers were flying high on the mind-boggling amounts involved, on the unambiguous statement by Wriston that "governments don't go broke" which everyone wanted to believe, and because of this they did not apply the same amount of care to third-world lending as they did to domestic lending. More significantly, they had few markers by which to assess country risk. Indeed, until Wriston and Costanzo hired Irving Friedman to lead the brain trust behind FNCB's country risk unit, no-one at the bank had any clear idea of what the bank's overall exposure to any one country might be—a danger exacerbated by the internal strife between the corporate division, and country heads who complained that their ability to book loans, and thus earn profits for the bank, had been curtailed. Friedman imposed a country limit of 5% of the bank's total loans, and set up a research unit that became so rep-utable that Citicorp was soon considered a form of Third World debt rating agency.

The danger—and faulty thinking—lay in the fact that even Fried-man had no way of assessing the other banks' total exposure, and the banks did not concert. Therefore, FNCB's loan percentage to one country could be well within the limits assessed as safe by the risk unit, while the aggregate loans incurred by that country with other banks rendered it in fact dangerously over-exposed. Another major problem was they they had little control over how governments chose to spend the money that was lent to them. Wriston explained: "If we, as a private institution, let political judgments influence our lending, then we are meddling in the internal affairs of other countries. If not, we are accused of aiding and abetting societies we do not believe in. It's a very tough nut." But it was mainly the drive for profits that led many bankers to dismiss as a formality the usual necessity of knowing the end-use of loans and debt equity ratios in the name of some elusive notion of political neutrality.

Despite these red flags, Third-World lending peaked in the seventies and the nations involved seemed on their way to developing the infrastructure necessary to rise to the level of the industrialized nations of the Northern Hemisphere; the petrodollars were absorbed and recycled, and the imbalances caused by the oil shock worked their way through the marketplace. In 1977, Citibank and other US banks such as Bank of America, Morgan Stanley and Manufacturers Hanover, were hailed as heroes for easing the world away from the brink of economic collapse.

Wriston never acceded to his coveted dream of being Secretary of State, but he nevertheless "presided over the largest transfer of global wealth since the Marshall Plan, effectively making Citibank a private sector extension of the State Department at Foggy Bottom," according to Philip Zweig. A decade later, he and his counterparts would be reviled for provoking the Latin American defaults on loans of the mid-eighties, and edging the world back to the brink for their unscrupulous and speculative loans.

◆   ◆   ◆

For Cedric Grant, FNCB's "Mideast gusher" was a veritable boost to his career: from a backwater banking region, playing less than second fiddle to more glamorous Latin America, Saudi Arabia become the primary focus of money-hungry international businessmen. The effects began to be felt by mid-1974 as Arabs started looking for ways to invest their new-found wealth. Cedric began opening numerous PIC accounts in London and in the Channel Islands, a maneuver that enabled Saudis to discreetly buy real estate in Britain under a company name without exacerbating the British fear of an Arab-possessed UK economy.

Unfortunately, establishing PICs for the purpose of purchasing real estate did not generate the amount of business that headquarters expected from the influx of money into the region. Cedric's clients would make the purchase, then leave only a small amount in the account to pay relevant bills, but would rarely supply them with further business. FNCB collected high commissions but major money was not pouring in. Cedric started to devise other plans to attract Arab wealth.

The first opportunity emerged at the Kentucky racetracks. Auction sales were held four times a year in Lexington, with bids rising in the tens, sometimes hundreds of thousands of dollars, but rarely higher. And horse-breeding and horse-racing were the type of exclusive and expensive hobby that would inevitably attract wealthy Arabs. Sometimes it was a passing phase; for others, such as the al Maktoums, it became a veritable passion. In early 1975, Mohammed al Maktoum, son of Sheikh Rashid, head of Dubai, purchased a yearling for $10.2 million dollars. It made front page news in the world of horse-racing, and turned the market upside down overnight. Soon the big auction houses were calling up FNCB asking them for the Middle East expert. They wanted to know who these big players were: frauds or for real? Would they pay up or renege? Arabs had been known to arrive by private jet, limo to the auction, bid several million for a horse, then change their mind because someone in their entourage suggested that it was a bad deal. They would leave without paying, and the horse would become unsaleable. Furthermore, the presence of wealthy Arabs gave con artists the opportunity to pass themselves off as members of the Saudi royal family without anyone being the wiser.

Cedric flew to Lexington, Kentucky, to meet with representatives from the anxious auction houses. He suggested first that the rules on horse auction bidding be translated into Arabic, and sent to all those dealing in horses along with the proposal to open a current account to the extent of several million dollars with FNCB London, which would then issue a letter of credit to their auction house of choice assuring them that the money was available in case of purchase. To the Arabs, he explained that this would ensure their protection against fraud, and would allow the auction houses to understand exactly who they had as customers and treat them appropriately with all the honor and service that they deserved. For the auction houses, it was an issue of security. From then on, the houses would call Cedric regarding a potential client to learn more about him. Cedric would try to weed out those who were serious, and those were taking a cursory interest in the fad of the moment. Unfortunately, there were very few of the former and many of the latter. It was such a fad, in fact, that by the time he'd set up the account system, there very few interested anymore, and the plan generated very little return on investment.

After the PICs and the horse-breeding, another opportunity came along when a very wealthy Sheikh tried to settle the bill for his daughter's birthday bash at the Dorchester on Park Lane in London with his American Express card, and had it rejected then cut up by a pimply-faced waiter who visibly had no idea of the affront he had just committed. Furious, the Sheikh called up Cedric at home to demand an explanation and request that, as his London banker, he come immediately to pay the bill.

It was a simple misunderstanding that should not have occurred, Cedric assured him a few phone calls later. The Sheikh traveled frequently and for extended periods of time, and his Amex bills had therefore piled up unpaid at home until American Express finally pulled the plug. Cedric spoke with the manager of the Dorchester, assured him that his client's account could largely cover the costs of the party, and a check would be remitted to him the following morning. He then suggested that the Sheikh write to American Express asking them to forward his monthly statements to FNCB and authorize the bank to debit his account for payment. In the event his account was not in credit, he could provide Cedric with the authority to have the necessary funds wired to London from his account in Riyadh.

Cedric fully hoped to extend this service to other clients—another FNCB personalized service that might generate income for the bank. He traveled to Brighton a few days later and met with American Express executives to expose his plan, whereby clients' statements would be forwarded to FNCB and Cedric would personally ensure the settlement within two business days. Since American Express charged no interest, they would be able to reduce the cost of lost interest for the grace period during which the payment was not settled. This was the clinching argument for the Amex executives who realized they had nothing to lose and much to gain, especially considering the 14% interest rates prevailing at the time (and heading higher).

He also had little difficulty in selling the idea to his clients. They would no longer have to worry about unpaid bills, nor face embarrassing rejections and card cancellations. Many of them left over $50,000 in their current accounts that the bank could place for interest, and by the time Cedric left London, the business was operating for over a hundred top accounts. He was also responsible for helping Prince Abdullah ibn Abdul al Aziz, fourth in line for succession to the throne after Prince Fahd, acquire the first American Express Gold card ever issued in the Middle East.

◆   ◆   ◆

These incidents highlighted the fact that a private banker did not only provide asset management advice; he was also expected to assume the roles of consultant, travel agent, educational advisor (for the clients' children heading to college in the United States), and friend. In one case Cedric helped save the life of client's son when the boy was diagnosed in Saudi Arabia with brain tumor. The doctor suggested London as the best place to have the operation, and since Cedric was the only person whom the boy's father knew there, he asked for his help. Cedric called the bank doctor and forwarded him the son's files. Everything was rapidly taken care of: the son was immediately booked into the appropriate London hospital, his plane from Saudi Arabia was met with an ambulance at the airport. Surgery was scheduled and a room in a convalescent home was reserved. The client deposited a four million dollar check with FNCB to cover the costs, and from then on was able to dedicate his full attention to his son while the bank took care of all the details.

Many Saudis turned to Cedric as their banker primarily because he was a familiar face in the region and a person knowledgeable in the geography and culture of the land. In contrast to the mass of bankers flocking to the money like fat city pigeons to a toss of bread loaves, Cedric was seen as someone who had been present and interested in the country when business in Saudi Arabia had been far more difficult to run for a foreign company. His extensive first-hand knowledge of the country became a precious commodity: he was often solicited to give speeches to companies interested in entering that market, and his credentials showed in the massive folds of his passport.

Said Aburish, a former agent in the Middle East, wrote in a remarkably frank book about doing business in the region, called *Pay-off: wheeling and dealing in the Arab world*: "In the early seventies, the massive increase in oil prices gave the words 'Middle East' and 'Arab' a special connotation in countries as distant as Taiwan and Brazil. [...] It became a blazing torch towards which international traders trekked. [...] Their lack of preparation and ignorance showed. They slept in taxis because there were no hotel rooms to be had. They arrived without essential entry visas. They tried to sell beer where Islamic laws forbade it. Recognizing their disadvantages, they sought for someone to help them with the Middle Eastern business. What they wanted were intermediaries, people who knew the area and were connected with a government authority prepared to promote their companies, their products and services."

Cedric would start his own speeches explaining some basic elements of Arab culture and mentality: "Don't come in on a Thursday, walk in the door, and say you want to meet so-and-so because you're leaving on Sunday morning. The Islamic weekend starts on Thursday afternoon. Before you do anything, send a letter to your bank and your commercial attaché at your embassy with your planned objectives—who you want to meet, what you want to achieve—and coordinate with them. Give yourself plenty of time for your visits, double your expected timeline, because appointments, plane and hotel reservations can be changed on a whim, and international phone lines are still dicey at best…" And he would launch into the story of Prince Talal who kept a plane waiting on the tarmac so that he could finish a bridge game. "In our eyes, Arabs have a strange sense of time—they have trouble with strict schedules, and have a hard time saying no, which often results in two meetings scheduled at the same time. Business in the Middle East is also more often than not conducted with an agent, a middle-man who expects a commission from the deals he handles. The system, as it is set up, makes this necessary—it is not corruption. Still, for Americans faced with the US government's growing desire to crack down on what they consider bribes and kickbacks, you must consider the costs involved in the use of an intermediary as consultancy fees.

"Intermediaries have contacts with ministers and members of the royal family, and can often make or break your contracts. And they are a Saudi's connection to the twentieth century and Western mentality: a Prince may be much wealthier than the average intermediary, but the agent—often Palestinian, Lebanese, Syrian or Jordanian—is more worldly and cultured.

"But with the amount of money involved these days, you must be extra-cautious: don't sign an agent until you know exactly who you're dealing with—another reason to coordinate with your bank and embassy. Islamic mentality encourages the display of money. so you can recognize an effective agent by the amount of money he throws around; he will be noticed. But even with an honest agent, things can go awry—other companies are using other agents, and more often than not, it's not you against them, but your agent's main contact and the other company's agent's contact. Find out who the agent's contacts are, and make sure you learn which minister or member of the royal family is effective in the area of business you are interested in. Simply having a royal connection is not enough."

Cedric never tired of giving these conferences. Like a teacher honing his subject, the more he spoke about the Middle East, the more he felt he learned. Cedric enjoyed imparting his knowledge of a region which he had grown to like immensely, and in which he felt almost at home. From a career nadir in 1971, he had reached an apex four years later. This was the moment when Cedric truly began to consider himself an international private banker.

9

Sometime in the first few months of 1974, the French left-wing magazine *L'Express* tapped into public frustration over the cant, flashy, and often crass behavior of members of the Saudi royal family when traveling abroad, and revealed the massive $23 million in debts which Prince Fahd had amassed during his gambling binge in Monte Carlo with arms dealer Adnan Khashoggi. Prince Fahd was immediately summoned to explain himself to King Faisal, and he is rumored to have claimed mistaken identity, that another Fahd was responsible for those debts—King Faisal dismissed the affair. Within Saudi Arabia the news was stifled, and the Saudi government retaliated by ostracizing France and refusing French nationals' requests for visas and canceling business contracts.

When Cedric was asked to settle mounting gambling debts later that year for Prince Salman, he faced the three most hand-wrenching months of his career in London in the attempt to avoid a similar incident hitting the UK and jeopardizing his relations with the royal family. Prince Salman, son of King Abdul Aziz ibn Saud, full brother of Prince Fahd, and Governor of Riyadh, had met Cedric on several occasions. In addition to being approximately the same age, Cedric had found him to be a very outgoing and honorable individual, which explains his attempts to cover the Prince's losses despite the fact, Cedric realized with horror, that Salman did not even have an account with the FNCB branch in London.

Prince Salman arrived one Sunday afternoon in London and proceeded to rack up a four hundred thousand dollar debt in Sterling equivalent at the Ladbrokes casino. Salman's secretary, who knew Cedric from his time in Saudi Arabia, assumed that since Salman had a substantial account with FNCB in Riyadh, Cedric would be happy to settle the Prince's debts with the casino. At nine o'clock on Monday morning, a check from Ladbrokes arrived hand-delivered on Cedric's desk, to be honored under British law within forty-eight business hours otherwise the debt would be claimed in open court, allowing the press to grab hold of the story. Every option that Cedric debated led to a dead-end. He could not debit Salman's account in Riyadh without the Prince's authorization, and after hours of fruitless phone calls to all the most likely hotels in London, it appeared that Salman had disappeared into the British countryside and was unreachable. Neither could Cedric set up a debit account in London for Salman, since British law forbade any foreign national from having an overdrawn Sterling account.

He called up Robbie Meyjes in New York to give him the rundown, and a conference call was immediately organized with Al Costanzo. Cedric suggested that they open a Dollar account and debit it for half a million. That way he could open and credit a Sterling account with an amount sufficient to cover the Prince's debts, and remain within British law. His plan was met with heavy breathing on the other end of the line.

"How do you intend to open the account without documentation?" Costanzo asked.

"I know the guy. It can be done."

"But what if he refuses to settle the overdrawn dollar account? He would be entitled to."

Cedric paused before answering. "It's a risk I think we should take. This is no Prince Talal. I can't guarantee anything a hundred percent, but I think that he is simply not aware that we have no account open for him here and that we can't settle his debts. As soon as he is made aware of the situation, he'll settle. He's one of the more honorable members of the royal family, and as Governor of Riyadh, he's key to our success over there. He has his finger on all the foreign deals: visas, contracts, stuff like that. He can make business there a whole lot easier for us if we do this right. But if we pull the plug, and because of us some scandal makes him look bad with Faisal, he'll blackball us on everything from bid bonds to bringing in staff. He could even shut us down."

Finally Al Costanzo gave him the green light, but told him in no uncertain terms that he was on his own if the operation backfired and Salman didn't pay back. Cedric didn't know whether to celebrate or throw up from the pressure, and Salman's actions over the next few days would not make it any easier for him to believe that he had made the right decision. The check with Ladbrokes was settled Monday evening, but more then followed: Prince Salman, still unreachable, continued to rack up debts, and by the end of the week Cedric found himself with an overdrawn dollar account, which he had opened without Salman's express consent, of $2.2 million. He got little sleep that weekend.

A week later, Prince Salman's assistant came to see Cedric to tell him that he was in trouble: the Prince was out of money. "A simple cash flow problem," the assistant assured, but they needed help. On the verge of a conniption, Cedric wasn't sure whether to kiss the man for finally allowing him to get in touch with the Prince, or kick him back out on the street for putting him through the proverbial wringer. "You're in trouble?!" he raged. "I'm in deep shit!" Cedric showed Salman's assistant copies of all the checks, statements and documentation, and pressed the folder into the man's hands, urging him to talk to the Prince and have him credit his new (and very overdrawn) Dollar account. Salman's assistant gave him the Prince's word that the debts would be settled upon their return to Saudi Arabia.

Once back in Riyadh, however, the Prince stalled, as Cedric said he wouldn't. Eventually, however, the gamble paid off. After three sweat-drenched months, the debt was covered and Cedric even made the bank money, charging the Prince double the going interest rates as payment for all his heart-wrenching. A few months later, on a trip to Riyadh, Prince Salman personally thanked Cedric for his handling of "that delicate matter."

Prince Salman would not be the only member of the royal family to give Cedric a few sleepless nights. Prince Talal, the black sheep of the al-Saud family, decided one evening, while sojourning in London, to visit Ladbrokes with one of his sons for an evening of fun. The manager directed him to his private high stakes room where he amassed nine hundred and forty thousand dollars in winnings. When he decided to call it quits, the casino remitted him a check for just over eight hundred thousand dollars. Talal naturally asked what happened to the difference, and the manager explained that his son had lost over a hundred thousand.

"My son is of age. Did I say that I would cover his losses? Did I give you that permission?"

The distraught manager could not say that the Prince had. He had simply *assumed*—an assumption, Talal pointed out, which the casino should not have made. Legally, Talal was entitled to receive full payment for his winnings, and the casino would have to write off over a hundred thousand pounds in bookkeeping. Talal refused the check that was presented to him, and told the manager that if he had any problems, he should call his banker in London, Mr. Cedric Grant. He wanted his full winnings, but he wanted the matter settled discreetly.

After a few hours of late night discussions, Cedric worked out a deal with Ladbrokes to notify him whenever a big Saudi client came in to gamble so that they could coordinate their efforts and make sure that whatever the results of their gambling might be, the fall-out could be handled without undue pressure and publicity. In the mean time, he assured the manager that he would speak with Talal the next morning.

"I refuse to go back there until they give me my full due amount," Talal told Cedric pointblank the moment he stepped past the security guards into the Prince's plush suite at the Hilton.

"Ah, your Highness…Please consider for a moment. You are Ladbrokes' best—their favorite—client. They do not want to lose your business, and will do everything in their power to right the matter They made an assumption that might be considered understandable from their point of view, but which they certainly should not have made. And which they will certainly not make again! However...Your Highness must understand that for Ladbrokes to remit you almost a million dollars on top of writing off a hundred thousand dollar mistake could create problems with the British gambling commission." Cedric was playing the publicity card, dangerously perhaps, but he knew that even a Prince in less than favorable standing with the Saudi royal family wished to avoid publicity at all costs. Talal said he would consider the matter, and waved him out dismissively. A few days later, the Prince returned to Ladbrokes, won again, and relinquished his claim to his son's hundred thousand dollar loss.

By the mid-seventies, Cedric's career and standing within the bank were waxing nicely. In the wake of the OPEC oil embargo and ensuing flood of wealth into the region, Walter Wriston paid a visit to King Faisal in late January 1975. His main objective was to convince the Saudis to lend thirty-year funds to bolster Citicorp capital. Though the mission failed, Wriston's visit was resounding success for Cedric's stature in the Middle East.

His name was mentioned right from the start when, at a dinner party organized in the Chairman's honor, Prince Salman immediately asked: "Where's Grant?" to a confounded Walter Wriston sitting next to him, before launching into how much he appreciated Grant's help and discretion in handling delicate banking matters, and how much he respected a Westerner who understood so well the Saudi culture. The following day, Wriston had his hour and half meeting with King Faisal. Though the king spoke English very proficiently, he always used the services of a translator, most likely to allow him time to debate his answers. On the occasion of Wriston's visit, the translator was Khalid Anani, a friend of Cedric's from his time in Saudi Arabia whom he had met at one of Omar Saggaff's parties, and at US Embassy social functions to which young US educated Saudis were invited. Khalid had always kept fond memories of their time together, and, as a junior making his way up the ranks within the Ministry of Foreign Affairs, Cedric had had the opportunity to help him in a career turn or two. When Wriston withdrew from his audience with King Faisal, Khalid snuck up to him and said: "Oh, by the way, give my best to Cedric Grant. He's one of our favorite people."

Upon his return to New York, Wriston wrote a letter to Cedric about his trip to the Middle East, and thanked him for being such a great representative of the bank, letter which Cedric forwarded to Robbie Meyjes with a note saying, *I think we're making progress here…* The news also circulated rapidly within FNCB, and shrouded Cedric from then on with a unique aura of invincibility. Branch managers who had previously been reticent about, or even condescending towards, his efforts to expand Private Bank services in Africa, India and the Middle East, positively fawned over him during his subsequent trips.

In 1975, King Faisal was assassinated by one of his disgruntled (and presumably crazed) nephews. Prince Khalid acceded to the throne, but he was in ill-health, and he had little stamina to handle the internecine fighting within the ultra-religious rightwing faction. It soon became apparent that Crown Prince Fahd would be the power behind the throne.

Business continued "as usual", and business for the MEA division of the Private Asset Management Group was finally booming. Cedric's American Express payment plan had resulted in FNCB making millions of dollars on large non-interest-bearing current accounts. Prince Abdullah's large dollar deposit, and the constant flashing around of his Amex gold card, encouraged Prince Salman to also request a gold card and open a large account. A slew of others followed: the big money that Meyjes and Cedric had hoped was now pouring in. "Finally feel like a Private Banker, Grant?" Meyjes asked him during one of the budget meetings in New York.

Cedric would have, if he hadn't personally been on the verge of financial disaster.

Bank housing policy for its overseas staff was quite simple: the bank paid officers' full rent, and deducted a fixed amount based on New York rates from their salary, an amount that remained constant around the world regardless of their actual rent. In London, however, the woman in charge of finding housing for new arrivals, Barbara Otto, heavily encouraged bank officers to buy. So Cedric took out a £40,000 mortgage at 6% interest and bought a house in Cobham, Surrey, a fifteen minute walk from the train station that would take him directly to Waterloo Station, a stone's throw from FNCB's offices on the Strand. When the time came for the Grants to relocate, they could sell the house, pay back the mortgage and pocket the anticipated benefits. He was not the only international officer to do so.

Initially they came out ahead: the 6% interest payments on the mortgage loan were less than the fixed rent deduction imposed by the bank. Over the next few years, however, interest rates gradually rose to 14%, and by 1975 they were paying more than half of their after-tax income towards non-tax-deductible interest payments. To make matters worse, real estate speculation had caused a market glut, and housing prices stagnated, the value of the dollar had plunged since the collapse of Bretton-Woods (international staff was paid in dollars with only slight compensation for variations in foreign exchange values), and Britain was entering its worst period of social unrest and economic distress since the end of World War II—declining economy, rising inflation and unemployment, an acute power crisis, crippling labor strikes, and IRA terrorist bombings.

Embittered by the desperate state of their diminished financial resources, those members of FNCB London's international staff who had arrived after 1971 presented a united front to the bank, and requested that it remedy the situation. After weeks of haggling and pressure, the London country head finally accepted to buy back their houses and compensate them for the difference between interest payments and the rent that would have been deducted if Barbara Otto had followed established bank housing policy. They were able to breathe again. And in March 1976, the Grants were able to afford their first skiing holiday in the Swiss Alps. Cedric's memory and opinion of the UK would forever be tainted by living there in the Seventies. He had very few qualms about telling people how much he loathed Britain.

◆   ◆   ◆

Ever since the name of FNCB's holding company, First National City Corporation, had been changed to Citicorp, Wriston yearned to change the name of FNCB to a variation of the original short and sweet name it had had in 1812: City Bank. The idea involved a logistical nightmare of revising thousands of forms and signs on hundreds of branches around the world, but Wriston pushed ahead. He hired a design firm to create a logo and submitted his plan to the board of directors. To his surprise, his wish was granted in February 1976, and on March 1st, FNCB officially became known as Citibank.

Alongside this dream, and to present a visual proof of FNCB's dominance of the world financial market, Wriston had plans for a new office tower in midtown Manhattan. Since the turn of the decade, he had given permission to an agent to quietly acquire an entire city block between 2nd and 3rd Avenues and 53rd/54th streets, and once they owned the land, Wriston launched a contest for the new building. The winner was the Cambridge, MA, architectural firm of Hugh Stubbins Jr. who had been recommended by Operations Chief and reckless Consumer Banking powerhouse prodigy, John Reed, who envisaged the new Citicorp Center not only as the bank's headquarters but as a veritable neighborhood Mecca.

The building was finished late 1977, and Wriston's new slanted-roof skyscraper in the form of a number '1' dominated the mid-town Manhattan skyline. He was toasted as the savior of an East Side resurrection of the city, from porn shops to shopping chic. With memories of New York City's near financial collapse still fresh in the minds of the city dwellers, Wriston took out full-page color ads showing a counter-shot photo of the building with the caption: "Why is Citibank staying in New York? We grew up here."

The skyscraper's literally shaky start, however, only reached the ears of the public many years later, and is now sidelined to bank history oblivion. But in the first few months of operation, Hugh Stubbins Jr. and Citibank flirted with disaster. When the building was virtually finished, and already open for business, an engineer discovered that the building would not be able to withstand high wind loads. Though the velocity necessary to cause such a skyscraper to collapse was very high, such winds—called once-in-a-century wind loads—had been known to occur. Wriston quickly implemented a series of contingency plans to protect Citibank from culpability and the public from possible harm. Working around the clock for a month, workers tore down walls and installed steel plates in the core column to reinforce the structure and eliminate the danger. When it was all over, Robbie told Cedric over dinner that everyday before the work was completed, he would walk into his office with the jitters. All day he could hear the walls groan and creek like a haunted house in pain...

In the mid-seventies, Citibank was experiencing even more profound changes than a name-lift and a new home at 399 Park Avenue, the seeds of which had been planted almost a decade earlier.

Throughout the sixties, the banks' operating expenses had risen at a near-debilitating rate of 18% per annum. It became difficult to imagine how FNCB could remain competitive, much less achieve Wriston's target of 15% annual growth earnings. Compounding this problem was a massive pile-up of paper work in the back office which emphasized FNCB's ineffectiveness and caused embarrassing situations such as the inability to produce a simple checking account statement for United Parcel Service, one of its oldest customers. When Wriston acceded to the helm of the bank, he knew that he had to quickly dote the institution with an effective and technologically advanced operating system.

Enter John Reed, fresh from his success in devising a budgeting and management information system for the Overseas Division. He took control of the entire systems management group for the bank, and possibly for the first time in banking he employed mathematical models and scientific methodology to analyze the flow of checks and papers into bits and bytes. He was fascinated with computers, and over the next few years would spend billions of dollars attempting to automate FNCB's operating system through a subsidiary he set up called Transition Technology, Inc., a virtual research and development arm of the bank.

The going was far from smooth and encountered near catastrophes along the way. Eventually, however, Reed managed to transform Citibank's back office mess into the most technologically advanced and efficient one in American banking, thereby accelerating the move towards an electronic payment system throughout the United States and around the world. "Citibank was not the first to offer cash machines," Zweig writes in *Wriston*. "That honor was claimed by Chemical Bank, which installed the first cash-dispensing machine on the outside wall of a branch in 1969. But that technology had severe limitations. In developing its own system, Citibank became in the effect the R&D branch of the American banking industry. Under Wriston, Citibank spared no expense in its quest for state-of-the-art hardware and software. [...] Reed saw the use of this technology as a way of extending Citibank's reach beyond geographic boundaries and of breaking down the legislative and regulatory barriers that generally limited banks' relationships with consumers to the confines of the home states."

The new automation technology, the plastic ATM and credit cards, and the telephone were the cornerstones of consumer banking, Reed said. And facing strong opposition, he set about developing it rapidly. In a meeting in September 1975, he set the goal for the consumers to generate 25% of total earnings. And Reed had the right idea: consumer banking would become the financial foundation of Citibank in the next decade. But he also heralded a new type of banker, in fact a manager who was only vaguely attached to the banking mentality from which Wriston—despite his ambition, his novel ideas, his attraction to risk-taking—had emerged. And his style of management would enforce a new cutthroat mentality, which would extend beyond the confines of consumer banking and spill into every corner of Citibank, including the exclusive one of Private Banking.

The cost of Reed's rise to stardom could be seen in his broken marriage and in those of his employees dedicated enough to follow his blazing trail that ate lives like a column of army ants in Liberia. Zweig writes, "Citibank abandoned any pretense of being warm and cuddly. Cost savings, automation and technology were king, and people were merely 'heads' to be lopped off. Reed's technocrats had little patience with the thousands of often undereducated minorities who performed many of the low-level clerical tasks at Citibank headquarters. People who worked ten to twelve hours a day, seven days a week, to get things done got thrown out like Kleenex. They weren't brains or college grads, MBAs and all that. They were good workers who were there when the going got rough. By the mid-seventies, Citibank was pitting profit center against profit center, international against domestic, the back office operative against the customer man, old-time relationship bankers against a new breed of transaction bankers. Citicorp was expanding so rapidly that it was losing touch with its constituencies, its correspondent banks, corporate customers, and retail customers."

Wriston could claim that he was in a tough bind, having consistently portrayed the image of the Citibank employee as an individual for which the bank cared—and how could Cedric disagree when Wriston had paused in his high-level meanderings to inquire as to his health after his bout with hepatitis and malaria, and to that of his wife's? But Wriston was also firmly committed to the profit earnings growth target: he embraced Reaganomics with gusto, oblivious to its cruel side effects, admired Michael Milken and would most likely agree with Boetsch's "greed is good" motto for the eighties..

He would have to confront, however, the ethical consequences within Citibank of such unbridled expansion and profit centeritis: the temptation to take shortcuts that compromised the company's avowed standards, if they didn't actually transgress the letter of the law. The first most visible result of the competitive pressures to make profits at any cost was the Dave Edwards affair. Cedric had met David on several occasions, and would never quite believe Citibank's claim that David was out to ruin the bank. Years later, when they met up again through a mutual friend, and Cedric asked him in veiled terms for his side of the story, David told him: "I've put it behind me and don't ever want to think about it again. Not to mention talk about it. I thought I was doing the right thing at the time, in the beginning, Wriston gave me that much. Afterwards…Well, I would never gone up against Citibank if I'd known how ruthless it could be, and the amount of power it could muster…"

While reviewing the year-end trading results for 1975, Dave Edwards noticed a discrepancy that led him to believe that a Belgian Citibank forex trader was receiving kickbacks. The ensuing investigation, however, revealed no wrongdoings. Edwards was not convinced, and as his own research advanced, he discovered that Citibank loans were being booked off-shore overnight in low-tax (or no-tax) jurisdictions such as Nassau, and then reclaimed the following day. The idea was to dress up a profit center for internal management reports and pay minimal taxes on earnings, while claiming a loss in high-tax jurisdictions. This was effectively parking transactions and hiding daily exposures which far outstripped national limits from the competent authorities in countries such as Switzerland, France and Italy.

The matter festered, and in July 1976 Edwards returned to the States on a leave of absence. Everyone he turned to within the bank either turned a blind eye or put the pressure on him to give up his "crusade". Tom Theobald, the newly appointed head of the International unit, circulated a memo that portrayed Edwards as a troublemaker whose allegations were insignificant—any infractions that might have taken place were minor and involuntary, the result of misinterpretations of the arcane and confusing laws regulating foreign exchange markets around the world. David Edwards did not give up.

In February 1978, he was fired from the bank. Four days later he sent to Citicorp directors and top officers a one hundred and six page report, infamously known as the "Blue Book", that documented Citibank's parking transactions and forex manipulations. Edwards would even go so far as to claim that Citibank, and its collusion with other US banks, were responsible for the plunge in the dollar in the Seventies. Wriston immediately ordered an investigation. But in July 1978, Edwards sued Citibank for wrongful dismissal: the suit was thrown out by the New York Supreme Court after a lengthy and costly legal battle.

While Citibank investigators toured branches in Europe, questioning auditors, traders and lawyers on local laws and practices, the bank attracted the attention of Ralph Nader, and in 1979 it was forced to admit that Edwards's allegations were being investigated by the SEC. Wriston masterfully discredited Nader, but it was obvious that his appreciation of deregulation and dismissal of government intervention in the market place had come up against a worthy opponent. In the end, US authorities deemed that Citibank had taken the necessary steps to avoid the renewed possibility of employees venturing out of the gray zone of forex regulations in which the bank operated, and did not press the issue. It was a minor handslapping reprimand for what was essentially unethical, but not illegal, behavior. Citibank described its activities as managing its tax positions rather than attempts to evade taxes, and vowed that it would remedy the situation: the bank subsequently urged its employees to better follow the letter, not just the spirit, of the laws under which they were operating.

There was, however, an event that occurred during the SEC investigation of the Edwards affair—a show of power, a display of arrogance, a bruised ego—that would cause Citibank incalculable harm almost eight years later. During the congressional hearings lead by Congressman Dingell in June 1983, Wriston showed impatience with, and was disdainful of, Dingell's perceived inadequate knowledge of banking affairs. Almost a decade later, when Citibank was strapped for cash and desperately searching for capital, Dingell would get his revenge by pushing the bank's solvency problems to the forefront of business news headlines by stating that "Citibank was technically bankrupt", with disastrous results.

◆   ◆   ◆

Bankers do not have a widely held reputation for eccentricity, and therefore, considering the career—and the institution—to which he had now dedicated more than fifteen years of his life, Cedric could certainly qualify as an oddball. For a banker. Given the chance he would much rather dress in a sweater and slacks than in a three-piece suit. He could talk for hours on traveling, philosophy, and Middle Eastern culture, whereas talking about finance outside of a bank meeting exhausted him. He'd backpacked around the world alone for two years, he'd gorged himself on caviar on the Trans-Siberian Railway, and he'd driven a Land Rover across the Sahara…

In February 1977, he took up jogging. Not just the round-the-block evening stroll, but the long-distance, knee-crunching, endorphin-pumping, marathon-like jogging—and all because of an inebriated dinner function bet that he made with a colleague named Larry Smith. Six months later, during a sweltering month of August, they both endured high humidity and suffocating pollution to finish the Athens International Marathon in under four and a half hours. They would go on to run over twenty marathons together, while Cedric would complete close to one hundred and twenty races over the next twenty years.

Among the thousands of Citibank employees worldwide, there were undoubtedly a few others who could be considered "eccentric". But Robbie Meyjes would later say that he only met one other who gave Cedric a good run for his money: Bob Ellis. Robbie would also claim responsibility for bringing the two together.

Ellis started working for Citibank soon after the end of WWII. His great passion was flying, and when he lost his plane in an emergency landing near Panama, where he was posted, he bought an odd-looking Beachcraft stagger-wing plane with an enormous engine in the nose and painted entirely gold. It was his baby, and he nurtured its gold encasing and intricate innards as such. When Bob learned of his transfer to Abu Dhabi in the mid-seventies, he had no idea where it was. So he pulled out a map, and realizing that it wasn't even close to being on the same continent as Columbia, he had a moment of panic at the thought of abandoning his baby. But this was a plane!…And no matter that Abu Dhabi was halfway around the world—he would fly there!

Ellis was by nature a friendly and hospitable man, and in Abu Dhabi he got on famously with the ruling family, that marvelled at his Beachcraft stagger-wing—within six months of his arrival, he was known throughout the Persian Gulf as "the man with the golden airplane". In 1978 Bob Ellis was slated for transfer to New York and the issue of what to do with his plane came up again. By this time, he'd met Cedric, another man quite fond of planes, and still fond of flying them. On one of his Middle Eastern trips with Robbie Meyjes, Cedric arranged to spend a few days in Abu Dhabi, and for a full weekend he and Bob went over the myriad logistical problems involved in the two of them flying across Asia and the Pacific, which would give them the satisfaction of being the first to fly a "Staggerwing" Wast to East around the world, The main problem was the Hawaii to Los Angeles leg, especially with regards to fuel: an extra person in the plane would take up precious space and weight.

They made the mistake (or perhaps—as fate would have it—the fortunate choice) of finalizing their plans in Cedric's hotel room. Just as they were charting their course, Robbie Meyjes—tired of sitting alone in the restaurant downstairs—walked in on the two boys surrounded by a few bottles of beer and an array of navigational maps and charts. Cedric and Bob fell over one another in their excitement to tell Robbie their plan.

"Are you absolutely stark raving mad? I am not going to lose my two best Middle Eastern bankers in some hair-brained scheme to fly some aerial equivalent of a Molotov cocktail half-way around the world." To no avail: Bob and Cedric were adamant.

The next day, they were scheduled to meet the client that Cedric loved to hate. Prince Talal was considering a chunky investment of three hundred million dollars to give Adnan Khashoggi a three-to-one leverage to buy commercial real estate in the United States, and a few days earlier he had called Citibank London requesting Grant's presence immediately. Cedric told Talal that he was currently in Abu Dhabi with his boss, a most knowledgeable man in financial investment, and that he and Meyjes would be happy to fly over and meet with him. Talal wanted sound investment advice and he would get it.

Robbie and Cedric were ushered into a small house previously occupied by some of the servants (though still larger than the Grants' home back in London) that Talal was using until the work on his palace was completed. Cedric had praised Meyjes highly to the prince, and Talal was now eager to meet with this Harvard Grad and premier financier. While Meyjes waited for his first meeting with the prince, he filled his pipe to the brim and puffed away reflectively. He wasn't sure how their client would react to his advice that this was not an ideal time to invest in real estate.

They had been waiting for fifteen minutes when Prince Talal entered carrying a phone and dragging behind him what appeared to be a mile-length of cable. He greeted Cedric and Meyjes cordially and, in a departure from Arab custom, launched into business talk almost immediately: "I've heard much about you, Mr. Meyjes, and am looking forward to hearing your views on my planned investment."

"Well, Your Highness, after closely examining the plan, and after deliberation with my investment staff, I believe that—"

At that moment the phone in Talal's hand rang, and without apologizing for the interruption, he picked up the receiver and proceeded to speak for the next ten minutes. Nonplussed, Robbie looked at Cedric, but if it was help or advice he was seeking, it was not forthcoming—in all of his meetings with Saudi clients, he had ever been confronted with such a dismissal. Talal looked up, made a vague hand gesture indicating that Meyjes should continue his presentation, but did not interrupt his phone conversation.

When at last he hung up, Robbie barely had time to gather up steam again before one of the prince's servants entered the room and handed him a letter. Again, without saying a word, Talal tore open the envelope and read his letter at length while Meyjes continued to talk—for the first time in his life stumbling on his words as he tried to gauge their effect on Talal who showed no signs of listening. As for Cedric, he was like a schoolboy witnessing the headmaster's embarrassment, and he could barely suppress his laughter.

Talal finally set aside the letter and seemed willing to listen to Meyjes's arguments as to why he should not invest in the real estate deal. But it was not to be—Robbie's presentation was yet again marred, this time by the sound of a lawn-mower right outside the living-room window. Now Cedric felt like he was acting a silent part in a sketch out of Monty Python's *Flying Circus*; he could only imagine what was going on in Robbie's mind. Eventually the lawn-mower moved away and Meyjes's presentation came to an end. Without any allusion to the various disruptions, Talal said: "The real estate market is soft and prices are high…I think your arguments are very sound, Mr. Meyjes. I have decided not to invest." And with little more ado, they were thanked and dismissed. On the flight back to Abu Dhabi, Cedric kept imitating Meyjes's expressions and Talal's insouciance, while Robbie just rolled his eyes.

The following day it was Robbie's turn to laugh: Bob loaded his golden airplane with all the gasoline it would need to fly halfway to Singapore. But barely twenty minutes after take-off, the plane started to shake so severely that he was obliged to land immediately in Abu Dhabi. Cedric's spirits sunk as he realized that they would never be able fly the plane back to New York.

◆   ◆   ◆

By 1976 doubts began to surface as to the smooth sailing of the pet-rodollar recycling machine. Citibank and other creditors had little con-trol over how the money was spent, and it soon became apparent that much of the money was being wasted. When Citibank officials flew to Zaire to inspect the airport for which loans had been made, they dis-covered that the ground hadn't even been broken. President Mobutu's corrupt regime had absorbed several billion dollars to buy off tribes and pad Mobutu's private account in Switzerland. Loan defaults by Third World countries such as Zaire in mid-1976 was not Wriston's only trouble—there were non-performing US real estate loans which had climbed from virtually nothing in 1970 to over one billion in 1976, and in 1977 Citibank experienced its first earnings decline in fif-teen years.

Wriston remained unperturbed. Defaults and non-performing loans did not seem to greatly affect the judgment of most international bank-ers, who generally considered that they had weathered well the oil shock of 1973. In 1978, as turmoil in Iran was mounting against the Shah, Costanzo got wind of another oil price hike when Sheikh Ahmed Zaki al-Yamani, the Saudi oil minister, invited Costanzo, along with several other top US executives, to meet with him in London, where he shared OPEC's desire to further boost oil prices, explaining that "the United States had failed to take adequate conservation measures". In mid-December 1978, a schedule of price hikes in quarterly install-ments was announced, to total 14.5% by October 1979, the rational-ization being that the OPEC surplus of the past two years had already vanished.

And so—no lessons learned—the lending frenzy began anew in a year that *Euromoney* called "The Year of the Gunslinger". This time around, US federal authorities began to examine more closely the banks' total exposure to developing nations in light of the regulation prohibiting banks from lending more than 10% of their capital to any single borrower. Few measures were taken, however, and those that were remained favorable to the bankers' greed and unchecked lending. And everyone still continued to assess country risk and limits by focusing on individual nations.

In the Summer of 1979, cigar-smoking, dry-humored Paul Volcker arrived in Washington as the new head of the Federal Reserve Bank, a nomination to which Wriston contributed—a contribution which he would later regret. Very quickly Volcker announced a dramatic shift in the way the Fed would conduct policy in a drastic attempt to win the war against inflation: a tight monetary policy with staggering increases in interest rates, seeking to control the supply of money rather than the cost of money. Philip Zweig describes the overhaul as "one of the most revolutionary in the annals of central banking" and, in its impact on the economy, one of "the most significant events of the postwar period."

In the first quarter of 1980, interest rates rose by five percentage points, throwing the United Stated into the deepest recession since the 1930s—but arguably keeping inflation low ever since. It also set the stage for the economic expansion of the Reagan era and beyond. Interest rates broke the 20% mark amidst a sluggish economy, and the damage was felt not only in the US, but even more severely in the Third World, where debtors were suddenly forced to pay back loans with real dollars based on high interest rates—not rates close to inflation with cheapening dollars. The difficulty in paying back loans was exacerbated by plummeting commodity prices, which further burgeoned Third World trade deficits and lowered their ability to earn dollars. In two years the world would face the worst financial crisis since the Thirties, and it was too late to do anything about it.

Cedric barely noticed the second oil crisis of 1979. Accounts were bulging, new ones were being opened, and he continued to travel extensively. But he was now the number one expatriot staff member with regards to time spent in London, the Private Bank division in London was running smoothly, and he wanted a new challenge. His thoughts turned to Geneva, Switzerland, as the natural "next step". He was also motivated by the fact that much of his business was being re-allocated to Switzerland where he had no control over it, since clients' preferences for secrecy and large deposits made Geneva a primary choice. On a personal level, Cedric wanted out of England. Badly! In contrast, Switzerland shimmered like Paradise on Earth—cleanliness, hard-work ethics, efficiency, neutrality and prestige. On this last aspect especially, London—despite its status as world financial center—could not compete in Cedric's field of work. Switzerland was, after all, the cradle of private banking.

One of his new employees to arrive in the late seventies, Ralph Krebs, was a Swiss native with whom Cedric got along so well that he soon made him his deputy. In the Summer of 1978, Cedric arranged for an informal meeting with Jean-Pierre Cuoni and his wife in Gstaad. Cuoni was still head of the European region of the Private Bank, and Cedric told him that since his Middle East and African activities were so connected with Switzerland and the rest of Europe, it seemed sense-less to separate the headquarters of the two regions. He suggested the move to Geneva. "I wouldn't do it as your superior, of course, that would make no sense, Jean-Pierre. And I realize that you would gain very little from me coming in as your partner. So I suggest placing my division under your supervision—I would maintain basic control of MEA but report to you as my superior," he added as an enticement, flattering Cuoni's ego: without him, he could not obtain a work per-mit.

Cuoni agreed. Robbie Meyjes, however, flatly rejected Cedric's pro-posal. Essentially Robbie agreed with Cedric's argument, but he was worried about Cuoni: "He's hard enough to handle as it is. If MEA came under the European division and Cuoni's control, he'll become a bloody egomaniac."

The battle waged for over a year. Finally, when Meyjes learned that he was to assume a new posting in Paris—while John Fogarty replaced him at the head of PAMG—he finally relented.

Annette visited several French schools for Nicole and Eric, deciding that here was an invaluable opportunity to make them bilingual and that her knowledge of French would enable them to get through their first year of school until they mastered the language proficiently. Cedric set about getting his work permit, thinking that perhaps he should make Switzerland the last stop in what was now almost twenty years of moving about for his career.

10

Though Wriston would not retire before 1984, he wished to allow the board of directors to evaluate three candidates' performance—Theobald, Reed and Angermueller—over a span of several years, and he began to plan the transition as early as the late Seventies. According to Phillip Zweig would turn out to be one of the most highly scrutinized, and some say destructive, succession races in the history of American business.

Thomas Theobald, 44 years old, a capable manager and quintessential corporate banker, emerged as the front-runner as head of all institutional, corporate, and government business, primarily because of the stronger emphasis placed on more stringent financial controls after the David Edwards debacle. But he lacked the vision, imagination and temerity of John Reed, the forty-year old managerial whiz who was placed in charge of all of the bank's business for individuals. Though he struggled to make the consumer business profitable, he was considered Wriston's protégé and favorite. Trailing behind these two was Hans Angermueller, fifty-five, head of all legal and external affairs, who figured he had been thrown into the race as a diluent, to reduce the tension between the other two contenders.

The three-way competition filtered down through the layers of the Citibank organizational chart, pitting friend against friend in a corporate civil war. As Zweig writes: "To many, this was the last stand for the old Citibank culture, politicizing the institution like no other event before it." By the early eighties, instead of 'revamping the entrepreneurial spirit', Vojta's re-organization and the succession race had turned Citibank into more of a political bureaucracy than a corporate enterprise.

In July 1980, Annette and Cedric settled into a comfortable existence in Geneva as the world was poised to tackle the new decade with Reagan and Thatcher leading their economic revolution, one that Wriston backed enthusiastically. He soon became part of the Reagan inner circle of economic advisors who made up the Economic Policy Coordinating Committee, and the only one who could claim to have day-to-day practical experience operating in the global financial markets. These twelve men formed the "board of directors for the development of Reaganomics."

At the dawn of the Eighties, however, the United States was set to enter the severest recession since the Great Depression. Citibank was already experiencing large credit card losses, lower profit earning, an indebted consumer business, and a choking funding squeeze due to mismanagement and a down-spiraling economy, exacerbated by external regulatory forces set up by Carter before he left office. In large part, Citibank was being kept on life support by several of Wriston's financial innovations, such as the negotiable certificates of deposit and commercial paper, which allowed them to keep bringing in liquidities.

The "pots and pans" method, a parenthetical anecdote in the history of the Bank, also enabled them to raise money in a surprisingly simple way. By giving away toasters and other appliances to new depositors, Wriston claimed that the Bank was able to rake in $1 billion in 1979. By 1981, however, the Fed cracked down—Citibank was not stingy, and the value of these gifts was far above the $10 and $50 limits imposed by the Federal Reserve. After a series of fines and embarrassing disclosures, Reed put an end to the practice.

Citicorp still outperformed its money center brethren, even though its shares were trading for a mere five times earnings, compared with twelve times just a few years before. And for the next decade, Citibank would in effect be continuously staving off a debilitating credit crunch. Monstrous stumbling blocks such as Third World debt and real estate loans would very quickly overshadow the enthusiasm generated by

Reaganomics and the leveraged buyout craze of the mid-to-late eighties.

Negative fallout from the cross-border loans was beginning to be sorely felt as Reagan ascended to the Presidency, and the old guard at Citibank—the last of the real bankers before the managers set in—was on its way out. Ed Palmer and Reed's mentor, Bill Spencer retired, and Wriston—whose own retirement loomed only a few years away in 1984—kept the three-way succession race alive by not naming a president to replace Spencer. Instead, he appointed John Reed, Theobald, and Angermueller respectively to vice-chairmen and director, while rank-and-file scrambled to distribute their favors evenly, unable to determine who would win the race.

The mega-bankers, including Wriston, had never looked upon their Third World borrowers as anything but individual countries with unique risk profiles. In the spring of 1982, the notion that they would all wind up as economic basket cases within months of each other was a worst-case scenario that had never even been contemplated. When Argentina invaded the Falklands in April 1982, it was one of the most indebted of Third World nations with loans totaling about $40 billion. Together with Mexico and Brazil, debt totaled nearly $200 billion, and became known as the "MBA problem". If MBA had been IBM with similar debt, Citicorp and the rest of the US banking system would have been underwater. Commercial banks pulled the plug on trade and short-term credits, sending the problem into a vicious cycle that made the danger of all three countries defaulting simultaneously very real.

By the fall of 1983, the IMF rescue package to Mexico seemed to have taken effect—the country was pumping 2.8 million barrels of oil a day and presented a surplus balance of payments—and Wriston was celebrating its recovery. Brazil, however, was another matter. In February, the IMF had signed off on $5 billion in loans—the biggest bailout ever of a Third World country—but the austerity measures were not going over well. Just as Mexico seemed to be recovering, millions of Brazilians were unemployed, sick and destitute, and workers were rioting in the streets. The LDC debt crisis was far from over, and all Citi-corp and the other banking institutions could hope for was to overcome each crisis as it erupted, while buying time to bolster reserves and fight its way out of the quagmire.

◆   ◆   ◆

Back in Geneva, Eric and Nicole were absorbing French like only nine and eleven year-old sponge-like brains can do. Annette was brushing up on her own French to help the kiddies with their homework, and worked as a freelance translator for a company that advertised vineyards and wineries in France for export to the UK and other EEC countries. As for Cedric, he was reaping the benefits of almost two decades of hard work and goodwill—and a dash of good timing—as a private banker in Switzerland, head of Citibank Private Bank's Middle East Africa division.

The United States might have been experiencing high inflation and high unemployment, but Switzerland remained an island of economic paradise, with a stable consumer index and an unemployment rate that was almost embarrassingly low. Far from the turmoil of Latin America, and despite the dip in Saudi Arabia's oil revenues, Cedric continued to enjoy booming business and extensive first-class travel. There were a few dark clouds on the horizon, however. New clients were consistently knocking on the lacquered front door, but the lack of competency in the Investment Division meant that too many established clients were losing money and slipping out the back door. The ubiquitous bickering and fighting between booking centers meant that Cedric spent much of his time and energy trying to get his colleagues within the Private Bank to assist one another rather than stab themselves in the back, as they tried to grab profits and make budget for their own personal advancement. Fortunately there were the clients, who continuously made his job worthwhile.

In the early Seventies, Prince Talal ibn Abdul Aziz al Saud came to Geneva to tend to some legal matters. He contacted what he thought was a prestigious law firm, but which turned out to be a small operation with a very similar name. Talal accepted that they handle his affairs, however, and eventually the firm directed him to Citibank to open a series of Liechtenstein Anstalts. The Private Bank in Geneva then proceeded to lose on the Prince's investments in high-risk placements. Talal pulled his portfolio from Citibank and took his business to Chase Manhattan.

In July 1980, the same month the Grant family moved to Geneva, one of Prince Talal's sons decided to invest in Switzerland. He approached the same law firm used by his father, and asked them which bank his father dealt with. The lawyers answered: "Well, he used to be with Citibank, now he's with Chase Manhattan." So Talal's son decided to use the services of Citibank to avoid confusion with this father. A short while later, Prince Talal's son's lawyer walked into the Citibank lakefront property at 16, Quai Général-Guisan, and opened an account for a Liechtenstein Anstalt named "Kingdom Establishment", into which he deposited a million dollars. The son's name was Prince Alwaleed Bin Talal Bin Abdul Aziz Alsaud.

Cedric met him for the first time four years later, when his client arranged for a quarter of a million dollar loan through Citibank Geneva to float the publishing business of one of his friends in Paris. Citibank Paris agreed to the loan, with the assurance from Geneva that the amount had been blocked as collateral in the client's account. But it was a verbal agreement that avoided costly letters of credit—so when Prince Alwaleed's friend defaulted on his loan, and Kingdom Establishment refused to authorize the wiring of funds from Geneva to Paris to cover the debt, Cedric was called in to resolve the issue.

He met with Alwaleed at the Georges V, a hotel that the Prince would later own. He found him to be, at twenty-seven, every bit as arrogant as his father. Almost immediately, the Prince told him—in remarkably good English, with a trace of an American accent acquired at university in the U.S.—that he expected the bank to assume responsibility and write off the loss, since he would soon become the Bank's biggest depositor and largest shareholder, and the biggest client of Citibank Private Bank.

Even though, by 1984, Alwaleed's construction company in Saudi Arabia was involved in a series of lucrative deals reaping in huge commissions, his statement still remained that of an inflated ego. And though this ego would turn out to be more than justified, Cedric found little immediate reason to placate it. Since Prince Alwaleed refused to pay, however, Citibank would freeze the amount in his Geneva account, and the matter could drag out for years. Not a very palatable option either.

Finally Cedric looked up at his client, and said: "Your Highness, I've spent some time at Columbia Business School, and I just can't see a way through this. I know you've attended business school in the States also, and you are undoubtedly smarter than I am. I would love to write off this loss as you're asking me to do, if only you could show me how to present it to our internal and external auditors, and to the Swiss and French government officials and tax authorities, so that it would be accepted…"

The psychological gamble worked: After a moment of reflection, Prince Alwaleed gave his authorization for Citibank Geneva to wire the funds to Paris, and accepted the loss as his own. The following year, Cedric's deputy, Ralph Krebs, started to report monthly deposits to the Prince's account from ABN-Amro bank in the Netherlands in the region of $50 million dollars, though almost all of that was quickly wired into Prince Alwaleed's accounts with UBS and Credit Suisse.

◆   ◆   ◆

After fourteen years at the helm of what was now the world's largest bank, Wriston retired. Before doing so, he had managed to help sweep the "MBA" issue under the carpet, and declare victory over the LDC crisis. Though there were of course ongoing problems, but Citicorp shareholders continued to heap praise on the Chairman as he presided over his last annual meeting. And everyone waited with baited breath to hear the nomination of his successor. After he returned from Philadelphia with barely three months left before he would enter what he called "statutory senility", Wriston decided it was time to make his decision known and declare the winner of the horse race that had preoccupied Citibankers and the financial press for nearly four years.

As Angermueller had sensed, the real race was between Theobald and Reed. Theobald's backers pointed out correctly that Reed had never made a loan in his life; he knew computers and assembly lines, whereas Theobald understood money and markets. Reed was a big-time gambler over the long-term, but with little knowledge of financial markets to lead the Citibank juggernaut. Reed's supporters, on the other hand, pointed out that Wriston himself hadn't made a loan in years, and Theobald had never spent any time in consumer banking, which by 1983 accounted for an large percentage of the bank's profits, as predicted by Wriston.

"Project Merlin", the ten-year plan set in place by George Vojta, the matrix management engineer and creator of the World Corporation Group, to revamp Citibank's entrepreneurial spirit and refocus the source of the bank's earnings on consumer banking and middle-market companies, was showing the first signs of success. And it was probably this last factor that tipped the scales in Reed's favor. His technological drive was finally paying off huge dividends: Citibank had become a vast cable machine, "the greatest nexus of information flow in the world," said Wriston. In his view, computers, satellites, electronic funds transfer technology, and trading screens had begun to render obsolete the distinctions between banks as places to make deposits and get loans, brokerage firms as places to buy and sell securities, and thrifts as places to save money and obtain mortgages. Technology was making the consumer savvy and well-informed, and Wriston and Reed had seemingly anticipated the changing nature of banking, and were now capitalizing on their advance. New York deposits skyrocketed in the early eighties, with its share of deposits doubling, thanks in large part to the branch-wide installation of ATMs. And the credit card business, one of the cornerstone's of Reed's consumer division, had finally gone from money drain to cash cow, thanks to the Marqette law which allowed Citibank to relocate its credit card business to South Dakota and charge 19.8% interest rates. The move boosted Reed's consumer division by bringing in close to $100 million dollars in 1981 alone. According to Phillip Zweig, Wriston pulled John Reed aside one evening soon after his return from Philidelphia, and told him: "I'm recommending you to run the place".

The world of banking from which Wriston retired was markedly different from the one he had entered thirty-eight years earlier. Comparing Wriston to J.P. Morgan and Bank of America founder A.P. Gianni, the *Wall Street Journal*'s Charles Stabler wrote on August 30, 1984, that the risk-free world of banking that existed in 1967 when Wriston became president had been transformed to a risky, aggressive, innovative, and exciting enterprise. Although high interest rates, technology, high energy costs, and the collapse of the Bretton Woods monetary system had a lot to do with this, Stabler said that "the adaptation of banks to this revolution, and even the encouragement of it, is Walt Wriston's doing." His choice for Reed made it clear that he did not consider it essential for a Citibank Chairman to be a lender. The notion that the chairman of a bank should be a manager was, however, a novel one in American banking in 1984.

When Wriston retired, Citibank was, among other superlatives, the biggest aircraft and shipping lender, the most important foreign exchange trader and cash management bank, the top banker to multinationals, and the ultimate loan syndicator and swaps dealer. During Wriston's reign, Citibank had overtaken Chase and Bank of America to become America's largest banking institution and its premier corporate lender. It was becoming, by default, the only truly global bank. In 1983, the last full year before Wriston retired, Citicorp earned an impressive 16% return on equity, making it the year's most profitable money center banking company.

Wriston was nevertheless leaving the institution on shaky ground and, some would say, in shaky hands, writes Philip Zweig. For one thing, he would bequeath to his successor a company that was insufficiently capitalized to withstand the knocks it would take over the next eight years at the hands of Latin nations and other deadbeat borrowers.

During the long reign of Louis XIV, France waged numerous battles on all fronts and rose to an apogee of cultural greatness that made French the international language by the turn of the eighteenth century, spoken in courts throughout Europe and even Russia. The legacy, however, hid shadier sides of debt and discontent. If Wriston was Citibank's Sun King—battling bank regulations and the traditional view of banking on all fronts, to lead Citibank to the supremacy of American finance—then Reed was Louis XV and Louis XVI wrapped into one: the spendthrift extraordinaire, followed by the good-willed manager trying to save his head and country from the ravages of the guillotine. Unlike the unfortunate French monarch, however, Reed would ultimately succeed—but not without considerable pain and bloodshed along the way.

◆   ◆   ◆

In 1967, El Haj Omar Bongo became the elected president of Gabon, the third largest oil producing state in Africa. Three years later he became a client of Citibank, and over the next twenty-five years would develop an extensive relationship with the private bank division, including checking accounts, loans, money markets, times deposits, and investments.

One Sunday morning in 1985, Cedric got a panicked call from Herb Stetzenmeier, Country Head of Gabon: the President's staff had decided to cook lamb in the bathtub of the Mandarin Hotel in Hong Kong and triggered the smoke alarms. Water sprinklers went off on the entire floor and caused close to $300,000 worth of damage to the carpets and furniture. Afraid that the President would run off without covering the expenses, the Mandarin Hotel contacted the Hong Kong authorities, who then threaten to ground Bongo until the amount was settled. Unfortunately, President Bongo was expected for a State visit in another country within two days, and if Citibank was unable to come up with the cash, he faced a major political embarrassment.

Cedric woke up Winston Kung in Los Angeles, the West Coast representative for the Private Bank, and asked for his boss's number in Hong Kong. Marie Travis was head of the Private Bank division there, and she and Cedric knew one another by reputation. He dragged her out of bed at six o'clock on Monday morning, gave her Stetzenmeier's scant explanations, and Travis reacted immediately. She called the bank driver, woke up several money brokers with whom she had had the opportunity to do business on several occasions, and presented them with checks drawn on Citibank Hong Kong. She managed to round up the three hundred thousand dollars within two hours and handed the check to the Mandarin Hotel, thereby avoiding a highly publicized and embarrassing restraint order for President Bongo—he was ecstatic.

Soon after his return to Gabon, President Bongo put an end to the impending investigation regarding leaks from Citibank Gabon about the size of his account and the origins of his funds, and moved just over $50 million from Citibank Bahrain to newly opened accounts in New York. President Bongo required extreme secrecy in the handling of his account, provided in part by the shell companies, Tendin and Leontine. Mirroring Wriston's words—"damned if we do, damned if we don't"—an internal document recommending a 1986 loan to Bongo stated: *This is a highly confidential transaction given the identity of the borrower...The only risk really associated with this credit is the so-called 'political' one, i.e. the supposedly negative consequences which may result from public knowledge of the credit transactions. A stigma is more likely to*

*be attached to the large deposits the client has with us overseas if this were
to be known.*

Arrangements made over the next ten years by Citibank Private
Bank kept knowledge of the Bongo accounts within a small circle, until
a 1996 inquiry by the Federal Reserve Bank of New York revealed the
existence of several accounts of questionable origins.

◆   ◆   ◆

By 1988, Prince Alwaleed's transactions were taking up more and
more of Cedric's time, and it allowed him to remain out of the main
fray of the omnipresent internal political strife of the Private Bank, and
away from Hubertus Rukavina, the new Country Head for Switzerland. Like Belgium attempting to stay neutral in World War Two,
however, Cedric would fail to remain untouched by the machiavellian
triangle involving Steve Crabtree, Eric Daniels, and David Gibson, the
man who'd replaced Steve Fogarty as global head of Citibank Private
Bank in 1987.

Steve Crabtree, a graduate of Bowdoin College and Harvard Business School, joined Citibank after completing his Peace Corps mission
in Ethiopia. He was sent to Calcutta, Liberia, and Pakistan. During his
time there, he met Cedric at a Middle East Africa conference in Istanbul, and both connected immediately. He was transferred to Dubai as
head of corporate banking, and Cedric met up with him again when he
was marketing the UAE. Then Crabtree went off to Puerto Rico,
where he was eventually and found himself effectively out of his job.
When Cedric learned from his boss in London, Nick Greville, the head
of the Europe-Middle East-Africa (EMEA) division of Citibank Private
Bank, that Crabtree had applied for a job within the Private Bank, he
fully encouraged Greville's decision to hire Crabtree as his deputy.
Over a breakfast meeting in London, he convinced Steve to accept the
position—his international banking background in the Middle East
and Africa made him a valuable asset.

Eric Daniels was in charge of the retail sector of the Private Bank, the on-shore marketing—targeting the French in France, the Germans in Germany, Italians in Italy, etc., to keep the money locally. However, though he was not in charge of England, Daniels remained in England, Cedric—like others—believed that Gibson had decided to replace Greville with Daniels as head of EMEA. After barely a year, Greville was proving to be a great marketer but a terrible manager—he wouldn't listen to advice and took no heed of the internal fighting going on among his personnel and the various booking centers as they fought for profits and lost business to other banks. Since Gibson had hired Greville, a close friend of his, he felt that he could not get rid of him without a valid reason. Daniels was in London to provide that reason.

Daniels and Crabtree became good friends during the latter's stay there. Cedric suspected that at some point Daniels roped Crabtree into his scheme by promising him a better position once he replaced Greville. Sometime in early 1988, Crabtree convinced Greville to organize an offsite meeting for EMEA Private Bank senior officers. When Cedric received the memo outlining the offsite, he and the new Geneva Branch Head, Simon Coulter, couldn't believe their eyes: Steve had organized the meeting to take place in Venice, with wives, at high season. Not only would the cost be astronomical, but it was the worst way to deal with the division in-fighting. The presence of wives would wreck havoc and make blunt talk impossible as everyone tip-toed around the important issues with cocktail niceties. He and Simon called Greville to give their point of view.

"No, no," Greville said. "Steve tells me it's the ideal solution for team and morale building."

"There is no team, and little morale to build *on*, Nick! Steve hasn't been with us long enough to know that, and you're not listening to me! What we need," Cedric emphasized, "is to sit everyone in a room and have it out. Then maybe we can start building a team."

"No, no, Rick, you'll see. It'll work out."

He hung up. "This is a disaster in the making," Simon said. And Cedric could only agree.

The meeting took place: four hundred dollar rooms, lavish dinners at posh restaurants, gondola trips, first-class airfares…Clashes, bickering, snide remarks, underhanded comments…Gibson—the guest of honor—went berserk. Upon their return to London, Gibson had dinner with his friend Greville and fired him on the spot, allowing Eric Daniels to take over.

Shortly thereafter, Daniels removed Simon Coulter as head of the Geneva branch, and replaced him with his friend Crabtree. Coulter was reduced to running the training program, and the Referral Agents Program that Cedric had set up when he moved to Switzerland, designed to hire previous Bank associates to do client networking in exchange of a percentage of the net revenue for any client they referred to the bank. Within six months, Crabtree had managed to create a thick atmosphere of insecurity within the Geneva branch. By late 1988, sixteen people had left or had been fired, and Crabtree replaced them with his own connections.

In early 1989, Prince Alwaleed met with Cedric in Riyadh to discuss investing in US money center banks. He wanted to focus on the United States because his mind worked in dollars, the economy was barreling ahead, and the stock market was rebounding well from the crash of 1987. Cedric and his colleague Steve Klemme in New York compiled information on Morgan Guarantee, Manufacturers Hanover, Chase Manhattan, Bankers Trust, and Citicorp, and sent it to the Prince. He began buying shares up to a 2.5% stake in a select few.

Around the same time Prince Alwaleed became Chairman of United Saudi Commercial Bank and hired an ex-Citibanker named Jerry Kangis as his Senior Executive. To the Prince's liking, Kangis used Citibank's operating, policy and budget manuals for inspiration, and USCB soon became a virtual mirror-image of Citibank. Everyday,

Alwaleed was surrounded by a simulacrum of Citibank's colors, logos, and literature, and USCB used Citibank for most of their transactions.

By mid-1989, he began to consolidate his purchases in Citicorp. In a personal letter to Cedric, he expressed his desire to expand globally, and had found that Citibank best served his interests. Cedric was soon in frequent contact with Phil Stieboldt in the Investment division, responsible for buying shares for the Prince through their Luxembourg subsidiary, not only because of its low trading tax, but because this enabled him to cable the order to New York in the name of Citibank Luxembourg, and keep Prince Alwaleed's identity secret. Cedric would then have the Geneva branch credit Luxembourg's account in New York.

Cedric sensed that Alwaleed was planning a big leap forwards. Sometime earlier, the Prince had called him to complain that Forbes Magazine had left him off their Billionaire's list. He told Cedric to call the Senior Editor and tell him that Prince Alwaleed Bin Talal Bin Abdul Aziz Alsaud was now a billionaire. "But Your Highness, you don't want anyone to know you're a billionaire," said Cedric. "Imagine—kidnapping of children, extortion, etcetera." But the Prince insisted. Cedric asked him for a letter authorizing him to disclose the Prince's wealth, and called the Senior Editor of Forbes Magazine in New York to convey the message. Forbes wrote up a special article in a following issue, and Cedric knew that the Prince would soon be ripe for even greater publicity.

Steve Crabtree, however, would foil his plans to maintain a front-row seat to the event. Rukavina, Country Head of Switzerland, and Eric Daniels did not get along. Crabtree, had to report to Daniels through Rukavina, a situation that satisfied no-one. The only way around the issue was Cedric: as head of Middle East Africa for Citibank Private Bank, he was—in the muddle of Citibank's twisted hierarchy—Rukavina's equal and dealt directly with Daniels in London. It was only on matters concerning Citibank Switzerland that he reported to Rukavina.

Therefore, in order for Crabtree to circumvent Rukavina's authority and report directly to Daniels, he would have to usurp Cedric's job as head of the Middle East-Africa division of Citibank Private Bank.

11

The differences between Reed's governing style and that of Wriston became rapidly apparent soon after the former's ascension to the "throne". Though the Citibank culture of the eighties was an apt reflection of Reed's business methods—emphasizing savvy style rather than substance—Reed lacked Walt's aplomb and assertiveness. By 1990, in an economy once again headed for downtown, his background as a manager rather than a banker left him apparently too inexperienced to run the nation's largest bank, struggling with Third World debt and uncapitalization.

In March 1987, Brazil did the unthinkable: believing it could gain some leverage over the banks, it declared a moratorium on $121 billion of its debt. Reed now knew that he had to take drastic measures to protect Citibank and relieve the pressure of cross-border debt: he decided to set aside $3 billion in reserves. It was, effectively, the biggest loss in the history of the corporation. When the news was announced to the public, the stock plummeted. It also put pressure on other banks to follow suit, leading to a $10 billion dollar loss in that quarter for the banking industry as a whole.

On the bright side, the Individual Bank was posting an increase in earnings of 41%. Citicorp Savings had turned around, and the Investment Bank division had developed a capacity to trade and distribute securities around the world. Following on the heels of economic rejuvenation was an unbridled enthusiasm in real estate, for which there seem to be no limits as to how high prices could go, and Citibank threw itself into the race with gusto.

Though the traditional institutional lending business was in the doldrums, the merger, buyout, and junk bond markets had skyrocketed. The tax law changes in the early eighties had given a powerful new impetus to debt financing, and it was a heady time for dealers and traders: junk-bond king Michael Milken would make a $550 million end-of-year bonus in 1987 alone...While working for Drexel Lambert, Milken created a new use for junk bonds, persuading executives to issue them to restructure their companies, and speculators and investors to buy and trade them. This allowed corporations, which had previously been unable to borrow, to leverage capital. Within a few years and almost single-handedly, Milken opened up a new spectrum of the American capital markets. Under Drexel's leadership, the amount of junk bonds on the market swelled to $200 billion nationwide, and the bonds became an important underpinning of pension plans and a popular mutual fund investment.

Milken and Wriston shared very similar views—Milken admired Wriston's penchant for risk-taking, and Wriston viewed junk bonds as a device that, much like his own negotiable CD, enabled capital-starved companies to tap the markets. They claimed that it was another way of trimming the corporate fat and restructuring corporations. Others called it amoral: destroying the painstaking and rewarding process of building a company, watching it prosper and profit for the shareholders—then mercilessly replace it by leveraging capital to buy out a company, and sell it off in pieces to pay off the debt and make a quick fortune—even break the law in the process. Those at the top, like Wriston, were not exposed to the human toll exacted by hostile takeovers. His wife hated them: Kathy Wriston had lived through leveraged buyouts as director of Federated Department Stores. "She's seen the human carnage, which is substantial," Wriston said.

Citibank backed virtually all the LBO kings—with Manufacturers Hanover and Bankers Trust, it virtually controlled the money vats fueling the takeover machine. But hungry for fees, it sidelined the relationship banking that had made it prosper: Citibank supported Ronald Perelman's unsuccessful takeover attempt of Gillette, despite the Bank's longstanding corporate relationship with the razor manufacturer; it also got involved in the RJR Nabisco takeover, though Reed sat on the board of Philip Morris...

Then the stock market crashed on October 19, 1987, and the junk bond bubble burst with the conviction of Levine and Boesky, the indictment of Milken, and the eventual demise of Drexel Burnham Lambert. The leverage buyout frenzy continued through 1988, however, most noticeably with the $17 billion attempted coup against RJR Nabisco, as Wall Street found it difficult to recover from the market crash, and turned to one guaranteed source of income: takeovers. But by 1989, a host of US corporations found themselves heavily indebted due to extensive junk bond holdings, and Ron Perelman's takeover of pharmaceutical giant Revlon was the first to result in bankruptcy, while the total of defaults and debt moratoriums by October 1989 was valued at $4 billion.

It would not be long before the real estate market would follow the same downward spiral, and push Citibank to the brink of bankruptcy. Reed now understood the dangers of confusing style with results, and realized perhaps that Citibank's last real banker had been his mentor, Bill Spencer. Office vacancy rates soared as the decade of greed neared its end, yet buildings were still going up. Developers, and the banks that had financed them, were victims of the time lag. In 1986, real estate looked like an excellent investment; three years later, after zone planning, gathering permits, negotiating with contractors, and initiating the construction, the market was on the verge of collapse.

By 1989, Citibank's per share earnings were roughly a quarter of those of the previous year. Then, in the first quarter of 1990, the real estate market plunged, and loan defaults were inevitable. Citicorp's perception of its real estate portfolio swung 180 degrees: write-offs of $100 million became commonplace, and outstandings swelled to $13 billion: nearly 43% of these were non-performing. Ironically, a portion of Citicorp debt had even been reduced to junk bond status.

The search for liquidities was no longer a desire, but a dire necessity, and at a time when the country faced a new recession, the pressure was on to raise capital…

Just as it seemed that the situation for Reed could not get any worse, Congressman John Dingell played the revenge card for Wriston's haughty attitude during the David Edwards affair by public declaring that Citibank was technically insolvent and "struggling to survive". While desperately seeking capital, Reed was forced to engage in spin control, and might not have made it without help from FDIC chairman William Seidman, who had no desire to see Citibank go under water.

Reed fell back on the easiest short-term method to raise cash: reduce labor costs. In 1990 alone, eight thousand employees lost their jobs. Reed was also forced to eliminate dividend payments entirely, the first interruption since 1813. Many were now speculating that the Board of Directors would demand Reed's resignation for his poor performance as a chairman. Others claimed that governing Citibank was an impossibly huge task for just one person, and rumors circulated about a possible split up.

Citibankers had always been assertive and sure of themselves. Brash and brazen, they had seen criticism from other banks turn to admiration. Now they were plagued with self-doubt and uncertainty about the survival of their institution—and they garnered no sympathy from others. The sense of belonging to a family had disintegrated entirely. If Citibank under Wriston could afford to be the benevolent father looking after his prodigal sons, Citibank in 1990 was the drunken stepfather slapping the kids around for under-achievement…Citibank's internal competition may have worked when business was growing; as Citibank faltered and jobs were eliminated, the backstabbing turned vicious.

And in 1990, Cedric experienced this as much as anyone. The aura of invincibility that had shrouded him since 1975 had all but vanished.

Saudi Arabia had been eating up its reserves for a while and was no longer the prime business target. Wriston was gone, and no-one paid much attention to something as elusive as reputation. Trust among colleagues was non-existent. In 1989, Cedric could hardly have pulled off the coup he managed with Bongo only four years earlier—someone down the line might have suspected that he wanted to get rid of them. Someone certainly seemed to want to get rid of Cedric, and it was a man he had recommended himself to the Private Bank, Steve Crabtree.

◆   ◆   ◆

In 1984, Cedric managed to convince the CSGI division not to sell off the Citibank branches in the United Arab Emirates, since the Bank represented the only US presence in the country. In May 1989, Cedric was invited to the 25th anniversary of the UAE branches, as well as Steve Crabtree, since he had worked as corporate head in Dubai. The day before they left, on a Friday night, Eric Daniels called Cedric at home to tell him what a great job he was doing for the MEA division of the Private Bank. It was a pleasant surprise for which Cedric was grateful.

He had managed to convince Rick Braddock, President of the Bank and former head of CSGI, to attend the re-opening of the branch in Abu Dhabi that had been renovated for the 25th anniversary. He also arranged for the presence of the Deputy Ruler of the UAE, Sheikh Saif bin Mohammed al-Nayan, and together they met Braddock at the branch. At the subsequent ribbon cutting, Braddock mentioned in his speech that the branch personnel had one person to thank for their jobs: Rick Grant.

The next morning, Cedric flew to Dubai where he met up with Crabtree for the celebrations—Cedric was on Cloud Nine—and they arranged to have dinner the next evening. Immediately Cedric sensed that Steve was acting strange—distant, aloof, and void of his usual humorous banter. Just as the main course had been served, Cedric asked him what was eating him.

"Well...Daniels appointed me the new head of Middle East Africa. So I guess that means you'll be reporting to me..."

"In what capacity?" Cedric asked. But it was a knee-jerk reaction. Crabtree's statement hadn't sunk in.

"I suppose as Head of Africa...?"

Cedric pushed away his plate and stood up. "I bring you in and this is how you repay me? By taking my job? Thanks a lot, Steve. Thanks a lot!"

Cedric assumed that this was Daniel's way of removing his buddy Crabtree from Rukavina's supervision—and he was just a sideline casualty. Chris Rogers was already Head of Africa, and there would be no point in him reporting to Crabtree via Cedric: he was left out to dry, with no room left for him in the Private Bank division which he had helped start from scratch. Cedric was not only angry, hurt, and disgusted by the maneuver, he was also irate at the manner in which it had been done.

When he returned to Geneva on Wednesday, he called Daniels in London immediately: "Don't say a word. I just want to tell you how pissed I am. For getting rid of someone, there is protocol. You should be fired or demoted by your boss, not your junior. And to set me up on Friday with all those congratulations, knowing that you were sidelining me—you're a flaming asshole, Daniels!" To add insult to injury, Chris Rogers did not even have the decency to come to him to explain that the new hierarchy would not work—a fact with which Cedric could only agree—but went directly to Crabtree and said that since Grant was out of the loop, he would bypass him from now on.

Cedric had been replaced, without another job having been offered him. But neither had anyone in the Bank specifically fired him. He expected it to happen, but decided he would not go down without fighting. The timing couldn't be worse—Nicole was ending her first year at Wellsley College, and Eric was set to start at Duke University in the fall. Not inexpensive schools. Even if he found another job, Cedric would lose his international staff status, the house rent payments would no longer be covered, he would have an effective salary decrease of almost forty percent; and the price of the Citibank stock which he had purchased for his retirement and to pay for his kids' education was going down the drain.

There was no point in asking Crabtree what his new job might be; it was implicit that he had none and was expected to leave. Steve would amble into his office on occasion to say, "Hey, Cedric, there must be some great jobs out there…" and Cedric would reply that he was looking at some possibilities…Indeed he was looking around, but he was now fifty-five years old, a redline for early retirement, and his banking knowledge was "limited" to client relations and Middle East Africa. After twenty-five years in the bank, he'd established an enviable network of acquaintances and friends for whom he did favors and who did favors for him in return, people who helped him in areas where he had little knowledge. He relied on, and lived off this network, and he could imagine that without it, he might not be able to handle the responsibilities expected of him in another bank. He was afraid he would lose any new job within six months of starting it—and besides, Cedric enjoyed his job immensely, it was an area in which he felt fully competent and in charge (within Citibank) and he had no particular desire to branch out into something else and enter a new working environment at his age.

So the other option was wait and see what the bank would offer him to leave. Cedric had helped build the Private Bank franchise from the ground up, only to be summarily dismissed, and he decided that the bank owed him: there was no way he'd take off without two years' salary. But no offer was forthcoming, and Cedric was left dangling for months with little work to do. He masked his indignity and maintained a positive outlook. He helped people where they needed help, and soon he was often solicited for his knowledge. He took business trips to maintain client contacts, he resolved problems between tellers and clients; and by assisting other managers with their client background data, he kept abreast of much of what was going on in the Bank.

Cedric refused to be beaten. He took advantage of his loose situation to come into work late, return home early, take a five-week trip to go trekking in Nepal in November 1989…And yet still no-one said anything. In the mean time, the atmosphere in the Bank was deteriorating rapidly with the continuous inflow of Crabtree's business buddies. Cedric's friend Ramoni, Head of the Saudi Arabia division of the Private Bank reporting to Crabtree, mentioned that he planned to leave also, and together they coordinated their job searching, figuring that they could place well as a team at another bank.

Ramoni did not have Cedric's patience, however. While Annette and Rick were vacationing in the south of France at Cap Antibes, Ramoni called Cedric to tell him he'd found a great job, and Cedric told him to go ahead and accept it. The job offered to Ramoni stipulated that he take his whole team with him—secretary, assistant, and two other officers—leaving a vacancy that no-one but Cedric could fill: Crabtree had been able to piss off or fire enough of the wrong people so that no-one was left with competent knowledge of the Middle East, especially Saudi Arabia, and certainly none whose expertise could even begin to compare with Cedric's. When Crabtree learned of Ramoni and his team's departure, he went ballistic; and when he saw Ramoni that same afternoon in the halls of Citibank, he threw him and his four associates out of the bank, and told them that he never wanted to see them in the building again.

Two days later Cedric got a panicked call from Steve asking him to take over Ramoni's job. Cedric made him plead—but he finally took the job. Saudi Arabia had represented eighty percent of his work as head of MEA, and the most rewarding. He would have to report to Crabtree, but that did not disturb him in the least. And he now had the upper hand by helping Crabtree yet again after the ignominy Steve had forced on him. Another fringe benefit of their mutual dislike of one another in the business arena was that Crabtree became even more secretive, and kept Cedric out of loop on all matters that did not concern Saudi Arabia. Any situation that made Cedric see less of Steve at the bank suited him fine.

So by early 1990, Cedric was back placing time deposits, renewing fiduciary placements, discussing investment options, researching real estate...His largest client was now Prince Alwaleed Bin Talal. Although the Prince's account with Citibank approximated only $150 million, the young man was now a billionaire, and between September and November 1990, Alwaleed raised his ownership of Citicorp stock up to 4.998%, the limit beyond which he would be required to disclose his identity.

While Saddam Hussein was facing down George Bush in Kuwait, Cedric flew out to visit the Prince and discuss his desire to acquire yet another 5% of Citicorp shares. Cedric knew that this was the moment he had sensed a few years earlier—Alwaleed was ready to come out of "hiding" and take the financial world by a storm. Sitting in the Prince's high-tech luxurious tent-compound outside Riyadh, Cedric told his client that he should not buy the shares through the open market—the effect would be diluted by the mass of daily trading activity. What he should do is have Citibank issue new stock, thereby infusing sorely needed capital into the sick and cash-starved institution, and make a bang on the market. Both Prince Alwaleed and Citibank would get the publicity they wanted, and needed. Prince Alwaleed Bin Talal was seduced by the idea, and in November, he charged Cedric with the mission to fly to New York and tender his offer at the highest levels of the Bank.

Cedric met first with Rick Roesch, in charge of Public Affairs, then with Paul Collins, the Vice-Chairman in charge of raising capital for the bank—but if he expected to be greeted with gasps of admiration and wan smiles of relief at the prospect of relief from Citibank's credit crunch, he was sorely disappointed. They were only modestly pleased.

Paul Collins flew out to meet the Prince with Cedric in December to negotiate the issuance of over sixteen million shares worth of preferred convertible stock—a capital injection equivalent to a five-year loan, time after which the Prince could exchange the stock for common shares. The amount would edge his ownership of Citicorp to just under a total of 15%, at a convertible price of $16 per share.

Discussions continued in the shadow of the impending Gulf War, but Citibank appeared abstrusely lukewarm on Prince Alwaleed's proposal. The Prince submitted yet another a proposal on February 1. Ten days later, he still had no news. Cedric did not understand Citibank's attitude either, and in a conversation with the Prince, expressed the opinion that perhaps his client's proposal—however welcome—was just a drop in the ocean compared with the amount of capital they needed to raise. Furthermore, the Prince was restricted by the Federal Reserve as a foreign investor, and could not legally own more than 10% of a US bank without a special permission from the Fed. If there was some way, however, that the Prince could sell off his 5% share of common stock, and increase his proposed interest in the preferred convertible stock to 9.998%, he would present Citibank with a capital infusion of just under $600 million. That just might grab their attention.

The next day, Prince Alwaleed sent a letter to Paul Collins, with copies to Cedric Grant, President Rick Braddock, and Chairman John Reed:

Pursuant to our attempts to reach an agreement on Citicorp's convertible preferred offering, it is time to consummate an agreement as soon as possible or for each party to pursue other avenues.

I have to inform you, not only as a serious investor in the convertible issue, but rather as a major shareholder of Citicorp, that I am extremely disappointed with the path Citicorp has taken to date.

In order to formalize an agreement on the convertible preferred, I had my advisors provide you with a detailed proposal. At this time, I am disappointed with the progress, or should I say the lack of progress of negotia-

tions. Mr. Collins, there must be an agreement reached on this matter soon. The present market conditions are quite favorable to me and it is not prudent for me to permit these opportunities to dissipate.

As a major shareholder of Citicorp's shares, it is my selfish interest to assist in any possible way to enhance Citicorp's quantitative and qualitative position, and as you so succinctly stated in the letter of December 14, 1990, a private purchase by me of Citicorp's convertible preferred will "...eliminate some of the current uncertainty that now exists relative to Citicorp and the adequacy of its capital position...", and such a purchase will actualize my philosophy of establishing a long term relationship with Citicorp.

As I have stated to you, a formal offer was submitted on my behalf by my lawyers Hogan and Hartson, to Citicorp on February 1ˢᵗ, 1991. It was clearly requested in that letter that a meeting should take place within a week in an attempt to resolve both the economic and legal issues. Unfortunately, no movement from Citicorp's side is evident to date.

It seems to me that the wrong "side" is pushing for this deal to go through. Rather than me pushing for this transaction, I was expecting Citicorp to be pursing it more aggressively (not to mention more professionally).

In a last attempt to consummate an agreement and to uphold my commitment to Citicorp, I am proposing an additional option for negotiations. Namely, to sell all my 16,610,550 of common stock in the open market (at a reasonable time so as not to depress further the price) and to concentrate purchasing all my 9.99% through the convertible preferred issue. As you may know, with my new proposal, you would be able to cover between 50% to 60% of the convertible offer (assuming an offer of 1 billion dollars). I am sure you appreciate the coup on Citicorp's part to have this percentage committed. However, my offer is contingent that the terms offered to me are most favorable and are based on the proposal you have received on my behalf on February 1ˢᵗ, 1991. Needless to say, this offer is contingent that the final negotiations begin immediately.

The Prince was pushing the deal despite Citibank's distance because the opportunity was too great to play the highly publicized role of the White Knight, with America's number one bank playing the damsel in financial distress.

Prince Alwaleed's letter finally seemed to make an impression. Reed got involved, assurances were made, a compromise of 11% gross was reached on the dividend rate, and a deal seemed imminent...Then

Cedric found out why Citibank had been playing hard to get for the past two months; and perhaps why it was not so much the Prince's letter than other external factors that explained the bank's turnabout and prompted Reed and Collins to suddenly get terribly enthusiastic over the Prince and his offer: on one of his trips to New York, Cedric learned that Bob Troxler, a Private Bank colleague working out of London, had been working on a deal for a capital injection by the Kuwaiti royal family. But once Desert Storm had been unleashed, the deal became moot.

Cedric understood Reed's reticence now, his desire to wait for the Kuwaitis to come through. And as Troxler had pointed out elusively, a Saudi Prince might not be quite as clean and dependable as the Kuwaiti government. Cedric himself was unsure how Alwaleed had amassed such a huge fortune in such a short period of time—from a $30,000 loan and a mortgage on a house given to him by his father, Prince Talal, in 1979 (as well as the $15,000 monthly stipend from the government as a grandson of Abdul Aziz ibn Saud), Alwaleed had broken the billion dollar mark almost ten years later. It was an issue that would be highlighted much later by both *The Economist* and *Business Week*. His investments outside Saudi Arabia didn't add up to several billion, and his affairs within the Kingdom remained veiled in opacity. Cedric did not question Alwaleed's integrity, and certainly not his ability as a businessman, but there was also the possibility that Alwaleed was fronting for other Saudis—a real threat since Prince Alwaleed had certified that his fortune was his alone, that no-one else was contributing a penny to his investment in Citibank. This problem was exacerbated by the BCCI scandal, which made the Federal Reserve wary of another Middle Eastern owning such a large share of America's biggest bank.

◆   ◆   ◆

The Bank of Credit and Commerce International erupted in early 1991 amidst disclosures of illegal foreign ownership in First American and National Bank of Georgia, through front men such as Robert Altman and Ghaith Pharoan, as well as suspicions of money laundering, fraud, bribery and corruption, drugs and arms trafficking, support of Pakistan's nuclear arms program as well as terrorism, management of prostitution, commission and facilitation of income tax evasion, smuggling, illegal immigration, illicit purchases of banks and real estate...BCCI was an international bank with an aggressive marketing strategy. And handily, by fracturing its corporate structure, record keeping, regulatory reviews, and audits, it was able to evade ordinary legal restrictions on the movement of capital and goods as a matter of daily practice. In creating BCCI as a vehicle fundamentally free of government control, Chairman Abedi developed an ideal mechanism for facilitating illicit activity by others. Among BCCI's principal methods for committing crimes were its use of shell corporations and bank confidentiality and secrecy havens, the layering of its corporate structure, use of front-men and nominees (i.e. Pharoan), kickbacks and bribes, intimidation of witnesses, and the retention of well-placed insiders to discourage governmental action, such as President Carter aide, Bert Lance.

In 1977, BCCI developed a plan to infiltrate the U.S. market by secretly purchasing U.S. banks while opening branch offices of BCCI throughout the US and eventually merging the institutions. In one of these plans, Ghaith Pharoan acquired 7% of National Bank of Georgia; in another, Bert Lance and former Middle East CIA liaison, Kamal Adham, assisted in BCCI's take over of Washington Based Financial General—which was eventually approved by the Fed in 1982—later renamed First American. Sheikh Zayed, ruler of Abu Dhabi, named his two sons as investors in Financial General to keep individual shareholding under 5%. Then in 1985, Ghaith Pharoan purchased Independence Bank, approved by the FDIC despite their knowledge of the fact that he was a shareholder of BCCI and was placing a senior BCCI officer in charge of Independence.

Cedric began to feel wary of BCCI during his tour of duty in London in the late seventies. Their presence there was highly visible, and their money broker offices were often established in the most prestigious corner buildings in the City. One day a Saudi client told Cedric that BCCI was paying much higher interest than Citibank on a similar time deposit. The spread was far too high and made Cedric suspicious—he knew that Citibank sometimes edged up their own interest rates by a quarter of a point to attract depositors, but not by anything close to what BCCI was paying. At a subsequent policy meeting, he raised the issue and said that something was fishy. Other officers voiced similar opinions—because of its high interest rates, BCCI was luring away Citibank clients, and also suspicious were its recent hiring of ex-Citibankers who had been fired because of dubious professional ethics. The decision was made to sever relations with BCCI, a decision that was transmitted to Citibank worldwide. Cedric heard nothing more about the affair until it blew open in 1991.

By 1985, the CIA had extensive information on BCCI, which it provided to the US Treasury and the Office of the Comptroller of the Currency, but which it failed to report to the Federal Reserve and the Justice Department. And the CIA continued to use BCCI and First American for its operations, even with the knowledge that both institutions were fundamentally corrupt and criminal. These activities included payments to Panama leader Noriega through the Panamanian branch of BCCI, and laundering payments to Afghan rebels though BCCI branches in Pakistan.

By 1986, the Justice Department and the Treasury were also aware of BCCI's criminal connections, and the State Department knew that terrorist Abu Nidal was using the bank to finance his operations in Europe. Finally, the Customs Agency was working with the US Attorney's office in Tampa in Operation C-Chase, an undercover sting operation designed to expose drug money laundering in South Florida, which ultimately targeted BCCI.

During a hearing on General Noriega's drug trafficking and money laundering, BCCI was identified as facilitating Noriega's criminal activity. In March 1988, the Foreign Relations Committee authorized the issuance of subpoenas to BCCI and those at the bank involved in handling Noriega's assets. Service of the subpoenas was delayed at the request of the Justice Department and the US Customs Service, due to concern that its service could interfere with Operation C-Chase.

The sting was finally carried out. However, federal prosecutors in Tampa handling the indictment of BCCI in 1988 failed to recognize the importance of the information that they received concerning BCCI's other crimes, including its apparent secret ownership of First American and other US banks. The January 1990 plea agreement between the bank and the US Attorney permitted BCCI to avoid trial, and had the effect of discouraging BCCI officials from telling the US what they knew about BCCI's larger criminality.

It 1989, the Bank of England had learned of BCCI's involvement in the financing of terrorism and in drug money laundering, and undertook limited supervision of BCCI in response. In early 1990, BCCI auditors at Price Waterhouse (UK) advised the Bank of England that there were substantial loan losses, numerous poor banking practices, and evidence of fraud, which together had created a massive hole in BCCI's books. The Bank of England's response was not to close BCCI down, but to find ways to prop it up and prevent collapse. Sheikh Zayed, ruler of Abu Dhabi, was a major shareholder and effectively controlled BCCI at this time. In April 1990, the Government of Abu Dhabi, auditors from Price Waterhouse (UK), BCCI, and the Bank of England, colluded to reorganize BCCI over 1990 and 1991 to keep the UK branch afloat, rather than advise the public of what they knew and provoke a run on deposits. This would, of course, later cause substantial injury to innocent depositors and customers of BCCI who continued to do business with an institution which each of the above parties knew had engaged in fraud. Under the agreement, Abu Dhabi guaranteed BCCI's losses, while Price Waterhouse agreed to certify the bank's books.

Meanwhile, Senator John Kerry of Nebraska, chairman of the Subcommittee that had investigated BCCI, was appalled at the plea agreement reached with the US Attorney in Tampa. He claimed that a $14 million fine was insufficient punishment for an institution which had a corporate policy of laundering drug money. In Spring 1989, he authorized Subcommittee Counsel Jack Blum to provide the information collected to the Justice Department. But they failed to move on this information, which Blum then forwarded to NY District Attorney Robert Morgenthau. His subsequent criminal investigation was critical in stopping the intended reorganization of BCCI, planned and backed by the Bank of England, Abu Dhabi and Price Waterhouse, in which the extent of BCCI's criminality would have been suppressed.

In early 1991, Cedric received a phone call from Larry Smith, the man with whom he'd run his first marathon in Athens, Greece. He had left Citibank, and was working as the personal US financial advisor to Khalid bin Mahfouz, head of the National Commercial Bank in Saudi Arabia, and another major shareholder of BCCI. Larry wanted Rick to place $50 million in a time deposit in the name of the account "Eastbrook", presumably owned by Mahfouz. Unaware of Mahfouz's connection to BCCI, Cedric welcomed the money, and proceeded to make the investment.

A short while later, Larry called Cedric again to ask him to break the deposit. Cedric acquiesced, and had the Treasury send the money back immediately. When Crabtree found out about this recent transaction, he went ballistic. "Don't you know Mahfouz's money has been blacklisted? He's a major shareholder of BCCI! His assets have been frozen—you should never have allowed that deposit to be broken!" No, Cedric hadn't known, Crabtree had never circulated the blocking order. Furthermore, though Treasury *had* been notified, the blocking order was in the name of Mahfouz, while Cedric's time deposit order was in the name of Eastbrook, and Treasury had not made the connection.

Cedric knew that he was about to take the heat. Crabtree sent a mail to Rukavina exposing Rick as responsible for releasing this money despite the blocking order, and effectively making the Bank liable for a $50 million loss. Cedric was immediately summoned to Zurich, and he felt once again that he was being set up for dismissal. His dealings with the Prince and Reed gave him a certain amount of assurance, but these were no longer the Wriston days and no-one was safe from being tended the pink slip—he needed help. During the meeting in Zurich, Rukavina and the legal department hardly gave him a chance to explain, and he soon understood their wrath—they already had a billion dollars of Mahfouz's money sitting in the Channel Islands, making everyone very nervous, another fact that Crabtree had omitted to mention to him. Liability for $50 million was secondary to the attention that Cedric's handling of the money could draw to this offshore account.

Cedric called Larry and told him that he was in big trouble. His friend told him not to worry: Eastbrook was not owned by Khalid bin Mahfouz, but rather by his brother, and was therefore was not covered by the blocking order. He sent a notarized affadavit that certified this fact, and Cedric presented it to Rukavina—thereby avoiding repercussions for everyone by exposing the whole affair as a misunderstanding.

The Federal Reserve finally initiated a formal investigation of BCCI and First American on January 3, 1991—an aggressive and diligent investigation which led to the decision to force BCCI out of the U.S. and divest itself of First American.

◆   ◆   ◆

In mid-February 1991, Prince Alwaleed sold off his stakes in the other US money centers, and transferred all his monies, totaling around $700 million, from UBS and Credit Suisse in Geneva to Citibank. In the mean time, Reed and Collins met with the Secretary of Treasury of Federal Reserve, as well as Chairman Alan Greenspan, to obtain their verbal agreement on the deal. Though Reed was under scrutiny by the Fed for all of the problems he faced with Citibank, they agreed to the principle of the deal, but stated that this did not allow Prince Alwaleed to forgo submitting the necessary documentation to the Federal Reserve for approval of 15% ownership of Citibank; if that were to fail, he would have to sell off his 4.998% share of common stock, just as Cedric had suggested earlier, and Alwaleed had confirmed in his letter to Paul Collins.

On February 25, the crowning moment of his career, Cedric received a letter from Prince Alwaleed authorizing the transfer from his account to Citicorp New York of US$590m, transfer to be effective on Thursday, 28 February, "upon receipt of the certificate of ownership of the preferred issue" by his lawyers. Cedric would later claim that it was the most important day in his life to date after his wedding and his children's births. No news had been leaked, and when the deal went through without a hitch, the publicity fall-out was enormous. Citibank stock began to edge up almost immediately. And Cedric spent the day running around collecting and copying all the news clippings he could find—for the Prince, and for himself.

The victory was not yet complete: the Fed still needed to be convinced to allow Alwaleed to retain a 15% ownership—5% over the legal limit. Cedric spent several weeks after the deal collecting all the requisite background information on the Prince and his wealth. He scuttled back and forth between Geneva and Washington, D.C. Boxes and trunks of material were sent, phone calls were exchanged, and the parties involved engaged in a constant questions-and-answers routine. The Fed was not convinced. Jack Roach, the Citibank Senior Legal Counsel, arranged a meeting with Cedric in New York, and explained that Senior Fed representatives had informally expressed their doubts: despite the wealth of information, the widespread opinion was that this was not all the Prince's money; there was no way to prove or disprove the fact, so the suspicion remained. "And you know what that means..." Jack ended. Cedric certainly did: Amidst the emerging scandal surrounding the Arab owned BCCI, the Fed might have trouble publicly justifying a special permission for a Saudi Prince to own 15% of the country's largest bank. "If anything surfaced later..." they repeated.

"It wouldn't," assured Cedric. "Prince Alwaleed might have been educated in the US and speak English without an accent, he remains Saudi to the core. Though he is a savvy and westernized businessman, that doesn't preclude him from doing business the Saudi way, especially in his own country. That might mean that he could seem on occasion unscrupulous in our eyes, but it doesn't mean he's dishonest. I doubt very much that he'd aid and abet money laundering."

"But it could be from other members of the Royal Family?"

"No. He might be elusive as to how exactly he accumulated his wealth in the Kingdom, but that's because he's presumably aware of how the United States views Middle Eastern business practices. I think he's too proud to front for anyone. And from the way his trusts are set up—I've never seen money returned to anyone else. A lot of it comes in, but the only amount that goes out is into investments made exclusively by himself."

"Then how did he accumulate such a fortune so quickly in the eighties? Business transactions in Saudi Arabia are hardly transparent. We only have his word that he made it in construction deals and real estate."

"He probably did...But those deals don't happen the same way they do in the States. Take the Jeddah airport for instance—back when I was handling the bid bond in 1968, the expected cost was $250 million; it was completed in the early eighties for $14 billion. That's not just inflation, let me tell you. There were huge commission payments, with everyone who could manage it trying to get their fingers in the pie. Prince Alwaleed is the son of Prince Talal, who is the favorite son of King Abdul Aziz ibn Saud's favorite wife. He has stature within the Kingdom, and a lot of connections. Combine that with a western education, business smarts and a truckload of ambition, and you've got a winning combination. Here's a crude and simplified example of how someone like him could have made his wealth: A bid is announced for a construction project, and three companies submit their bids: a Korean team, for $200 million; a German team, for $400 million; and a Saudi Prince's company, for $600 million. The minister overseeing the project, who happens to be the Prince's uncle—this all conjecture, remember, I'm just painting a simplified picture—calls in his nephew and asks: 'How come you've bid so high?' And the Prince answers: 'We hire the Korean team for $200 million to do the work; then you get $200 million, and so do I.' Then the Prince sets up the infrastructure to provide loans, equipment, rentals, transportation, insurance—anything the Koreans might need. From start to finish, he's putting money in his pocket."

"Is that legal?" Roach asked.

"Not according to our Foreign Corrupts Act, but it's the way business is done in Saudi Arabia. No U.S. company is involved in paying kickbacks or commissions. The method is perfectly acceptable over there—who are we to judge? And I'm not really bothered by the ethical considerations, because though the government is being charged three times the price, it's over-charging itself. That's just the way things are done there sometimes. Besides, we're not talking Gabon here, where oil profits are pretty much going into one man's pockets. A lot of money has been poured into the infrastructure of Saudi Arabia. In fact, it's now the seventh largest agricultural nation in the world! That's not bad for a desert nation."

Roach shook and nodded his head as if trying to solve an internal debate. "I understand your point of view, but it's not something that will convince the Fed. Especially since you have no proof. That's your intuition, and be sure that they'll be relying on theirs."

The day before Cedric was scheduled to receive an answer from the Fed, an article came out in *New York Magazine* covering foreign ownership of US banks, effectively putting up a danger flag. Cedric showed up the next morning with a copy of the paper, and the Fed representative simply nodded his head. Both knew the Prince would never be granted an approval, and he wasn't. A system was later worked out whereby Prince Alwaleed would sell off 4.998% share of his common stock gradually so as to fall below the legal 9.99% limit without disrupting the market.

Prince Alwaleed's timing with regards to his capital investment in Citicorp was impeccable, and his judgment sound: two weeks after securing the deal, a group of international investors bought a further $600 million of new preferred shares, and Citicorp's capital crisis passed. By 1994 the bank share price had soared and Prince Alwaleed had made a fortune, raking in a $100 million profit for the common shares he'd been obliged to sell. By 1995, his $590 million stake in Citibank was valued at $2.5 billion. He became one of the biggest and most liquid players in the global financial market, and Citibank not only edged away from the abyss but began once again to reassert itself as the largest financial institution in the United States.

Cedric felt fully vindicated for everything that had happened with Crabtree over the past two years. His star was waxing again, and now it seemed a pleasant and prestigious coasting to retirement—though he expected those last eight years to be far from boring or easygoing—as Prince Alwaleed's personal banker. Unfortunately, he would be wrong again.

12

"It's now coming back," Wriston said of Citibank in 1993. "It's the greatest franchise in the world. Probably no-one could have withstood what they've gone through." And as bank profits improved, regulators realized that they had come down too hard on the banks to begin with, and started to remove regulatory impediments which eased the credit crunch even further. Nevertheless, the urge to reap continually greater profits still stoked the coals of many decisions, and inevitably led to brushes with disaster. The result of Reed's desire to increase the Private Bank's share of Citibank's earnings to 20% meant that very few bankers refused dubious accounts—they refrained from asking "impertinent" questions regarding the clients' wealth, and often dismissed the "Know Your Client" rule.

John Reed would never convey the same convincing authority as Wriston, and even when accepting responsibility for mistakes made on the part of his personnel, it was apparent that he showed little of the oversight and control that Wriston displayed during the David Edwards affair. Reed's inability to govern the Citibank behemoth with the same iron fist became obvious at the end of the decade in two highly publicized ways: the merger with (though some would claim the take-over by) Sandy Weil's Travelers Group in 1998, to form Citigroup; and the Congressional hearings of November 1999 on Citibank's alleged involvement with money laundering in the Salinas, Bhutto and Bongo affairs.

Private Banks are particularly vulnerable to fraud and money laundering, because of the secret and personal nature of the business, and because of their specific expertise in effectively moving large sums of money around the globe and shielding client identity. The worldwide assets under management at the end of the millennium were estimated at over $15 trillion, with Citibank alone controlling over $100 billion. In developing a close relationship with their clients, private bankers often feel a loyalty that leads them to minimize warning signs, and discourages them from probing too deeply into the client's background to verify information about his or her assets, business dealings, and other sources of funds. In certain cases of dealing with heads of states, additional issues of etiquette and protocol are also of concern. The problem is exacerbated when internal pressure exists to reap profits at the expense of sound policy safeguarding the reputation of the bank.

This leads to the inherent contradiction of the private banker's role: developing a personal relationship with a client and increasing their deposits on the one hand; monitoring their accounts for suspicious activity and questioning specific transactions on the other. The pressure to perform and bring money into the bank collides with the requirement to refuse or close, or at least notify authorities about, large accounts of suspicious nature. "If I don't accept this account, someone else at some other bank will…" is a reasoning that can often run through the mind of even the most ethical of private bankers, under pressure to increase bank profits.

Two laws lay out the basic anti-money laundering obligations of all US banks. First is the Bank Secrecy Act which specifies that all banks must have anti-money laundering programs through the development of internal policies, procedures and controls, with an independent audit function to test programs. The second is the Money Laundering Control Act of 1986, which prohibits any person from knowingly engaging in a financial transaction which involves the proceeds of a "specified unlawful activity", including drug trafficking, fraud, theft, and bribery.

Citibank Private Bank had established particular policies to adhere to these requirements, notably obtaining due diligence information on a client—background, source of income, anticipated levels of activity—prior to opening an account, information which was then recorded in a "client profile" and updated annually. A global memorandum from Corporate Staff Relations, dated November 4th 1993, emphasized that Citicorp placed "a high value on integrity." Unfortunately, components within the bank also placed a high value on profit earnings, which would lead many directors to fuel the enthusiasm of their employees in opening accounts without effecting the appropriate 'due diligence'.

A prominent Mexican businessman and long time client of Citibank, Mr. Carlos Hank, introduced Raul Salinas to Ms. Amy Elliott in early 1992. Shortly thereafter, Elliott opened an account for Salinas, with the first deposit coming from Mr. Hank, supposedly for repayment of a loan. She set up a shell corporation in the Caymans called Trocca Ltd. to serve as the owner of record for accounts benefiting Salinas and his family, using "nominee companies" as company directors to ensure that Salinas's name did not appear anywhere on the Trocca incorporation papers.

Though this was not an uncommon request or procedure, Elliot did not follow many of the necessary procedures to protect the bank from harm. She was not aware that Salinas had held a government post; she did not ask him about his employment; she did not verify the existence of the construction company he had owned, and she relied on Mr. Hank's word that Salinas had just sold this company. Finally, she assumed that Salinas had "in the neighborhood of $20 to $30 million," based on her knowledge of wealthy Mexican families. So she waived the standard policy of requiring two references, figuring that Mr. Hank's word and knowledge of the Salinas's family was enough; and she failed to fill out the client profile in clear violation of bank policy, leaving it blank until 1995.

In mid-1993, Mr. Salinas told Ms. Elliott he wanted to move his funds outside of Mexico until after the upcoming 1994 elections. In a one-month period, almost $50 million flew out of the country. Nevertheless, Elliott still did not inquire as to the source of the funds, relying on her initial assumptions of the Salinas wealth and Paulina Salinas's previous divorce settlement, despite the fact that the deposit amounts through 1993 far exceeded the projected account potential of $20 million.

On February 28, 1995, Raul Salinas was arrested and imprisoned in Mexico for helping plan the murder of Jose Francisco Ruiz Massieu, deputy leader of Mexico's ruling Institutional Revolutionary Party, and Raul's brother-in-law. Later, Mexican authorities would add a count of "inexplicable enrichment." The following day, tape transcripts of telephone conversations between New York, London, and Switzerland, showed that the private bank's initial reaction to the arrest was not to assist law enforcement, but to determine whether the Salinas accounts should be moved to Switzerland to make discovery of the assets and bank records more difficult, a suggestion made by the Country Head of Switzerland, Hubertus Rukavina. Finally the decision would be reached to hand over management of the accounts to the Private Bank's legal department.

By November 1995, Elliot realized that Swiss authorities had frozen the Salinas's funds in their Swiss bank accounts. She reported this news to her superiors, and on November 14, 1995, Mrs. Salinas began the process of closing the Salinas accounts at the Private Bank. She was arrested the next day, following which arrest Citibank was included in the order to freeze Salinas Swiss accounts. On November 17, Citibank filed a Criminal Referral Form, but did not mention the Trocca accounts in London and Switzerland that amounted to $50 million.

Cedric learned of the developments in Mexico through the papers. Considering the rapacious attitude rampant within the Private Bank, he was not entirely surprised. Neither was he surprised to hear about the fall-out from the Bongo account—but when that news hit the papers, he was shocked to learn that Citibank was still handling the account.

By August 1996, Chris Roger's client profile still only offered Bongo's position as head of an oil producing nation as an explanation for President Bongo's business background and source of wealth, wholly inadequate after an eleven year relationship with New York. Rogers later wrote in a December memo that, *Gabon resembles a Gulf Emirate in that Oil accounts for 95 pct of revenues for a population of less than one million. It is clear therefore that Tendin Investments draws most of its wealth from oil, but we have no way of being more specific.* Later that summer of 1996, the private bank's legal counsel considered ending the relationship, but was concerned for the safety of the country officer in Gabon if they did so.

Though the client background information was updated to include real estate investments and financial instruments overseas, connections to French oil companies such as ELF, and oil ventures within the country, the bank had virtually no supporting documentation for this description. Mr. Rogers, therefore, claimed to have leveled some questions at Bongo's staff, and in an internal memo to Mr. Ober (senior officer in charge of the Bongo account), Chris Rogers wrote that, *Every year, an overall allocation, loosely referred to as 'security' or 'political' funds, is voted into the budget across the operating and investment categories. Although not spelled out for obvious reasons, these funds are understood to be used at the discretion of the Presidency.* For 1995, this meant $111 million, or 8.5% of the overall budget. A later memorandum, dated April 14, 1997, characterizes the $111 million in the 1995 Gabon budget as funds which "are at the disposal of the Presidency, without any limitation".

The Private Bank was plainly identifying Gabon government funds as a primary source of the income for the Bongo account. It is not surprising that this did not bother the Private Bank personnel who knew of the Bongo accounts—after all, the Royal Family in Saudi Arabia controlled all the oil revenues, and disbursed a substantial amount to their members each year. Furthermore, Gabon had the highest per capita income in Africa, low unemployment, and was a stable environment. For most, there were very few ethical considerations on that issue.

The information, however, was not correct. Mr. Ober, and later the OCC examiner, did not attempt to verify it. During the subsequent Congressional Hearings, Gabon budget experts from the IMF, a Library of Congress expert on African law, and Gabon budget experts from the World Bank, were unanimous in stating that no recent Gabon budget authorized the President to make personal use of government funds, certainly not to the order of $111 million.

Mr. Ober then claimed that the source of funding in the Bongo account to date derived from the $52 million deposit made in 1985, but that he did not ask President Bongo directly where the funds came from "for reasons of etiquette and protocol" and because he was "not sure what the reaction would have been." As for other deposits, Ober continued to say that they were related to oil interests, though he could not specify which ones.

In April 1997, a number of articles appeared in the press describing an unfolding criminal investigation by French authorities into corruption allegations involving the French oil company, ELF Aquitaine, and its subsidiary, ELF Gabon, over bribes to government officials. French reference newspaper, *Le Monde,* raised questions about President Bongo's role in the scandal, reporting that two Swiss bank accounts containing millions of dollars in allegedly improper payments by ELF had been frozen by Swiss authorities. Both accounts were linked to Bongo through his oil advisor Samuel Dossou.

An April 28, 1997, a citimail from Chris Rogers read: *I feel quite strongly that all of us need to be very thoughtful and selective about the press coverage we choose to interpret and share about our top customers...I am unable to interpret the current press allegations insofar as they might touch upon the Bank but would not be tempted to try because of the doubts it could raise in people's minds about our own relationship with our customer...[W]e ought to be extremely careful about sharing such information with regulatory authorities, because we can't answer for it...[W]e should stay as far away as possible from this mess, unless and until any one of us has firm or verifiable evidence which would lead us to suspect that the Bank's interests are at risk.*

Without Mr. Ober's knowledge or participation, someone determined that the head of the Private Bank should be made aware of the articles and allegations. President Bongo's accounts were therefore formally reviewed by Mr. Aziz in October 1997. The decision was made to leave it open, despite the emerging Bhutto scandal in Pakistan, the recent Salinas affair, and despite the Private Bank's awareness of allegations of bribery and criminal probe into Bongo.

On November 6, 1998, Chris Rogers emailed Salim Raza in Geneva, warning of the consequences of closing the Bongo accounts:*...the marketing fallout is likely to be serious....Sam [Dossou] gets his marching orders from Tendin....Tendin has been vitally instrumental in our franchise's success over the years.... The probability of this support being reversed indefinitely should be weighted seriously.... Tendin's family and friends extend far.... The impact on [private bank] marketing in Francophone Africa will be serious.*

Then in December 21, 1998, after another review of the Bongo accounts, Mr. Aziz suggested closing them, and made the decision to do so the following month—the accounts had inspired too many questions, required too much paperwork, and incurred too many "incremental costs." He made no mention of the ongoing criminal investigation into President Bongo or his other Swiss accounts which had been frozen.

In July 1996, Deepak Sharma, head of Citibank Private Bank's operations in Pakistan, was promoted to Regional Head of Asia. Before leaving, Deepak asked Cedric to take over management of his accounts, as one of the more senior officers in the Geneva branch. Cedric began a review of the accounts, and fell across Capricorn, Bomer and Marvil—all three opened by a highly controversial character named Asif Zadari, husband to Benazir Bhutto, ruling Prime Minister of Pakistan since October 1993. Zadari's reputation as a conniving skimmer and conscienceless middle-man was widespread in the Middle East, and Cedric was shocked to learn that Citibank was handling his accounts. By October, he'd learned enough—and read enough in the news about new scandals of murder and embezzlement and fraud—to convince upper-management to close the accounts.

Jans Schlegelmilch, a Swiss lawyer and long-time family friend of the Benazir Bhutto, approached Kamran Amouzegar, an Iranian private banker who worked in the Geneva branch, to open some accounts at the Citibank Dubai branch. An account in the name of M.S. Capricorn Trading, a British Virgin Island PIC, was opened in October 1994 to receive money and transfer it to Switzerland.

Citibank later stated in Congressional hearings that Mr. Schlegelmilch had claimed to be working for the Dubai royal family, and did not reveal that Zadari was the beneficial owner of Capricorn Trading. The account manager in Dubai performed due diligence on the royal family member who had signed Schlegelmilch's U.A.E. visa, and whom she therefore believed was the owner of the account. Two deposits totaling $10 million were made almost immediately from A.R.Y. International Exchange, a company owned by Abdul Razzak Yaqub, a Pakistani gold bullion trader living in Dubai. Then in December 1994, the Bhutto government awarded Mr. Razzak an exclusive gold import license. Ms. Bhutto would later claim that the previous payments did not come from Mr. Razzak, who would deny making any payments himself, and could have come from a third party using A.R.Y's exchange services. Zadari would later claim that by giving the sole monopoly to export gold bullion, his wife had put an end to the illegal import of gold into Pakistan that had prevailed since 1947. Most likely, cash was brought to A.R.Y, that then issued a cashier's check to be deposited on Capricorn's account at Citibank Dubai.

During their visit to Geneva in February 1995, Bhutto and Zadari met Steve Crabtree at a reception. On February 27, Schlegelmilch met with Amouzegar to open three accounts for Zadari in Switzerland. Deepak Sharma, head of private bank operations in Pakistan, and

Salim Raza, head of the EMEA division of the bank, agreed to sign the memo recommending opening accounts for British Virgin Island PICs Capricorn Trading, Marvel and Bomer Finance. Sharma was thrilled with the business—the money it could generate as well as the contacts it could provide—and was easily able to convince Philippe Holderbeke, head of Private Bank Switzerland, to sign his agreement.

The first transfer of funds came through in March 19, in the amount of $8.1 million, and then another on May 5, of $10.2 million, routed through Citibank's New York offices. Shortly thereafter, the Dubai account was closed. Schlegelmilch continued to receive quarterly payments of twenty percent of the client's net revenues earned by the bank under his standard referral agreement with Citibank Switzerland. And money continued to flow in and out of the three accounts. Eventually, Holderbeke signed a memo delineating restrictions to be placed on the accounts, including a $40 million aggregate limit, and required that the accounts function as passive, stable investments, without multiple transactions or funding pass-throughs. The need to place such restrictions showed concern regarding the sources of income, yet there was no consideration to close the account.

The public outcry over the Salinas scandal, and increasing publicity about allegations of corruption against Zadari in early 1996, prompted a review of the account, but Holderbeke, now head of EMEA, and Raza, Sharma and Amouzega, apparently concluded that these allegations were politically motivated and decided to keep the accounts open. The review did not, however, cover the accounts' transaction activity, a matter about which Holderbeke remained unaware.

In the Spring of 1996, Amouzegar asked that the overall aggregate limit be increased to $60 million, a request which Holderbeke rejected. Amouzegar proceeded to bypass Holderbeke's authority, and violate the restrictions on aggregate limit and multiple transactions. He had his approvals signed by Raza and Sharma, until the latter was transferred in July.

Cedric met with Schlegelmilch at the latter's request in early September, after taking over Deepak Sharma's accounts. He left with a very distasteful impression. Schlegelmilch was a heavy-set Swiss German with a slinky and dismissive attitude, and he brushed off Cedric's questions as to the origins of the Zadari funds. Cedric decided to take a close look at the accounts: he asked his secretary to pull all the files, and over the next two weeks went over them with a fine-toothed comb. He immediately noticed transgressions of Holderbeke's restrictions and the usurpation of his authority. The accounts had functioned more as checking accounts than passive investments accounts. He immediately recommended closing them.

On September 20, 1996, Murtaza Bhutto, leader of the Pakistani opposition, was gunned down by police in the Sind province by the political party of his sister, Prime Minister Benazir Bhutto. Their mother immediately accused her daughter and son-in-law Zadari of masterminding the assassination. By early October, press accounts of Zadari and Bhutto's alleged corruption, and Zadari's involvement in his brother-in-law's assassination, surfaced in newspapers around the world. Transparency International, a German foundation, had recently ranked the Pakistani government as the second most corrupt in the world behind Nigeria's. Zadari and Bhutto were soon accused of squirreling away billions while Pakistan wallowed in poverty and debt.

Cedric called Schlegelmilch to inform him of Citibank's decision to close the Capricorn, Bomer and Marvil accounts. Disgruntled but silent, Schlegelmilch signed a letter to Citibank on October 14 requesting that all funds be transferred to Banque Financière de la Cité in Geneva. In a memo dated October 11, 1996, Cedric confirmed Holderbeke's approval of the closing of the accounts, and requested the termination of Schlegelmilch's consultancy agreement with Citibank on October 31, "with any funds due him to be paid as soon as possible." Capricorn Trading would be the last of the three PIC accounts to be effectively closed on January 8, 1997.

No steps were taken, however, to inform US authorities by submitting a Criminal Referral Form or Suspicious Activity Report, or otherwise. The letter of the law was vague, and since the accounts were closed, Cedric considered that it was better to risk a potential, but not definite, hand-slap from the regulatory authorities in the U.S., than to risk exposing the bank to embarrassment through possible leaks if a report were made.

Nine months later, Bhutto and her husband were arrested, and the Swiss government cooperated with Pakistani authorities to have their accounts frozen at Citibank, UBS, Barclays and COBP (Cantrade Ormond Burrus Privée). Citibank took no action since the accounts had been closed, and maintained a strict no comment with the press when the affair was extensively covered in mid-September. Only in November, anticipating a New York Times coverage of allegations that Zadari held accounts with Citibank in Dubai and in Switzerland, did Citibank contact the Federal Reserve and the OCC. Dr. Livia Mueller-Fembeck from Citibank's legal office in Zurich, did, however, inform Swiss authorities on September 16, 1997, that the bank "no longer maintained any relations with persons [mentioned in the blocking order]."

In June 1998, Switzerland indicted Mr. Schlegelmilch for money laundering in connection with kickbacks paid by the Swiss companies for the award of a government contract by Pakistan. Zadari in July 1998, and Bhutto in August, were indicted for violation of Swiss money laundering laws in connection with the same incident. On April 15, 1999, after an 18-month trial, Bhutto and Zadari were convicted of accepting kickbacks, sentenced them to five years in prison, and fined $8.6 million. Bhutto denounced the decision as politically motivated, a position somewhat undermined by the previous indictments by a Swiss court that could hardly be accused of political motives.

All three affairs made worldwide headlines in 1999 when Citibank became the focus of Congressional Hearings on money laundering allegations. Cedric was asked to testify, but the bank refused to allow him to leave for Washington, D.C. Cedric spent a large part of the summer of 1999 in Maine, fully expecting to be subpoenaed, but he never was, though he would be mentioned in the hearings. John Reed was called in, and the Chairman admitted to mistakes having been made, to wrong-doing, to slips in internal controls, but not to a purposeful attempt to launder money. The general consensus by the end of the Hearings was that Citibank did have internal control policies to prevent its collusion in money laundering schemes, and had taken the necessary steps to close the fraudulent accounts, but had severely lacked in due diligence.

As other allegations shrouded other banks in New York and Switzerland in 2000, and no unusual punishment was meted out to Citibank, the Salinas, Bhutto and Bongo affairs were relegated to yesterday's news. Citibank—or Citigroup as it was now called—could once again breathe a sigh of relief at seeing its name and reputation maintained. John Reed, however, stepped down from the joint chairmanship in early 2000, leaving Sandy Weil in full charge of the megalith that was, yet again, the biggest financial institution in the world.

◆   ◆   ◆

Though he remained largely on the periphery of the scandals that rocked Citibank, Cedric's own career in the late nineties would veer quite far from the smooth-sailing he had envisioned when he became Prince Alwaleed's personal banker within Citibank Private Bank. For the better part of the decade, he led a team of accountants, investment bankers, market researchers and assistants to manage Prince Alwaleed's business. The premier financier of Saudi Arabia became a global player, and Cedric was continuously traveling to meet corporate CEOs, illustrious persons such as Rubert Murdoch and Michael Jackson, convening on the Prince's new yacht—formerly the *Nabila*, owned by Adnan Khashoggi then Donald Trump, a purchase which Cedric arranged—or in the Prince's high-tech desert outfit near Riyadh, and arranging for the myriad investments in which the Prince became involved: Saks Holdings in June '93, Euro Disney in October '94, Four Seasons Hotels in November '94, Apple Computer and Mediaset in March and July '95—the start of his foray into tech investments—then Netscape Communications, Motorola and News Corporation in November '97. The Prince had a knack for investing in troubled corporations which he believed had solid grounds for expansion, and see them indeed turn around and turn a large profit within several years.

Cedric also arranged for the liquidation of the Prince's Liechtenstein Anstalts. It was with a Liechtenstein Anstalt in the name of Kingdom Enterprise that Prince Alwaleed had first opened an account with Citibank in 1980. The time had come to move the Prince's assets into a more structured entity, since the Anstalts had dropped out of favor with the international banking community: they were now widely perceived by bankers and government officials for what they really were—phony shell companies, false entities, nothing more than poorly disguised current accounts. To help convince the Prince, Cedric engaged the knowledge of Citibank's Senior Trust Officer in Zurich, Thomas Salmon, and together they met with the Prince and his lawyers in Paris. Salmon explained that the Anstalts were only poorly regarded, they also did nothing to protect the Prince's assets in the case of inheritance. If he died, all his money would have to return to Saudi Arabia under *sharia* law. The Prince's lawyers confirmed, and so the Prince agreed to set up a trust and asked Citibank to handle it.

Paul Collins opposed his veto—the Prince already owned close to 10% of Citicorp, and he didn't want Alwaleed as the Bank's biggest individual shareholder, biggest individual client, and biggest individual trust. Cedric introduced the Prince, therefore, to his former colleague Jean-Pierre Cuoni at Coutts & Co., who set up a trust for the Prince in the Caymans. It was quite a heady experience for Cedric, and the gleam in Cuoni's eyes reflected the large satisfaction Cedric felt at disposing of several hundred million dollars with a fellow banker. He could afford to be generous, and it felt good.

But Cedric would have ridden the crest of his career for only six years.

Michael Jensen joined Citibank at the age of twenty-one, and had been a long time employee by the time he arrived in Switzerland, to replace the head of the PBG corporate finance division, which had been set up in Geneva to provide investment advice to its big clients interested in purchasing, selling or merging companies. But the division was floundering: Citibank Private Bank had little expertise, staff or connections in corporate financing, and clients usually preferred to solicit advice from market leaders such as Salomon Smith Barney or Lehman Brothers.

The treasurer of Prince Alwaleed's United Saudi Commercial Bank was an American with connections in New York within the top ten financial institutions. One of these connections convinced him to invest in Bear Stearns junk bonds—or more aptly called "kitchen sink bonds" since they were so devalued. The risk was high, but so was the yield, and the USCB Treasurer invested one billion of USCB's money into these bonds. Both had been duped, however, into thinking that the bonds were not interest rate sensitive, and when they rose, the Prince discovered to his horror that the value of his bonds had plummeted. He called Cedric in somewhat of a panic, and asked for his help in extricating himself and USCB from this costly mess. Caught in a bind, Cedric turned to Mike Jensen and his corporate finance knowledge to resolve the problem.

Together they flew to Riyadh on the Prince's private jet to explain how the situation could be resolved, and Jensen ultimately extricated United Saudi Commercial Bank from its position with a "meager" $200 million dollar loss—meager in light of the potentially more disastrous outcome. From then on, Cedric asked Jensen to accompany him on every meeting he had with the Prince, especially since Prince Alwaleed was moving ever more rapidly away from pure deposits and into global investments. Jensen was delighted to play around with the Prince's billion-dollar war chest. "He is the most liquid player on the world scene," Jensen would say in interviews. "The possibilities are enormous." Cedric maintained the personal relations side of the business, and transferred $50,000 monthly to Jensen to cover expenses in travel, research and staff.

When Prince Alwaleed needed background research on companies that interested him, Jensen and his team would deliver in-depth study reports and proposals. Once an investment was decided upon, Cedric would open another PIC in the Caymans that would own the shares. All the Prince's PICs had the same base name of Kingdom 5-KR: 'Kingdom' for Kingdom Establishment, '5' for his first wife's favorite number, 'K' for his son Khalid, and 'R' for his daughter 'Reema'. At the time, he was grateful that he could rely on Jensen for the corporate side of the business. Corporate finance was not his arena; handling the PICs and renewing the numerous time deposits required by Alwaleed's assets comprised most of Cedric's work. And it was work he enjoyed doing.

Sometime early 1997, Paul Collins called Cedric to tell him that they needed to reduce the size of the Prince's liquid assets in Luxembourg. Cedric, the Prince, and the Prince's lawyer convened to discuss how to best dispose of the $2 billion. "Whatever you do, I don't want it placed in subsidiaries!" Cedric gulped. Indeed, Alwaleed's lawyer turned to him and said: "But the money already is in one. Luxembourg is a Citibank subsidiary." The Prince was incensed: a subsidiary was only liable to the extent of its own capitalization; a branch was covered under Citicorp's global liability. However, a branch could not loan out to other branches or credit card operations, which is why Cedric had placed it in Luxembourg in the first place. But he had acquired the Prince's authorization beforehand, and when presented with his signature, Alwaleed calmed down. "Just get it out of there as fast as possible."

Since subsidiaries were unacceptable to the Prince, and Citibank branches were unacceptable to the Bank—and therefore Cedric—for liability reasons, Cedric devised another solution. He arranged to place $100 million in time deposits with other major banks—Banque Nationale Paris, Swiss Bank Corporation, UBS, Bank of America, Barclays Bank, ABN-Amro, Nat West, Chase Manhattan, Chemical, Bankers Trust, Société Générale, and Cititrust. The Prince accepted the proposal, pursuant to his desire to be a global player and use these large banks' global facilities. The money was wired through the Prince's Cayman shell companies, 5KR-10 and 5KR-11. Just as it had been a heady experience setting up a trust for the Prince with Cuoni, it was quite a power trip offering $100 million dollars to each of these various bankers. Those who had branches in the Cayman Islands and could accept the money, were literally fawning over Cedric.

◆   ◆   ◆

By 1997, the Prince was worth close to $12 billion, with a wad of available cash in the arena of $3 billion. The $590 million that he'd injected into Citicorp six years earlier was now worth just over $5 billion. Euro Disney, Apple Computer, and Saks Fifth Avenue had turned around, earning him the name of "Prince of Fallen Angels". He was investing in Korean conglomerate Daewoo, Donna Karan International, Planet Hollywood, and was the de facto manager of Michael Jackson.

Cedric was handling massive amounts of global investments, company documents, money flows, multi-bank deposits and renewals, interest rate negotiations…Each day the Prince required faxes of the major items in the *International Herald Tribune* and the *Wall Street Journal*, and DHL shipments every week of all the major magazines—*Time, Newsweek, The Economist, Forbes, Fortune 500*. This was his job: satisfying the Prince. And he did it remarkably well; his standing with the Prince was phenomenal: during a lunch talk with lawyers on board the Prince's yacht, Prince Alwaleed claimed that "Cedric remains my banker while both of us are still alive".

Cedric was worried, however, that he would no longer be able to go on vacation, or that if he fell ill (though he found that to be a ludicrous notion, having never missed a day of work since the hepatitis debacle in Liberia), the Prince's affairs would fall into chaos. So he involved Jensen in all aspects of the business, not just in the corporate finance work. Having a backup reassured him. Being the Prince's personal banker required being available 24/7, and though this was preferable to seeing Alwaleed take his business elsewhere, having Jensen to carry part of the workload seemed the ideal solution. In the mean time, however, Jensen's corporate finance division within the Private Bank was disintegrating from lack of work. Cedric saw this to his advantage: Jensen would have more time for the Prince. Jensen, on the other hand, might understandably have felt uneasy: if, for some reason, he was removed from working with the Prince, he would be out of a job.

In early 1998, Cedric attended an award ceremony in the Prince's honor for his philanthropic activities in Saudi Arabia. After the ceremony, Cedric suggested that since the Prince was now a world player, he should set up a philanthropic trust in which he could place $100 million. Alwaleed loved the idea, it appealed to his sense of grandeur. All the great men—Ford, Getty, Rockefeller—had set up a foundation. "Grant, I like it! You are considering me not only as businessman, but as a man of heart as well. A world philanthropist. Yes, do the research!" There were various forms of trust—from the permanent staff and annual allocation of funds of the Getty Foundation, to the specifically targeted aid of the Soro's fund. Cedric had two members of his team draw up proposals based on these foundations, and for every possible variation in between.

Shortly thereafter, Cedric had another idea. His affable personality had made him many contacts within the sphere of marathon runners, and one of them got Cedric interested in Operation Smile, which involved bringing US plastic surgeons to operate on children in developing nations who suffer from goiter, hare-lips, cleft palettes, and other malformations, while local plastic surgeons studied their techniques. The results were amazing, and Cedric believed he could convince the Prince to invest in Operation Smile so that the efforts could be extended to other countries. It was one of the poorest judgments of character and timing that he ever made.

One afternoon on the Prince's yacht, after a meeting with engineers about the hotel complex he planned on building in Riyadh, Cedric was honored with an invitation to join the Prince and his family for lunch. Cedric bought up the subject of philanthropy, and exposed his idea on Operation Smile. "Your Highness, if you inject even three to five million dollars, you could pick the countries, the children—it is a great opportunity to do an amazing amount of good." Cedric pulled out some before-and-after pictures of the operations in the Philippines and showed them to the Prince.

How could he have forgotten how much the Prince admired beauty? He ate frugally, exercised regularly, and abhorred fat. Deformity even more so. The pictures that Cedric showed him could not fail to disgust him. He pushed them away and said to Cedric: "Grant, you've ruined my lunch." Suddenly Cedric realized the extent of the faux pas that he had committed.

He soon recovered, however, and resumed his almost casual demeanor with the Prince. Unlike everyone else who surrounded Alwaleed, Cedric could only be his natural self, and would often try and break through the Prince's ubiquitously serious mien. "Relax, Your Highness, loosen up! You're wealthy, young, smart and handsome—enjoy it!" Once in a while he even managed to get the Prince to crack a smile.

Then he committed his second faux pas.

Prince Alwaleed would often discuss policy items with his advisors during a brisk hour-long walk. On one of these occasions, as the Prince and his entourage were preparing to make the 4mph stroll along the Cannes boardwalk near where the yacht was moored, Cedric remarked:

"Your Highness, you must be aware that research has shown that aerobic exercise near traffic—breathing in exhaust fumes—is equivalent to smoking a pack of cigarettes. It's four pm, rush-hour, probably not the best idea…" He'd miscalculated again: Prince Alwaleed did not appreciate being told that what he was doing was unhealthy.

In August 1998, Cedric and Mike Jensen were scheduled to meet with the Prince, but when Cedric arrived shortly before ten on the Prince's yacht, he discovered that Jensen was already in a private meeting with him. When the Prince finally appeared to greet Cedric, he took one of his aides aside and had him tell Cedric to leave immediately.

Cedric could not imagine what had been said between Jensen and Prince Alwaleed, and he assumed that there must have been some misunderstanding. So he swallowed his pride and joined the meeting on the yacht despite Alwaleed's injunction. The Prince didn't even look at him; and they would never speak again.

He knew he had two options: distance himself from the Prince's business and allow Jensen to wallow in far over his head; or remain and help Jensen in the back office. In the first case, he would diddle around the Bank until official retirement—fifteen months away—a dismal prospect hardly deserving of his career; the second option would allow him to continue the work that he enjoyed. He was dealing at the time with over twenty different people associated with the Prince—bankers, lawyers, doctors, real estate reps, tax agents, telecommunications, his wife's assistants—and was running all the PICs. Cedric finally realized that salvaging his pride and getting revenge on Jensen weighed light in the balance of remaining in the bank doing nothing—if indeed he were allowed to remain and not asked to retire early. He also realized that the back office work was the side he enjoyed most. If he never saw or spoke to the Prince again, he still maintained personable relations with Alwaleed's assistants. And he was no longer woken up at 3am on a Sunday morning. He could leave that hassle to Jensen.

So Cedric stayed.

◆   ◆   ◆

In the end—with his ability to see the good side of every-thing—Cedric realized that Jensen had done him a great favor. Until his fall from grace, he had not realized how tense and stressed he had been. Suddenly the Prince was no longer calling him day and night to attend to his every whim, asking him for the dollar-yen rate on the spot or to get in touch with John Reed within thirty minutes…Cedric had his life back. On top of it, he maintained his independence within the Bank, and remained outside the ring of constant bickering, in-fighting, power-struggles, and back-stabbing that was still pervasive. He had never wanted to become a Senior Executive plagued with administra-tive problems; he had never really expected to reach this high in the corporate structure. By the end of 1999, Cedric had achieved a sense of inner peace with regards to his career, and he could look back on his thirty-eight years of service to Citibank with pride and pleasure. Who could ask for more?

And then it got better—a sugar-sweet retirement and aftermath.

Though Cedric would have continued working for years, the Citi-corp-Traveler's Group merger meant another reorganization, and since Cedric had passed the age of sixty-five in March 1999, he was offered a severance package with eighteen months' salary and full benefits—one that he could not refuse.

Four months later, the bank asked him to return to manage a newly opened branch of Cititrust in Mauritius for a client who had made a substantial fortune in the Internet start-up frenzy. It consisted in little more than visiting the branch for a week every month or two to main-tain appearances, and it seemed to Cedric the perfect and most appro-priate way to begin his retirement.

In January 2000, Cedric had the pleasure of seeing old friends and colleagues convene for an unofficial retirement party in Robbie Meyjes's New York apartment: Jimmy Griffin, Kerry Hemming, Peter

Sperling, Jean-Pierre Cuoni, and a host of other personalities from the various stages of his career, including Walter Bigelow Wriston. Cedric had crossed paths with Wriston several times since the latter's retirement in 1984, at different official and unofficial functions, and every time—like this last time in Meyjes's apartment—he'd clapped Cedric around the shoulder and smiled.

"I hired this kid in 1962," he'd tell the audience. "Cedric came into my office with twenty-five cents in his pocket and said he wanted to start working right away. I knew he'd go far."

0-595-26817-X